The Retirement Challenge

The Retirement Challenge

What's Wrong with America's System and a Sensible Way to Fix It

MARTIN NEIL BAILY

BENJAMIN H. HARRIS

OXFORD
UNIVERSITY PRESS

OXFORD
UNIVERSITY PRESS

Oxford University Press is a department of the University of Oxford. It furthers
the University's objective of excellence in research, scholarship, and education
by publishing worldwide. Oxford is a registered trade mark of Oxford University
Press in the UK and certain other countries.

Published in the United States of America by Oxford University Press
198 Madison Avenue, New York, NY 10016, United States of America.

CIP data is on file at the Library of Congress

ISBN 978-0-19-763927-6

DOI: 10.1093/oso/9780197639276.001.0001

9 8 7 6 5 4 3 2 1

Printed by Lakeside Book Company, United States of America

This book is dedicated to our families. To Vickie Baily and Jessica Harris for their support during the writing of the book, and to our children and grandchildren, current and future, in the hope that they will have better choices as they face their retirement challenge.

CONTENTS

LIST OF TABLES AND FIGURES

TABLES

FIGURES

We wrote this book to reset the policy conversation around retirement. For years, the retirement conversation in policy circles has focused largely on "fixing" Social Security and Medicare, each of which has a trust fund that will be exhausted in the coming years. To be sure, Social Security and Medicare pose daunting challenges, but American's overall retirement challenge is much broader.

As we explain, a sound retirement requires changes throughout the current system—from private insurance to retirement saving accounts to the labor market for older workers. Fortunately, all these changes are undoubtedly achievable. Indeed, we can dramatically improve the retirement system through a series of incremental reforms that largely preserve the current system.

As we also explain, retirement policy is about much more than retirement. Because retirement programs are a large part of the federal budget, retirement is about fiscal choices—and the policy tradeoffs inherent in spending trillions of dollars a year to achieve retirement security. Because the savings of American workers provides capital for investment that expands the economy, retirement policy is about macroeconomic growth. And because economies depend on labor, both in terms of the number of workers and the skills of older workers, retirement policy is about the labor market.

Retirement policy is also about equity. We believe strongly that anyone who spends most of their life working deserves to retire toward the end of it and not retire in poverty and hardship. We also believe that middle-class workers who have spent decades in the labor market and have made responsible choices along the way deserve a reasonable degree of prosperity in retirement.

Ultimately, however, retirement is about happiness. As people get older, they derive happiness from doing what they love outside of work, a retirement system that offers more hours of leisure makes people better off. But a sound retirement system isn't just about enabling older workers to spend more time in retirement: it's also about security. It's about a system in which workers know that they can turn their savings into a steady cash flow in retirement, older Americans can age comfortably in their own homes, and older workers can decide when to retire.

In sum, we wrote this book to change American retirement in a way that makes people better off throughout their working lives and after.

That's the "why," but we also want to explain the "how." In short, we wrote this book with a lot of help. The effort was launched with generous grants from the Alfred P. Sloan Foundation and the Laura and John Arnold Foundation (now Arnold Ventures LLC), which provided funding to the Brookings Institution and the Kellogg School of Management for us to elicit policy reform ideas from some of the nation's top experts in retirement policy. We commissioned top economists and lawyers to propose manageable policy reforms that would improve the retirement system.

Our first event, in January 2019 at the Brookings Institution, for which we commissioned papers, focused on policies to enable people to work longer. Notable economists Robert Clark and John Shoven argued for Social Security reform to incent workers to continue working. Alicia Munnell, a titan in the field of retirement, and co-author Abigail Walters, proposed reforms to both encourage people to work longer and to better understand issues related to retirement. Jim Poterba, a world-renowned economist and retirement expert gave a masterful exposition of the current retirement system and where it stands.

Over the next two years, we held three more events and commissioned more papers. The second event was at the Kellogg School of Management and focused on annuity reform. We returned to Brookings for our third event, which focused on reforming reverse mortgages. By the time we reached our fourth event, for which we focused again on policies that would encourage people to work longer, COVID-19 was in full swing, and we were forced to hold the event virtually.

To help guide our work, we formed an advisory board that included experts from academia, industry, and advocacy organizations. We met with the board several times a year and relied on the board to guide our selection of topics and of the experts from whom to commission papers.

The work built on itself. We wrote papers to frame the discussion around each event to provide an overview of the relevant economic issues and help participants at the events and readers of the reports understand the current state of play around each topic. We wrote many op-eds on retirement policy, with one of us contributing regularly to the *Wall Street Journal* and the two of us jointly writing pieces for CNN.com, *Fortune*, and other outlets. We appeared on radio shows, spoke on podcasts, and discussed issues with the media. We spoke with Congressional staffs, other economists, and experts in the field.

We felt the time was right to combine the lessons we'd learned into a book, and the Smith Richardson Foundation generously provided funding for us to do so. We found a brilliant editor in Lawrence Haas, began writing, and, in the midst of the pandemic, retreated to our home offices to continue working on the manuscript.

As we were writing, we seemed to be aiming at a moving target. On some days, America's retirement system seemed to be changing before our eyes. Long-term care facilities were hotbeds for transmitting COVID-19, and residents suffered heartbreaking rates of death. The stock market crashed, albeit temporarily, and some experts predicted widespread declines in housing prices—which would sharply curtail the resources available for retirees. Unemployment soared for workers overall, and older workers left the labor market in droves. We wondered whether retirement as we knew it was ending and whether we were writing a book for an earlier time.

In 2022, just as it seemed that the world was returning to a (new) normal, Russia invaded Ukraine, there was a surge of inflation the like of which we had not seen in 40 years, and the stock market took a (temporary) dive.

When this book is published we very much hope that the war has ended and the economic upheavals will have eased or ended. But even if that is true, the scars will remain. Retirees may be more wary of institutional living, and some older workers may be less inclined to work face-to-face jobs. Savers will have been reminded of the uncertainty they face with respect to inflation and investment returns. Nevertheless, they will find that the post-pandemic retirement paradigm they are facing is nearly identical to that of pre-pandemic 2019. We still must improve. A new paradigm is needed and we hope that this book can do what the crises could not: help change the face of American retirement.

Martin Neil Baily
Benjamin H. Harris
Washington, DC

Katherine G. Abraham
Distinguished University
   Professor
University of Maryland

Robert L. Clark
Professor
North Carolina State University

Thomas Davidoff
Associate Professor
University of British Columbia

Laurie Goodman
Vice President of Housing
   Finance Policy
Urban Institute

Steve Goss
Chief Actuary
Social Security Administration

Seth Harris
Former Visiting Professor
Cornell Institute for Public
   Affairs
Deputy Assistant to the President
   for Labor and the Economy

Susan Houseman
Vice President for Research
W. E. Upjohn Institute for
   Employment Research

Christopher J. Mayer
Paul Milstein Professor of
   Real Estate
Columbia University

Stephanie Moulton
Professor and Faculty Director of
   Research
Ohio State University

Alicia Munnell
Peter F. Drucker Professor
Director, Center for Retirement
  Research
Boston College

David Neumark
Distinguished Professor
University of California, Irvine

James Poterba
President, National Bureau of
  Economic Research
Mitsui Professor
MIT

John B. Shoven
Charles R. Schwab Professor
Stanford University

Beth Truesdale
Research Associate
Harvard Center for Population and
  Development Studies

Abigail Walters
Former Research Associate
Center for Retirement Research
Boston College

Debra Whitman
Executive Vice President and Chief
  Policy Officer
AARP

1

Overview

Individuals and families face a new economic reality: since the turn of the century, median incomes have grown at only half the pace of the prior 15 years.[1] As a result, annual pay increases are becoming rarer for many workers, who in turn are finding it harder to make their rent or mortgage payments and cover other basic expenses. Moreover, medical and college costs rise each year. Roughly 80 million Americans have debt with a debt collector, suggesting they're living close to financial ruin.

The pandemic-driven economic downturn of 2020 was America's second deep recession in a generation. The first—known as the Great Recession—began at the end of 2007, imposing severe harm on businesses and families that dragged on for years even after the economy began to recover from the recession. Unemployment peaked at 10 percent in October of 2009, with more than 15 million people out of work. Incomes shrank, stocks fell by more than half, and the housing market collapsed. Millions lost their homes, and almost all homeowners suffered a sharp decline in home values.[2] The economy quickly recovered, but by 2022 there were new problems including a surge in inflation, a 20 percent market decline, and the threat of a third recession.

Slower overall economic growth and at least two recent recessions have imposed a huge financial burden on many families when it comes to saving for retirement. Not everyone is facing financial problems, of course. Some middle-income families have found ways to build substantial retirement accounts, while many affluent households have enjoyed robust income growth. But a broad segment of the middle class has struggled with little growth in their incomes even if they were able to continue working, while others were forced to retire earlier than they planned due to the recessions.

The financial burden on families to save for their retirement comes at a time when the nation's retirement landscape is changing in big ways. Companies are phasing out pension plans, and governments are scaling back their pensions. Families must not only save, but they also must manage their investments and figure out how to live during their retirement on what they socked away. They do not know how long they will live, or if they will need expensive care, or have to pay for high medical bills.

Even though families are assuming a much bigger role in their retirement planning, government programs—namely, Social Security and Medicare—still play a critical role in Americans' retirement security. Financially, however, these programs face major challenges. Slow economic growth, large tax cuts, and a rapid rise in the number of people collecting Social Security and Medicare benefits have combined to drive very large annual federal budget deficits, adding trillions of dollars to our federal debt. Meanwhile, the Great Recession, the pandemic-driven recession, and the federal policy responses to both added trillions more to the debt, pushing it to a level that's roughly as large as the annual economy itself. At some point, such massive amounts of red ink will put more political pressure on the nation's leaders to constrain the growth of federal "entitlement" programs, notably Social Security and Medicare. The programs surely will not vanish, but cuts to them may be a key part of any reform plan.

Nevertheless, America remains a very rich country that can address its retirement challenges. Low-income families have Social Security, Medicare, and Supplemental Security Income to help them avoid poverty. Middle-income families still have incomes that can cover basic needs with a bit left over, and they recognize that they must save and invest. Even though the stock market has suffered setbacks, it has risen a lot over the long term, helping savers build wealth for retirement and other purposes. But families at all income levels need more retirement help: they need access to solid retirement saving plans, and they need the ability to buy insurance policies at fair prices to protect themselves against too much uncertainty as they grow older.

RETIREMENT: FROM WHENCE IT CAME

In the grand sweep of human history, retirement is a relatively new concept. Not until the 1880s did Otto Von Bismarck introduce the idea in Germany, and not until the 1920s did US corporations introduce policies to support retirement in America—and, even then, they were rare. President Franklin D. Roosevelt and Congress established Social Security in 1935, and the program paid its first monthly benefits in 1940. At that time, a man reaching age 21 had only a 54 percent chance of reaching 65 and collecting benefits.[3] It wasn't until the post-World War II economic boom that retirement became an attainable aspiration for many of America's workers.

Today, retirement affects virtually all Americans, directly or indirectly. More than 46 million workers are retired, and tens of millions more are about to be.[4] Roughly a third of today's nearly $7 trillion federal budget is devoted to supporting Americans older than 65, and that share will grow to roughly half by 2051.[5] At the state level, soaring pension liabilities have jeopardized the stability of public finances.[6] Younger workers may be decades from retirement, but the decisions made by their older counterparts will shape the scope of their opportunities in the workforce and the extent to which future generations will support them in their own retirement. Moreover, the decisions of both working-age and retired Americans about saving and investing go a long way toward shaping economic growth.

Yet, as a concept, retirement has never fully fulfilled its promise. Social Security has stood as the bedrock of the retirement system and has helped countless retirees achieve a better life after work, but, for many, it doesn't supply enough money to maintain a prosperous retirement. Company pensions used to provide lifetime security for those fortunate enough to have them, but Americans these days are far likelier to do their retirement saving through 401(k)-like accounts. And while some current retirees are still collecting pension incomes, pensions were never available to all workers. Because companies have largely eliminated traditional pensions, workers have traded the lifetime security of a pension for the chance to earn the higher returns associated with riskier investments in stocks and mutual funds. The trade has paid off for some who saved diligently and invested well, but it has left others with far too little. And many retire with little other than their Social Security benefits.

As we will discuss in this book, researchers do not agree about how well or poorly Americans are preparing for retirement. Certainly, many households have accumulated significant financial assets in retirement ac-counts or other saving vehicles.[7] They have equity in their homes, and they may be able to earn additional funds by working part-time in retirement. Even these families, though, face significant challenges in managing their assets and ensuring that their income will cover their expenses for the rest of their lives.

Many other families are not saving enough.[8] A recent study from the Stanford Longevity Center noted that "the vast majority of American workers of any age will be unable to replicate and maintain their standard of living if they retire fully from working at age 65. This may be a crisis for those that are unprepared for a significant drop in family income or aren't prepared to work beyond age 65."[9] As we—the authors—judge the evidence, we think that large numbers of families approach retirement without adequate funds to ensure a secure retirement. Even if that does not amount to a saving *crisis*, there is certainly a widespread saving *problem*.

The saving shortfall, however large it may be, is exacerbated by inade-quate products and strategies to enable savers to turn their saving into a secure retirement. That is, people entering retirement don't have enough affordable financial and insurance products—like annuities, long-term care insurance, and reverse mortgages—to help make a nest egg last a lifetime. Instead, savers generally are pushed onto a path in which Social Security and Medicare are their only sources of guaranteed benefits (and "guarantee" is up for debate, as we shall discuss in the pages to come). Rather than plan adequately, they roll the dice to see whether their saving will cover their retirement.

Retirement, then, remains a mixed bag. Millions of workers enjoy a secure retirement that would have been unfathomable two generations ago. Retirement savers have stockpiled $22.5 trillion in assets and saved trillions more in their homes, businesses, and non-retirement financial assets.[10] But about half of workers enter retirement with tiny nest eggs at best and only Social Security at worst. The Federal Reserve Board reported in 2020 that 25 percent of Americans do not have any retirement savings. And Social Security, by itself, does not provide generous benefits. (The average Social Security benefit in December 2020 was $1,544 a month, according to the Social Security Administration.)

All told, we believe that America's retirement system works well for some and falls short for others, and a series of common-sense reforms by families, businesses, and government would improve it significantly. We wrote this book to provide a roadmap for making a mediocre retirement system work better for everyone.

NEEDED: A NEW PARADIGM FOR RETIREMENT

As noted, middle-class Americans used to rely on company pensions that provided a decent standard of living for as long as they lived and that, in many cases, also provided healthcare benefits that supplemented Medicare. Many families also saved for retirement, creating a nest egg to cover unexpected needs in retirement or to leave to their children. Some moderate-income families also had pensions through their unions, and those that didn't relied heavily on Social Security, often supplemented by part-time work.

Today, private pensions have mostly disappeared for young workers and are scarce even for those approaching retirement. Although the federal government and most state governments still provide traditional pensions, they are scaling them back and asking government workers to rely on their own savings for a greater share of their retirement. Policymakers also have, in effect, reduced Social Security benefits. In 1983, they gradually raised the age at which retirees can receive their full benefit, from 65 where it was first set to 67 for those born in 1960 and later. Many people take "early" benefits at age 62 or soon afterward, but those monthly benefits are lower each month because they start earlier in retirement, and, as a result, early retirees often struggle to make ends meet on low benefit levels. People are living longer, exacerbating the danger that they will run out of money. And healthcare has become very expensive, even for Medicare beneficiaries. Poor retirees too often must choose between buying food and filling prescriptions.

To be sure, not everyone retires without enough money. Companies that once had pensions now offer 401(k) plans and contribute to individual employee accounts. Families are saving for retirement through 401(k)s or other saving plans and reaching retirement age with adequate or more than adequate resources. These families often don't feel secure, however, because they don't know how long they will live, they're concerned that they'll need full-time care at enormous cost, and they've seen wild swings in the economy and the stock market. Many families hoard their retirement saving against future risk and, as a result, do not enjoy the comfortable retirement they deserve.

Meanwhile, the current retirement paradigm is poorly designed. The federal tax code offers hundreds of billions a year in tax breaks to encourage savings but, studies show, they do little to increase total saving. Income annuities, which offer guaranteed income for life, have never realized their promise, partly because Americans don't seem to understand their value and partly because the products are not well-designed to strengthen retirement security. The trillions of dollars of housing equity held by older households is difficult and costly to tap.[11] And no worker on the cusp of retirement knows how much she needs to save because she cannot answer the most fundamental retirement question of all: How long will I live?

Nevertheless, *if families, companies, and policymakers all took incremental steps to improve the retirement system, every American could achieve a more secure retirement.* We can build on what's working and make it better. Employers won't again be offering company pensions and retiree healthcare, but they want to do more to help their employees. Social Security is a success, and policymakers should strengthen it financially—and they need not make radical changes to the program to do so. Despite the wide political divide, policymakers from both sides of the aisle could agree on other steps that can help families transition into a secure retirement.

If implemented, our proposals would create a new retirement paradigm. Each step is feasible and could receive wide support. Together, they would bring a major, much-needed shift toward retirement security for all.

THE AGENDA FOR FAMILIES, COMPANIES, AND POLICYMAKERS

The retirement challenge is big enough that everyone with a stake in it—families, companies, and policymakers—must act. Simply relying on families to save more is unrealistic and inefficient; they may save too much in their working years, reducing their well-being just in case they live into their late 90s, or they may save too little and leave themselves poor in their old age. Companies must be part of the solution since they administer the main vehicles through which workers save for retirement and offer some of the most promising strategies for helping workers turn their saving into security. So, too, must policymakers be part of the solution, since they have jurisdiction over everything from Social Security to the tax code. As we discuss in greater detail in the pages to follow, here is a synopsis of what each party must do:

Families must act. First and foremost, families must make sure that they don't dip into their retirement funds prematurely unless they have no alternative. Second, they need a realistic retirement plan that recognizes that they may live for many years, perhaps into their 90s or beyond. Third, they must learn how to handle uncertainty—the uncertainty of returns on retirement saving, of one's lifespan, and of one's future health and whether one will need full-time care. Families need good advice to address these uncertainties.

Some workers don't have access to a 401(k) plan on the job, which makes their retirement challenge much bigger, but they still can manage it.

Workers can easily set up an IRA with a reputable financial company and put money in the account each week or month. Some workers get quarterly or annual bonuses, and companies can deposit them directly into a retirement account. As behavioral economists have concluded, workers find it much easier to save if the money comes out of their paychecks automatically. Families need access to automatic retirement savings, even if their employer doesn't offer it or they work on their own. Some families simply will have to set up retirement accounts themselves.

To be sure, many workers barely make enough to live on. We cannot expect them to save much for retirement. Low-wage workers, however, pay a lot in Social Security and Medicare taxes, and they deserve to get enough in benefits to enable them to avoid poverty while they live in retirement.

The best way for low-wage workers to prepare for retirement is to work as long as they can and not draw Social Security benefits until they must. Ideally, they would wait until age 70 to tap Social Security because that will benefit them greatly. A retiree who waits to start collecting at 67 instead of 62 receives a 30 percent boost in monthly benefits. Each additional year of waiting adds another 8 percent. By waiting until 70, the beneficiary receives 77 percent more than someone who starts collecting at 62. Some people, of course, aren't healthy enough to work into their late 60s or have medical conditions that may presage a short life. They should take benefits before 70. Everyone, however, should understand the tradeoffs involved in taking benefits and how to maximize the value of their Social Security.

Employers must act. Employers have exited the pension business en masse, viewing it as too costly and too risky. That is not entirely bad—if companies replace pensions with well-designed portable 401(k) plans or their equivalent. Workers with their own retirement accounts can change jobs or become self-employed without losing the funds that they've accumulated. Employers, however, must ensure that all of their employees are automatically enrolled in their retirement plans, and they should make their own contributions of at least 5 percent of an employee's salary (and preferably more).

Employees have the right not to contribute to 401(k) plans, but, whether they do or not, employers should counsel everyone to save for retirement.

Either way, employers should offer all of their employees the option to buy annuities with part of their retirement savings, offer them the option to buy long-term care insurance, and counsel them about the value of these insurance options.

Employers also should implement strategies to prevent discrimination against older workers and those with disabilities, who are often older. While physical endurance and mental capacity diminish with age, experience increases with age, and older workers are often more motivated to perform well than younger workers. For older workers, working longer can go a long way to helping them strengthen their retirement funds, but only if older workers can find suitable jobs.

Policymakers must act. Most importantly, policymakers must address the financial problems of Social Security and Medicare—both of which will run dry of their needed revenues in the coming years—while preserving their central role in retirement security. They can fix Social Security with a modest increase in taxes and reduction in benefits for more affluent recipients. While making these changes, however, policymakers must protect everyone against falling into poverty after a lifetime of work, even if they started collecting benefits at 62. A humane society will not let its oldest citizens live in poverty. Anyone who has spent their career on a production line or carrying boxes deserves to live in retirement with an income that is at least above the poverty line, if not substantially higher.

Medicare is a tougher problem to solve. The Affordable Care Act helped restrain the annual growth in Medicare costs, but that problem is far from solved. America's healthcare system has features that make costs excessive for both the young and old. Policymakers must not require retirees to pay more of their own bills for essential health services than they can afford on retiree incomes.

The tax code offers valuable retirement savings incentives. Workers can contribute to 401(k)-type plans and IRAs from their before-tax income, and the returns on retirement assets are exempt from tax as they accrue. Retirees pay back the Treasury for some of these tax savings because, when they withdraw funds from their plans, their withdrawals are taxed as ordinary income. Nevertheless, the tax code's retirement provisions cost the

Treasury about $250 billion a year in lost revenue, and their tax benefits go overwhelmingly to high-income taxpayers who typically do not need tax incentives to secure a retirement nest egg.[12]

Policymakers should change these tax incentives so they provide most of their benefits to low- and middle-income households. Policymakers, for instance, could provide the same per-dollar benefit for retirement saving for everyone, regardless of income. Low-income retirement savers also could receive an automatic federal matching contribution for every dollar they contribute, up to a certain amount. In fact, low-income households could receive federal contributions to their accounts even if they themselves can't contribute to them.

For these tax incentives to work, every household would need access to a 401(k)-type plan. Currently, nearly half of all workers don't have it. Some states are providing access to retirement accounts to state residents, and more may do so. A federal program, however, would eliminate problems that can occur when people move from one state that provides access to another that does not.

Laws that preclude discrimination against women and minorities are strong and effective. Court rulings, however, have undermined the effectiveness of laws against age discrimination. Plaintiffs find it very hard to prove discrimination, and, as a result, many cases are never brought to court and employers rarely face penalties when they discriminate. As we discuss later in more detail, policymakers should amend the law to give age discrimination the same status in the courts as other forms of discrimination.

Although, as we have said, employers should offer insurance products to their employees as part of standard retirement packages and explain their advantages for workers once they become retirees, policymakers must improve the markets for these products through legislation or regulation. For example, long-term care insurance is very expensive, and it only partially covers costs. As a result, few people buy it. Consumers should have a choice of standard policies that they can understand and that employers can offer.

WE CAN DO THIS

Our agenda is ambitious, and it requires widespread buy-in from a wide range of stakeholders. It requires that the president and Congress enact laws to amend the tax code, Social Security, and a host of other programs. It requires that companies alter their practices and take a more active role in their workers' retirements. And it requires that households act differently: save more, get smarter about their finances, and trade part of their 401(k) balances for insurance products.

These steps will not prove easy for policymakers, companies, or families to take, nor will they inevitably take them. But our agenda does not represent a radical change to the existing system. Social Security and Medicare will remain at the center of American retirement, and company retirement plans will remain the principal way that workers save. If policymakers, companies, and families do their part, we envision a much more secure and prosperous retirement system.

So, let's begin by taking stock of where we are. How well are we doing when it comes to preparing for retirement? That is a surprisingly difficult question to answer.

Retirement

How Are We Doing?

Is America facing a retirement saving crisis? Those who see a crisis note the near extinction of company pensions, low 401(k) balances for most workers when they retire, high poverty among older single women, soaring out-of-pocket health costs for retirees, and a Social Security Trust Fund that's expected to be exhausted in 2034.[1]

Those who do not see a crisis point to the trillions of dollars that Americans have saved collectively for retirement, a Social Security system that has provided important retirement benefits for decades, low poverty among elderly persons, massive public spending on programs that promote a healthy retirement, and research showing that most households have been able to maintain their standard of living after they stop working.

We would not use the term "crisis," but the retirement system has serious problems. Pensions, Social Security, and savings have been the traditional supports for families in retirement,[2] supplemented by the Medicare health insurance program. This system is still working well for most current retirees. For example, a study using data from 2012 found that median household income of those 65 and older was $44,400[3] (compared to just over $51,000, the median for all households), and the poverty rate was only 6.9 percent, lower than that of the general population.[4] But not all current retirees are doing well, particularly older, single women and people of color, and, while most retirees today seem to be managing, the future looks more challenging with pensions disappearing and Social Security stressed.

As we discussed in Chapter 1, the retirement world has changed, and many American families have not adjusted to the new retirement reality, are not saving enough to replace the pensions they would have had in the past, and are not well-equipped to manage the uncertainties they face. The very nature of American retirement places too much risk on the backs of retirees.

Along with the disappearance of traditional pensions, building an adequate retirement nest egg has become more difficult because interest rates have been so low. Funds placed in bank accounts or safe bonds like Treasurys will earn returns that likely will not even keep up with inflation. The stock market promises higher returns but with much greater risk. A mix of stocks and bonds may be best for most people, but interest rates that are low relative to inflation mean that retirement savers must either save more or take greater risks to reach a given financial goal.

Even those who have had healthy incomes and saved considerable retirement funds face substantial uncertainties. Rather than spending down their retirement nest eggs over time, many retirees feel forced to stockpile assets in case they live longer than expected, need extended care, or experience high health costs. A fundamental part of the problem is the very structure of retirement: the ways that people accumulate assets, including through individually owned 401(k) plans and home equity, do not give people protection against the array of potential financial risks that they will face in retirement. As a result of this flawed system, a significant fraction of the population is not prepared for retirement.

DEFINED-BENEFIT PENSIONS AND DEFINED CONTRIBUTION (401(K)-TYPE) PLANS

Traditional pensions started as a way to attract and retain workers, particularly during times of worker shortages. These pensions were based on a model in which employees stayed with a single company for much of their working lives and, when they retired, received a pension that was often structured as a percentage of the salary they received during the last few years of employment. The employer was responsible for funding the pension payments, which lasted until the retiree died, sometimes with a provision to support a surviving spouse. These pensions were known as *defined-benefit plans* because employees knew how much they would receive, at least in relation to their future salary. The company providing the pension carried the risk of financial market fluctuations and retiree longevity. The highest pension participation rates were by government workers and unions members, although large companies frequently offered pension benefits as well.

Starting in the 1970s, private companies moved away from traditional pensions and toward retirement plans in which the employer contributed a percentage of the employee's salary to a retirement fund. (For companies, these plans are termed "401(k) plans," based on a provision in the federal tax code. Other legal entities operate under similar provisions of the tax code, such as 403(b) plans for non-profits.) These individual retirement accounts are known as *defined-contribution plans* since the employee knows how much the employer is contributing, but then must decide how to invest the fund (usually choosing among a set of mutual funds that the employer suggests). Up to an annual cap, employees can add their own tax-advantaged contributions to whatever the employer puts in their retirement fund; in some plans, the employer contributes only a small amount or nothing at all and employees largely fund their retirement accounts.

Once the employee retires, he or she must manage their own retirement fund, decide how to draw the money out over time, and assess whether there will be enough to last their lifetimes. For this reason, 401(k) plans are often deemed riskier for the worker. While this may well be a fair assessment, workers with defined-benefit pensions also bear risk—such as the risk that their pension plan does not have the assets to make all payments or that they don't work for an employer long enough to gain benefits.

Generally, contributions to 401(k)-type plans come from before-tax income so that neither the employer nor employee pays tax on the amounts they place into these funds (up to a maximum amount under tax law). Once the retiree draws from their fund, however, they must pay taxes on what they take out (at that point, most people will pay a lower tax rate than they would have paid on their income while they were employed). To limit the tax break that 401(k) plans provide, retirees must make minimum withdrawals of a percentage of their fund each year—a percentage that rises with age. This required minimum distribution (RMD) starts when the individual reaches age 72, although of course they can start withdrawals earlier and draw out larger amounts. What remains in retirement funds when a retiree dies can be passed to their heirs, subject to complex tax provisions.

Self-employed workers, and workers without access to a 401(k)-type plan, can still make contributions to an Individual Retirement Account (IRA) with before-tax income. Furthermore, once an employee retires, the amount in their 401(k)-type plan is typically "rolled over" into an IRA account.

To encourage people not to draw on their 401(k) funds too early, the tax law imposes a tax penalty on amounts that account owners take out before age 59½, thus encouraging retirement saving and discouraging people from taking money out before they retire.[5] For savers facing an emergency, an extensive set of rules lets owners take "hardship withdrawals" or loans from their accounts. These rules are intended to provide a measure of emergency access while still preserving the accounts' purpose as a retirement saving vehicle.

We talk more about traditional defined-benefit pension plans versus defined-contribution (401(k)-type) plans later in this book, and we make some of the following key points:

- With traditional pensions, the employer makes the saving and investment decisions and then carries the investment and longevity risk. With defined-contribution plans, the worker carries those risks.
- Traditional, defined-benefit pensions were valued highly by workers but in practice they have not been the majority of private-sector retirement plans for a number of years, and, as we have said, these plans are being phased out in most firms.[6]
- An important advantage of 401(k)-type plans is that they let workers change jobs more easily and build up retirement

assets even if they move from employer to employer or are
self-employed.

- Another advantage of defined-contribution plans is that the
moneys invested remain intact even if the company goes
bankrupt. If a company with traditional pensions goes bankrupt,
however, the pensions are taken over by a federal agency, the
Pension Benefit Guaranty Corporation, and the benefits are often
reduced.
- A concern about 401(k)-type plans or IRAs is that affluent
families use them the most and get the biggest tax break from
them.

ASSESSING HOW WELL AMERICANS ARE PREPARED FOR RETIREMENT

It is surprisingly hard to assess how well-prepared Americans are for retirement. Economists use very different approaches, and it is difficult to
collect reliable data. You would think that a simple strategy would be
to speak with a sample of households and ask them where they stand.
Unfortunately, that does not necessarily produce accurate estimates. Data
from government sources like the Social Security Administration and the
IRS do not jibe with information from surveys, even when the surveys are
carefully conducted with in-person interviews. We will not burden our
readers with all the reasons why it is hard to assess Americans' preparedness for retirement, but it is worth highlighting the most important issues
and trying to draw a reasonable bottom line.

The Life Cycle Model

Economists seek a framework (or model) within which to examine savings and consumption decisions over people's lifetimes. They prefer the
life cycle model, which looks at what a rational household would decide

about how much to spend and how much to save to ensure that they have a sound retirement.[7] The life cycle model predicts that people save part of their incomes when they are working, build up a retirement fund, and then use the money to live on when they retire. The amount saved will depend on how long people stay in the workforce, how much money they make, and how they plan to spend their retirement. Rational households, the model finds, will smooth consumption over their lifetimes, keeping spending at a similar level across years but also saving to protect against running out of money in old age, at a time when it would be very hard to go back to work. Households must also budget for large foreseen and unforeseen expenses, like home repairs or an unexpected illness.

Data on household consumption show it rising as people's incomes grow in their peak earning years and then declining in retirement. That makes sense. Families with children consume more, and older people no longer need to pay for work clothes or the cost of commuting, and many of them own their homes and do not have to pay a mortgage. Older people spend less on food, raising concerns that they cannot afford enough to eat. That concern is valid for some poor older families, but generally the decline in food consumption comes because older people eat out less often than younger people.[8]

A 2006 paper by John Karl Scholz, Ananth Seshadri, and Surachai Khitatrakun built a sophisticated life cycle model that incorporated risky outcomes, like unknown earnings and unexpected health problems, to estimate an optimal wealth target for households with different characteristics. They then applied their model to roughly 10,000 households born between 1931 and 1941, using data through 1992. The results were striking.

American households born in the 1930s, they concluded, were doing a sound job of hitting their wealth targets. Only 15.6 percent of households were undersaving, and the undersavers tended to be short by only a few thousand dollars (typically, the gap was just $5,260 in 1992 dollars, or about $10,000 today).[9] Some demographic groups tended overwhelmingly to hit their optimal wealth targets. An impressive 95 percent of the highest-earning households tended to hit their optimal wealth targets[10], and married households also did particularly well.[11] A follow-up study by Scholz, Seshadri, and William G. Gale found that American households were not doing quite as well: when they looked at a wider range of birth cohorts (not just those born between 1931 and 1941) and updated the data to 2004, they found that roughly three-quarters of Americans were hitting their wealth targets.[12]

Is the Life Cycle Model a Good Guide to the Future?

On the face of it, the conclusions from this research seem to fit well with the findings that we reported earlier in this chapter showing that older households in 2012 generally had incomes not too far from the incomes of all households. But it is important to look under the hood: *How* have families hit their retirement targets? In the middle of the income distribution, households aged 65 and older get about half of their income from Social Security, about a quarter from traditional (defined-benefit) pensions, about 10 or 12 percent from continuing to work for pay, only 6 percent from IRA accounts, and 5 percent from interest and dividends. That is, retiree households are not relying on drawing down their retirement savings but instead are getting most of their income from employer or government programs and from continued work. At the bottom of the income distribution, as you might expect, Social Security accounts for around 80 percent of income.[13] Even at the top of the income distribution, IRA income is only 10 or 12 percent, and most of the income of these groups comes from pensions and earnings. Social Security is still important for all but the very top 10 percent of the income ladder, accounting for a quarter or a third of income. This does not suggest that the life cycle model was wrong, but it does suggest that we need to be careful in our interpretation. Historically, at least, Americans have relied on the government and employers to make the saving decisions and manage their retirement funds.[14] Surveys of household wealth confirm that most households have only modest amounts saved in retirement accounts or indeed in any financial asset.[15] Except for those in the top wealth brackets, retiree wealth comes mostly from the lifetime value of their Social Security benefits and from what they have accumulated in their family homes. (The notion of characterizing Social Security benefits as wealth is not entirely obvious. Economists often include expected Social Security benefits in household wealth because the benefits are structured like an annuity, which is a form of wealth.)

Since pensions are disappearing, one main source of retiree income will eventually dissipate, suggesting that households will have to assume much more responsibility for their own saving. Since many retirees hold much of their wealth in their family home, an important consideration for them will be how they take advantage of the home equity they own. (We address this issue in much more detail later in the book.)

Some middle- and upper-income households accumulate substantial financial assets for retirement, but they often don't use it in predictable ways. A large fraction of this affluent group does not draw down their wealth to live on in retirement, as a finding from academic studies shows; instead, they hold onto the money and watch it grow larger. Shockingly, they have more wealth at 85 than they had at 65![16] We do not know for sure why they do this, but one plausible answer is that they are worried they will need to pay for an expensive nursing home or in-home care at some point in the future. And they figure that if that turns out not to be true, then their children will get the money. There is nothing irrational about doing this, but it puts a different perspective on the life cycle model. Rather than using retirement savings to live more comfortably in their golden years, many families feel that they must hold on to their savings in case they face a huge expense in their last few years.

This tendency to hoard savings can extend even to obvious oversaving during working years. Saving is a virtue, but oversaving has a serious downside. It means that many people shortchange their happiness in their younger years, foregoing the happiness that can come from everything from a family vacation to a larger house. Beyond concerns about the need for nursing home care, these households engage in "precautionary saving" in case they live longer than average and run out of assets, forcing them to live solely on a Social Security check.

Behavioral Perspectives

If people try to follow the behavior that the life cycle model implies, that puts heavy demands on their ability to make the right decisions and do so while facing much uncertainty. Someone in their 30s or 40s has to look ahead 50 years or even more, factor in how much income they will make, consider the fluctuations in inflation and investment markets, think about their children's college expenses, and decide whether they will need end-of-life care and what it will cost.

Two psychologists, Daniel Kahneman and Amos Tversky, questioned whether it is correct to attribute this level of rationality to people and if actual behavior matched the life cycle model. They found that people often do not make good decisions when they face complex, uncertain situations. This contribution proved so noteworthy that Kahneman won the Nobel Prize in economics for his work.[17]

Economist Richard Thaler, who also won a Noble Prize, focused on savings and retirement decisions and found that many Americans are not saving enough to maintain their standard of living. Among other reforms, he advocates for company retirement savings plans in which employees automatically enroll unless they specifically choose to opt out. This call for automatic enrollment is part of a broader argument by Thaler and others that people will benefit if they are "nudged" to save more, including through saving plans in which the result of "doing nothing" is having part of your paycheck deposited into a retirement account.[18] Indeed, in instances when it's been tried, automatic enrollment has dramatically increased participation in savings plans.

An attendant problem, which is the focus of a later chapter, is why saving is so hard for so many. Economist David Laibson, a leader in this field, concluded that saving problems are the result of the overwhelming power of immediate consumption—a force so great for so many that it overshadows people's desire to protect their future selves. He suggests that people pre-commit to a retirement savings plan that locks them into saving.[19] Under Laibson's approach, we should protect our savings from the lure of the latest tech product or luxury car by setting rules for saving before we feel the inevitable pull to spend.

Other Approaches

These considerations suggest that a simpler, more pragmatic approach to assessing retirement preparedness may be appropriate. One such approach is the concept of replacement rates, whereby workers aim to accumulate enough saving to "replace" a particular proportion of their working-years income. One notable measure is calculated by Boston College's Center for Retirement Research (CRR), which, since 2006, has published a replacement rate-based measure known as the National Retirement Risk Index and which published its most recent measure in January 2021. The CRR uses this index to estimate the share of pre-retirement households that are saving adequately for retirement. The heart of the analysis compares CRR's "target" replacement rates with the replacement rates that households could expect given their current income and saving path. CRR assumes that replacement rates differ somewhat by marital status and income level, and the percentages differ by marital status because some household costs rise as the number of people in the household grows.

CRR then uses Federal Reserve information on consumer finances[20] to determine what fraction of Americans are "at risk" of being unable to meet their target level of consumption in retirement. The results are sobering. CRR estimated that for households that retire at age 65, 49 percent are at risk. This figure is down slightly from the 2016 estimate due to stock market and home price increases, but it is much higher than the 43 percent estimate of households based on 2004 data before the financial crisis. The pandemic and the inflation of 2022 have undoubtedly made the at-risk group larger also. CRR concludes that younger households are not preparing themselves for retirement as well as earlier generations did and are more in danger of being at risk when they retire: 58 percent of those in households in their 30s and 48 percent in their 40s are in the at-risk category. CRR did not have comparable data covering the COVID-19 pandemic, but it estimated that the percentage of all households in the at-risk category rose to 51 percent due to the effects of COVID-19.

Another simple way to assess retirement preparedness is to survey households. The results show a picture of a "glass half full and half empty." In April of 2019, a Gallup poll of working age Americans found that 57 percent of non-retired American expected to be able to live comfortably in retirement. That figure had risen substantially since 2012, when just 38 percent of non-retirees said they expected a comfortable retirement. And a long-running survey by the Employee Benefit Research Institute found that, in 2015, 58 percent of Americans were either very confident (22 percent) or somewhat confident (36 percent) that they would have enough money to live comfortably in retirement (based on their own definition of "enough"). Lots of Americans are comfortable with or confident about their prospects for retirement, this survey says, but 42 percent are not.

A 2020 survey (during the pandemic) reported by the Federal Reserve Board[21] found a more troubling picture of how people are doing. The survey found that only 36 percent of households thought their retirement saving was "on track," while 44 percent said they were "not on track" and 20 percent were not sure. There were sizable racial differences, with 42 percent of Whites saying their saving was on track while only 25 percent of Blacks said the same. The same survey also found that 26 percent of respondents reported they had no retirement saving.

The bottom line on retirement saving is that most of *today's* seniors are having their basic needs met, while many are thriving. Current retirees are still benefitting from traditional pensions while also enjoying reliable income from Social Security. There are certainly older Americans today who are short of money and struggling to find enough for food, medicine, and living expenses, but these are the exceptions. The best evidence suggests a low poverty rate among those older than 65 and adequate income among the majority.

The comfort of today's retirees, however, does not mean that *tomorrow's* retirees will fare as well or that the current system is perfect. The dearth of pensions for current workers means that there are many more questions about the adequacy of saving for future generations. Not all workers today have access to a retirement plan, like a 401(k), and many find it hard to contribute each month given their low wages and high day-to-day expenses.

Indeed, as the retirement system evolves toward individual accounts and away from company pensions, Americans will have to adjust to a world in which they manage their own retirement. In contrast to that of years ago, this system confers an enormous amount of risk on families that, in turn, respond by changing the way they save, consume, and invest. We have said that uncertainty plays a critical role in retirement planning, and, in the next section, we expand on this point and describe the importance of uncertainty on retirement, a theme that is pervasive throughout the book.

THE CRITICAL ROLE OF UNCERTAINTY

Much of the discussion around retirement saving and spending focuses on what amount each household should save. The complicated part of this approach is that no one knows what their future holds. Will they get sick? Live to 110? Pick the best performing stocks or receive a large inheritance? The right amount of saving for one person may not be enough another— and luck has a lot to do with it.

Perhaps the greatest uncertainty is lifespan: people simply don't know how long they'll live. Life expectancy, which is a well-known concept, is the average number of years that people who were born in a given year will live. We can make the same calculation for people at any given age. For instance, how long will someone likely live once they've reached the age of, say, 20, or 30, or 60.[22]

In the United States, life expectancy has been gradually rising, from about 50 years at the turn of the 20th century to close to 80 today. But progress has been stagnating in America (especially compared to other developed countries), with virtually no growth in the years leading up to COVID-19 and a small, sharp drop due to its impacts on mortality in

2020. While health experts do not expect COVID-19's impact on life expectancy to endure, the ongoing stagnation is more concerning.

The path of population-wide life expectancy is one uncertainty: at age 30, a person doesn't know how long people in her birth cohort will be living when she reaches retirement. Will medical advancements and healthier lifestyle make "80 the new 60," with much higher life expectancy in 2060? Or will stagnating, or even declining, life expectancies mean that lifespans will be less, on average, than expected?

Population-wide change in life expectancy is just one uncertainty; another is that, for a given life expectancy, people simply don't know how long they themselves will live, no matter the population-wide average. Social Security Administration estimates illustrate the size of this uncertainty. In 2017, the median 60-year-old man was expected to live to 82 and the median 60-year-old woman to live to 85.[23] But, as Figure 2.1 shows, the actual ages at which people would die varied greatly around those medians. Given the mortality patterns of 2017, about a third of men who were then 60 would live to 87 (i.e., 5 years beyond the median) and about 12 percent to 93 (11 years beyond the median). Among 60-year-old women, about a third would live to 90 (again, an extra 5 years) and about 10 percent to 96 (again, an extra 11).[24] Those with higher earnings have significantly longer life expectancies than those with lower earnings, and the longevity gap between them has been growing.[25] As longevity rises, the shares of men and women living to advanced ages will grow even more. (In 2020, COVID-19 cut life expectancy in America by 1.5 years.)[26]

To some extent, individuals may be able to predict when they will likely die. However, in reality, the evidence suggests that people are not very good at such predictions. In 1992, researchers asked people between the ages of 51 and 61 to assess the probability that they would live to 75, and they could express that probability from 0 to 100 percent in 10-percentage-point increments (e.g., 20 percent, 30 percent, and so on).[27] By 2010, as shown in Table 2.1, researchers could see how many of the older interviewees—those born between 1931 and 1934—had made it to age 75.

A large share of people reported probabilities of 50 or 100 percent. The more optimistic one was, the likelier that one would live longer.[28]

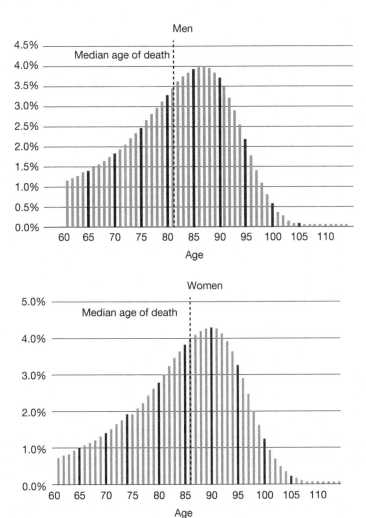

Figure 2.1 Distribution of projected age of death for men and women age 60, as of 2017.
SOURCE: Social Security Administration Period Life Tables.

Nevertheless, actual survival rates differed notably from anticipated survival rates. Among those who thought they had a low chance of living to 75, actual survival rates were consistently higher, sometimes by a lot. Roughly half of those who said they had no chance of living to 75 actually did. Among those who thought they had a 40 or 50 percent chance, the share living to 75 was considerably larger (69 percent and 75 percent, respectively).

Table 2.1 Chances of living to age 75, based on expectations: Weighted
tabulation of actual survival to age 75 by response to question
about subjective mortality expectation asked in 1992 of persons aged
58–61 years. Source: Abraham and Harris (2016).

Subjective probability of living to age 75	Actual probability of living to age 75	Unweighted sample size
0	49.2	218
10	59.9	65
20	64.6	107
30	71.2	130
40	68.9	110
50	75.1	702
60	78.4	168
70	80.9	284
80	80.1	434
90	82.5	222
100	78.2	664

Uncertainty over longevity and the difficulty of planning for it are even bigger for married (or cohabitating) couples. Because couples plan for the retirement of all household members, they must account for the probability that one or both will live to 80, or 90, or even older.

Uncertainty over longevity, of course, makes retirement planning exceptionally hard. Beyond that, unknown health costs, including for long-term care, can further complicate planning. Out-of-pocket spending for health services among 75- to 79-year-olds in 2003, for instance, averaged about $2,400, with those costs rising to nearly $22,000 for those who spent the most.[29]

Another uncertainty centers around healthcare costs. Nearly all those older than 65 are covered by Medicare or an employer-sponsored plan, but not all healthcare expenses are covered, and retirees must make co-payments. The biggest healthcare uncertainty arises for those who need full-time care in a nursing home or from a full-time, at-home care specialist. Those without significant assets, or who run through their assets, can be admitted to a Medicaid-funded nursing home. The quality of care in these homes is often not very good, so many families try to avoid them. As we noted earlier, upper middle-class families who have saved a substantial nest egg at retirement often do not use their savings for regular living expenses but instead hoard them, so they often have funds to help cover such healthcare costs and avoid a Medicaid-funded nursing home.

Another uncertainty is the return on investments. Stock returns can be especially volatile; over the past 20 years, the S&P 500 index has risen in 15 years and fallen in 5, with returns rising by as much as 29.6 percent and falling by as much as 38.5 percent, year over year. Interest rates matter, too, not just for holders of interest-bearing bonds but for retirees who want to convert their savings to annuities (whose price depends critically on interest rates). Interest rates also affect the costs that some retirees bear, including those who have incurred credit card debt or who hold a variable rate mortgage.

Tax policy adds an additional uncertainty. Its main source is changing tax rates, but other tax changes can affect retirement planning as well. Tax rates on both ordinary and investment income change the amount that a saver needs to save. Income tax rate cuts in 2001 and 2017, for instance, raised the after-tax value of retirement savings since contributions to retirement plans[30] were typically exempt from income tax, but withdrawals will largely be taxed at individual income tax rates.[31] Still more uncertainty comes from changes to the rules governing retirement plans, such as the 2019 change to annual required minimum distributions that let people draw down their retirement savings more slowly without facing a penalty.

One uncertainty that's particularly hard to quantify is the potential for changes to two major public programs: Social Security and Medicare. The Social Security Trust Fund is currently projected to be exhausted in 2034, meaning that it won't have sufficient funds to pay all the benefits owed to retirees. At that point, the government would have to cut benefits or raise new revenue, such as by increasing payroll taxes that finance Social Security or transferring funds from the Treasury. While a future president and Congress almost certainly will not let Social Security benefits for current retirees be cut without significant advance notice for retirees—the reforms that President Reagan and Congress enacted in 1983 are still phasing in today—there's no guarantee that policymakers will preserve the full benefits that the law currently requires. Similarly, concerns over soaring health costs could prompt reforms to Medicare, which could affect out-of-pocket health spending for retirees.

Housing is an underappreciated uncertainty. Home ownership represents one of the largest investments of retirees, with housing comprising about a fifth of total assets for households aged 60 and older. A golden rule of investing is to diversify, which means to hold a range of different assets that do not all rise and fall together. An owner-occupied home is an undiversified investment, a single piece of property, which makes it a risky investment. On the other hand, housing prices historically have been far less volatile than stocks. That convinced many people that real estate was a very safe investment despite the lack of diversification. The housing price decline of 2007 and beyond shattered many beliefs about housing's safety as an investment. There were sharp declines in home prices across many US markets, and prices remained depressed for some time. Housing risk does not just apply to homeowners. Roughly 22 percent of retirement-age households are renters, and, for these households, market rents comprise a large share of their spending. Rent increases can cut deeply into the standard of living of low- and moderate-income households.

Inflation poses a risk for retirees, particularly those who have purchased bonds as an important part of their retirement assets. Inflation erodes the value of most bonds, reducing their purchasing power. However, there are some mitigating factors that can reduce the effect of inflation on retirees. First, most older households get much of their income and in-kind benefits through Social Security checks and Medicare benefits, both of which are adjusted for inflation. Second, inflation has a marked impact on most debt, but relatively few older households are debtors since they've paid off their mortgages, student loans, and car loans. Third, some private sources of income, such as inflation-indexed Treasury bonds, are explicitly linked to prices. Nevertheless, for the small share of households that are either heavily invested in bonds or, conversely, that owe money through fixed-rate debt (like mortgages), inflation can be a meaningful risk to consider. Inflation had been very moderate for a number of years but in 2022 inflation jumped, causing distress to workers and retirees. This episode reminds us that inflation risk has not disappeared.

For older households, the various sources of uncertainty are compounded by the difficulty in mitigating their effects. Typically, younger households have more flexibility to increase their work hours if they need to address a shortfall in income; it's usually very difficult or impossible for an 80-year-old retiree to return to work if he or she needs more income to maintain their standard of living. Also, cost increases or income declines are often related to an event that permanently changes a household's financial outlook. A spouse's death often can mean sharp declines in Social Security, pension, or annuity benefits, while the need for long-term care can mean prolonged higher costs for care.

Much of this book addresses sources of uncertainty and how to mitigate them. For example, we later discuss how annuities—contracts that pay a given amount for life—can help people handle uncertainty about lifespan. And long-term care insurance can help address uncertainty about illness and need for care. As a general matter, one of the biggest criticisms of the current retirement system is that, outside of Social Security and Medicare, it presents few options for addressing uncertainty. In the third section of the book, we suggest how to change that.

SUMMING UP

Many of the issues confronting our country—and planet—seem out of control, if not hopeless. Retirement presents a more hopeful picture. Today's retirees are mostly doing well. Social Security has provided a reliable source of retirement income for 85 years, and Medicare provides essential health insurance to almost all older Americans. Some building blocks of a strong retirement system are in place, but it will take major changes to ensure that future retirement is secure. Social Security and Medicare's preservations are a top priority to ensure that no retirees are forced into poverty. But Social Security provides only a minimum level of income, and it is just one piece of the retirement puzzle. To ensure a comfortable retirement for most Americans requires a new paradigm in which households learn to save consistently, manage their funds, and deal with the uncertainties that all of us face. Employers and policymakers will need to help because most people struggle to do this on their own. The rest of this book is devoted to outlining this new paradigm.

A new paradigm for retirement, however, would do more than ensure a comfortable retirement for millions of Americans. It also would help spur more economic growth, as we see in the next chapter.

Retirement and Economic Growth

There is a profound connection between retirement and economic growth that moves in two directions. The rate of economic growth impacts retirement programs, while the retirement decisions of families influence the speed of economic growth.

The first of these effects is large, and we mention it at several points in this book. Specifically, economic stagnation due to slowing growth in the labor force and productivity puts a lot of stress on Social Security and Medicare finances. The second effect is smaller, though still important: rising household saving makes more funds available for investment, an important source of economic growth.[1]

We start by looking at the first of these effects: how the slowdown in economic growth has impacted the retirement landscape.

THE IMPACT OF SLOW ECONOMIC GROWTH
ON RETIREMENT POLICIES AND DECISIONS

Strong population growth has been a US trend. In 1700, America's population was an estimated 251,000, rising to 5.3 million by 1800, 76.2 million by 1900, and 331.4 million by April 2020.[2] Each generation of Americans has been larger than its predecessor, and the belief that this would persist was a factor in how policymakers designed Social Security's retirement program. In recent years, however, the population growth rate has slowed dramatically. Each generation is still larger than the one before, but not by much.

As discussed in greater detail in the next chapter, Social Security's largest component by far is the retirement program from which Americans receive benefits monthly, with the benefit level depending on each individual's work history and the age at which they choose to start collecting benefits (between ages 62 and 70). Workers pay payroll taxes on their wages to finance the retirement benefits of current retirees. For many years after the program started, tax contributions exceeded benefits paid, nourishing a substantial trust fund that reached $2.9 trillion in 2019.[3]

Over time, policymakers expanded benefits,[4] retirees lived longer, and, importantly, the rate of increase in the population slowed. After World War II, families had more children, and this fertility boost continued into the 1950s. In 1960 the fertility rate—the number of children per woman— was 3.65, but this fell to 2.01 by 1972 and 1.71 by 2019.[5] At this rate, the population would actually be declining over time, and it is only immigration that maintains population growth.[6] COVID-19 has caused an additional decline in the fertility rate, with the number of births falling 4 percent between 2019 and 2020.[7] With the pandemic continuing into 2021, we will have to wait and see whether births pick up once it is finally over.

The decline in fertility translated into a slowdown in the rate of labor force growth. The two do not move exactly together because of changes in the number of Americans who choose to work and the availability of jobs. The percent of the population that was working rose from 1960 to the mid-1990s with the influx of young people and the increase in women choosing to work. In 2008 and 2009 the Great Recession triggered a drop in employment, which then gradually recovered until 2019, although the aging of the population is causing a long-term decline in the ratio of employment to population and an increase in the number of people collecting Social Security benefits.[8] These demographic changes, in turn, have caused big shifts in the ratio of workers contributing to the Social Security Trust Fund relative to the number of people drawing benefits. In 1960, there were 6.1 workers paying into the system for each beneficiary, a figure that fell to 3.2 by 1980 and 2.6 by 2020.[9] In 2060, there will be only a projected 2.0 workers contributing for each beneficiary. (COVID-19 caused a sharp drop in employment, but we expect this will be mostly reversed by 2023.)

Largely due to the decline in the number of workers paying into Social Security relative to the number collecting benefits, the trust fund is now shrinking, and the Social Security Administration expects it to be exhausted by 2034. Of course, even after the fund is exhausted, there will be contributions coming into it and policymakers can supplement it with general revenues. Nevertheless, the demographic changes have put this key retirement program under stress.

Richer Than Their Parents?

Another important American belief has been that improvements in technology and productivity will drive income increases that make each generation richer than their parents. Over the long term, the economy has indeed brought affluence to millions, with living standards rising spectacularly especially in the decades after World War II. Recent years have seen a more mixed experience. Although technology seems to move with bewildering speed, productivity growth—the key driver of improvements in living standards—has been sluggish since the early 1970s, as we discuss later in this chapter. Furthermore, large increases in the cost of healthcare have meant that much of the improvement in worker compensation has been absorbed by the cost of health insurance premiums, leaving smaller increases in take-home pay. Also, the distribution of earnings has widened, so that workers at the top of the distribution have done very well but those lower down have seen only modest wage increases, if any. Most American households have had to adjust to a slow pace of improvements in living standards, and some have not been able to enjoy the lifestyles of their parents. What does this mean for retirement?

Slow growth in wages adds to the problem of slow growth in the workforce. As noted, Social Security is financed from the wages of workers, and wage growth across generations has made it easier to finance Social

Security retirement benefits. Now that earnings for most workers are only growing slowly, that puts more of a burden on each generation as they pay payroll taxes to support beneficiaries.

How private retirement saving has been impacted by slower growth is not clear. Private saving rates have varied over time and are lower now than they were at peak periods in the past, but explaining these changes has proven hard. There are offsetting factors. Smaller families create less of a financial burden on the parents. But many people find it hard to accept that their incomes are not rising over time or that they cannot live as well as their parents. Medical bills and housing costs have risen enormously and so have college tuitions. Many families, we believe, find it hard to save adequately for retirement, and a slowly growing economy has made it harder.

THE POTENTIAL IMPACT OF RETIREMENT SAVING ON ECONOMIC GROWTH

What is the best way to spur growth? In what is largely a two-sided debate, one side promotes more tax cuts so that individuals and businesses have more money to save or invest as they see fit. The other side promotes greater public investment in education and training, infrastructure, and other physical capital (such as equipment or software) so that people have the skills to do the increasingly sophisticated jobs of today and tomorrow, and businesses have thriving communities in which to locate.

Retirement policy can also help spur more economic growth. On its own, to be sure, it will not take sluggish growth and make it robust. But retirement policy can make a difference. That is because more saving—which a strong retirement policy would promote—makes more funds available in the economy for investment, and it reduces the need for foreign borrowing to secure investment dollars. In addition, the more years that Americans work—to increase their savings and better prepare for retirement—the larger the labor force will be. That is particularly important because a larger labor force is a key tool of higher economic growth, and the labor force is not expected to grow as quickly in the coming years as it did in the past, as we noted earlier.

In the rest of this chapter, we outline the connection between retirement policies and economic growth. Every other chapter focuses on individuals, in hopes of helping Americans achieve a more secure retirement. This chapter explains why more saving is helpful to the economy as well. We believe that this "macro" perspective is valuable because it offers additional motivation for creating sound retirement policies.

STRONG ECONOMIC GROWTH HAS BEEN ELUSIVE

America's economy has not grown at a consistently high rate in recent decades, in part due to slow population growth. Like other nations with advanced economies, the United States is experiencing lower birth rates, leading to slower growth in the population in general and in the labor force in particular. The labor force grew 1.7 percent a year between 1974 and 2001, but only 0.7 percent a year from 2001 to 2021; in the future, it is projected to grow only about 0.4 percent a year.[10] As the share of Americans working or seeking a job fell, COVID-19 caused a sharp drop in the labor force in 2020 that is only slowly returning to normal.

Slower growth in productivity also has constrained economic growth over the past two decades. After growing strongly for a quarter-century after World War II, the growth in labor productivity (what workers on average produce in a given time period) fell sharply in the early 1970s and has remained sluggish ever since, except for about a decade starting in the mid-1990s.

Together, the slow growth of the labor force and of productivity drive the slow growth in our economy's ability to produce. This concept, known as *potential gross domestic product* (GDP), measures the size of the economy if workers and capital are firing on all cylinders. (Economists use this measure to distinguish "ability to produce" from actual production, as the latter is influenced by the ups and downs of the business cycle.) Before COVID-19, potential GDP grew at only about 2 percent a year from 2002 to 2018, and the Congressional Budget Office (CBO) projected that it would grow by only 1.9 percent a year from 2019 through 2029 and would slow later in the decade. From 1950 to 2002, by contrast, growth averaged more than 3 percent a year.[11]

Slower growth has limited the rise in average living standards and made the nation's long-term federal budget challenge—huge annual deficits and ever-rising debt—even larger. As the population ages, more people become eligible for Social Security, Medicare, and Medicaid, and spending on each of those programs rises as a share of the economy. The rise in that share would be smaller, of course, if the economy were growing faster and the economic pie were expanding more. Meanwhile, slow economic growth limited the financial health of households because wages and incomes have grown more slowly. With wages and incomes only creeping upward, and with the costs of healthcare, education, and other crucial needs growing substantially, middle-class families have experienced a decline in their net wealth since the late 1990s.[12]

Retirement policy is one way to increase national savings. An effective retirement strategy should help ensure that working-age Americans set aside enough money to live comfortably when they retire. Those savings, in turn, can provide the resources for investment that will fuel stronger economic growth—everything from more funding for infrastructure to additional capital for businesses to spend on research and development. In the absence of sufficient US saving, the private sector and government have only two options for financing promising new investments: borrowing from abroad or forgoing the project. Relying on foreign investment can certainly benefit Americans, all else being equal, but it also means that a share of the gains will flow outside our borders; forgoing promising investment is a worse option because, then, productive products never see the light of day.

Retirement policy also should encourage people to keep working rather than retire too early. Life expectancy has risen, and most people are staying healthy longer and can keep working. That would improve the financial status of older households and increase the size of the labor force. By working longer, older Americans can help both themselves and the economy. By reforming tax and benefit laws, changing workplace incentives, and mitigating discrimination against older workers, policymakers and business leaders can change the calculus around retirement so that it makes financial sense for workers to stay in the workforce.

Should Policymakers Foster Higher Economic Growth?

We think so, though the issue can be surprisingly controversial. For several decades, some experts have questioned the value of economic growth,[13] arguing that the modern economy is unsustainable and we will soon run out of natural resources, such as oil and gas, raw materials, and agriculturally suitable land. With global climate change a more recent top concern, others have argued that by generating more pollution, economic growth has made that problem worse. Rather than promote growth, they argue, policymakers should promote a more balanced "sustainable development," meaning a policy that promotes growth without extinguishing scarce natural resources or reducing environmental quality.

Well, the world did *not* run out of natural resources. The productivity of farming soared, and we produced previously unimaginable amounts of food from each acre. We used less water per day in 2015 than in 1970—and with a population that is more than 50 percent larger. And the shift toward a digital economy means that we simply consume less *stuff*. The concern about pollution has proved prophetic, however, with greenhouse gases now mounting a very serious threat to the planet.

Does the pollution threat weaken the argument for policies to increase the pool of investment funds or create new technologies? We do not think so. We strongly support policies to reduce emissions and other pollutants, even if that sacrifices some amount of economic growth. But, in shifting from traditional energy sources to cleaner alternatives, the nation will have an even greater need for higher saving and higher rates of productivity. That is because a massive shift in energy production requires an equally massive investment in research and a retooling of the energy infrastructure. Indeed, funds for investment are a necessary component in the critical transformation to renewable energy and away from fossil fuels.

Should Policymakers Encourage People to Work Longer?

In France, in late 2019, workers launched strikes to protest retirement policy reforms that included an increase, from 62 to 64, in the age at which retirees could get their full retirement benefits. French workers are famous for striking, but Americans might have reacted similarly because raising the normal retirement age is unpopular with Americans as well.

In this book, we do not propose policies to force anyone to work longer. In fact, we argue that Social Security reforms should ensure that no one ends up in poverty after a lifetime of work, even those who decide to stop working at 62 and begin drawing Social Security benefits. Nevertheless, the nation faces some tough arithmetic.

In prior decades, with a higher birth rate and a younger population in general, there were many more workers than retirees in the United States and, with workers funding Social Security and Medicare through payroll taxes, the financing burdens on those workers were not great. As America's birth rate fell, however, the number of workers per retiree fell with it, raising the burden on the workers of today and tomorrow to support the retirees of their day.[14] Their burden grew even more with the increase in life expectancy, which means that workers are supporting more retirees for a longer period of time. Those who retire today at 62 may live 25 or 30 more years in retirement.

Meanwhile, the federal government is already running very large deficits. This was true before COVID-19, and deficits have ballooned even more due to the crisis. Few politicians have expressed credible concern about long-term deficits in recent years, but that will likely change at some point.[15] When it does, policymakers will seek to slow the growth of spending on all social programs—including Social Security, Medicare, and Medicaid, which do so much to cover the pension and health needs of retirees. Given these trends, we should seek ways to enable people to work longer as part of their retirement planning. That, in turn, will help a bit to offset the decline in labor force growth.

The rate of labor force participation (i.e., people who are either working or seeking work) is important because so much of economic growth is determined by the amount of labor that a country's workforce supplies.[16] Recent trends portend a steady decline in the share of Americans willing to work: labor force participation has fallen from 66.0 percent in December of 2007 to 62.2 percent in June of 2022—a 3.8 percentage-point decline overall and an annual decline of 0.4 percent.[17] Put differently, that decline in participation means about 5 million fewer workers in the economy—more than enough to dampen economic growth. And the pandemic has pushed down participation even further, by 2.4 percentage points between March 2020 and April 2020, before an increase as the economy recovered.[18] The medium-term trend is unknown.

Economist Jason Furman and his colleagues examined the sources of this decline since the end of 2007 and its modest recovery since around 2015.[19] Almost all of the decline, they conclude, is due to the aging of the population since workers in older age brackets have lower participation rates than those in the prime age bracket, 25–54. In short, the aging of America is reducing economic growth by about 0.4 percent a year.[20]

In an encouraging sign, workers who are older than 55 are generally working longer. As illustrated by Figure 3.1, labor force participation among those 60–64 was 57.3 percent in 2018, compared to 44.2 percent in 1987. The upward shift is greatest for those older than 75, with participation

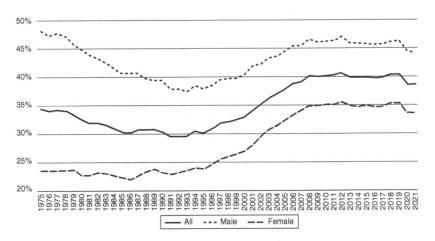

Figure 3.1 Civilian US labor force participation rates for those ages 55 or older, by gender, 1975–2021.

more than doubling between 1987 and 2018. People are choosing to work longer, realizing they need to save more before they retire and postpone the age at which they start collecting Social Security benefits.

The aging of the workforce will dominate labor force growth in the coming years but raising both labor force participation and the employment of older workers will mitigate that trend, helping to grow potential GDP.

INVESTMENT BENEFITS BOTH WORKERS AND THE ECONOMY

When workers or their employers contribute to retirement accounts, and when these funds are invested in a sound portfolio of stocks, bonds, and other financial assets, workers become invested not only in companies but in the overall economy. Even if contributions are small at first, consistent retirement saving will grow over time to significant sums, giving households an ownership stake in productive assets and making them wealthier.

To the extent that workers can accumulate assets that grow over time, they will benefit more from economic growth and perhaps reduce dissatisfaction with the economy as more workers enjoy the fruits of economic growth. Realistically, low-wage workers will not become millionaires through their 401(k) plans, but, with the help of policy changes, they can accumulate retirement assets that will help them considerably.

Consider a worker who earns $30,000 a year ($2,500 a month) and puts 2.5 percent of his or her monthly earnings ($62.50) into a retirement account. Suppose, in turn, that some combination of an employer match and a tax incentive doubled that amount to boost the total monthly retirement saving to $125.

If the funds were invested at a 3 percent rate of return (after accounting for fees and inflation), the worker would retire at 70 with close to $138,000[21]—not as a millionaire, but with savings equal to 4.6 times annual earnings and enough to help meet unexpected retirement expenses or supplement Social Security benefits. Over time, that worker will see these retirement assets grow and recognize the payoff from investing in the economy.

Meanwhile, retirement policy can boost the economy as well by helping to increase labor supply and savings. The debate over how to spur greater economic growth has tended to ignore this important point since, as we have said, it has focused on either tax policy (with an emphasis on cutting taxes) or on public investment, such as improving roads, ports, or schools.

When economists think about the drivers of economic growth, they typically separate the effect of capital investment on labor productivity growth from the effect of other sources of growth, such as technological change, new products, or improved operating efficiencies. These other sources are grouped together under *total factor productivity growth*, or TFP growth.[22] Figure 3.2 shows this breakdown for three periods starting in 1985.

- The first period, 1985–1995, shows slow growth of labor productivity, 1.28 percent a year, with contributions from capital

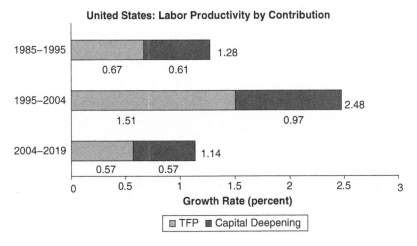

Figure 3.2 The contributions of capital deepening and total factor productivity (TFP) growth to the growth of GDP per hour worked.
SOURCE: OECD Productivity Statistics.

deepening and from TFP split roughly equally between these two
contributing factors.

- The second period, 1995–2004, shows much faster growth,
  2.48 percent a year, with greater contributions from both TFP and
  capital. The larger contribution came from TFP growth, which
  is often associated with advances in information technology, but
  increased capital investment in this period was also important,
  adding nearly a percentage point a year to labor productivity
  growth.
- The third period, 2004–2017, shows very slow growth, with
  reduced contributions from both TFP and capital.

Figure 3.2 shows the contributions to growth over periods of a decade
or more, which give us the best handle on longer-term trends. Economic
growth from year to year can bounce around a good deal because of short-
term booms and downturns. The past few years provide striking evidence.
A large tax cut stimulated the economy in 2018 and 2019, generating very
low unemployment and a modest boost to productivity. Whether this was
a sign of a longer-term improvement in productivity growth we will likely
never know, because 2020 brought COVID-19, and the economy tanked,
with employment and output both falling dramatically. It will take a few
years to restore normality, and only then will it be possible to determine
the trend of productivity growth.

We do know that getting the economy back on track will require a return to greater contributions of capital and technological change. TFP's
future growth rate is uncertain, but we expect it to increase from its tepid
pace of the past decade or so. The nation has witnessed extraordinary
advances in biology, materials science, and information technology.
Robots have massive productivity potential, and faster computers and new
software also have the potential to improve business operations. Faster
TFP growth is likely for some period in the future, and, to capitalize on it,
the economy will need greater investment. Greater growth requires new
capital spending, and new technologies will require new types of capital.

FUNDING AND INVESTMENT INCREASE

For business investment to increase, where will the extra money come from? Savers want to get the best returns they can find, allowing for risk, and they generally put their money into banks, mutual funds, and other financial institutions that manage it for them. Those savings are then available for investment. Competing for those funds are businesses that are looking to invest and a federal government that has been borrowing very large amounts of money in recent years to finance its budget deficits. The federal government has been borrowing so much, in fact, that it would have absorbed most of the nation's savings, crowding out business investment. That has not happened because America has tapped into another important source of funds—money from the global economy. Foreign governments, foreign companies, and other foreign investors have purchased US assets, including US Treasury bonds, corporate bonds and equities, American real estate, and companies of all kinds. One measure of that flow of money from overseas is called the *current account deficit*, which has been running at around $400 billion a year since 2010.

To fuel a sustained increase in US business investment, more investment funds must be available. One way to make more funds available is for policymakers to reduce budget deficits. With an aging population drawing on Social Security and Medicare, however, policymakers will find it hard just to keep deficits from growing larger. Reducing deficits by a significant amount would invariably force policymakers to raise taxes substantially, which may not be politically feasible.[23] Borrowing more from the global economy may be possible, but it will impose costs on our economy.[24] Moreover, likely there is a limit to how much foreigners will be willing to lend us. Interest rates have been very low for a number of years, making borrowing cheap, but that need not be true forever. In fact in 2022 interest rates increased substantially, suggesting we should not take low rates for granted.

That leaves private saving as a potential source of extra funds that could help finance an increase in investment.

We are under no illusions about how hard it is to increase saving, but it is worth trying. It is important for many families to increase their saving and, if they do, that will not only help these families, but it also will make more funds available for investment and, in turn, help drive more economic growth.

Boosting Personal Saving to Boost Overall National Saving

The personal savings rate has fluctuated greatly in the postwar period. Personal saving as a percent of disposable income totaled between 7 and 8 percent in the years preceding COVID-19, but in April 2020, the personal savings rate skyrocketed to 32 percent before falling again.[25] Previously, it was 10–15 percent in the 1960s and '70s but fell after that, dropping to 3–4 percent just before the Great Recession, when many people were borrowing to buy houses or converting their housing wealth to cash.[26] Thus, there is not a constant rate of saving. Families are choosing different rates of saving, which means that it should be possible to increase personal saving, such as by making 401(k) plans available to everyone.

Fairly small changes in savings rates can make a big difference in the total pool of savings. If, for instance, the personal saving rate in 2019 were 10 percent instead of 7.5, that would have generated 30 percent more saving, adding about $400 billion to the funds available for investment, which would have represented a very substantial contribution. Changing the savings rate is hard, and we do not know how big an impact it would make if everyone had access to a savings plan, but any success would be a win-win—a win for families and a win for the economy.

At some point, policymakers who want to boost savings will turn their attention to addressing the nation's rising budget deficits. And, when they do, they will invariably take a closer look at the fast-growing federal retirement and health programs that are so important to America's retirement system but also so central to the deficit challenge. It is to those programs that we now turn.

Entitlements

The Cornerstone of Retirement

Social Security, Medicare, and, for some, Medicaid, form the foundation of American retirement. Social Security, created in 1935 as part of President Franklin D. Roosevelt's New Deal, is one of America's greatest success stories, dramatically improving the lives of tens of millions of retirees by helping many live a comfortable retirement and protecting many others from poverty. It has provided a dependable stream of income for the vast majority of retirement-age people, paid every dollar promised to retirees, enabled people to retire earlier, and empowered savers and investors to assume more risk than they otherwise might have. It has also delivered benefits with impressive efficiency, using less than 1 percent of its funds to administer the program, according to the Social Security Administration.

Medicare and Medicaid, created in 1965, are the biggest achievements of President Johnson's Great Society. Medicare, a massive, federally run health insurance program, pays for a wide range of health-related services that include hospital care, physician care, certain long-term care, and prescription drug benefits. It is generally available to Americans at least 65 years old, along with some younger adults with disabilities. In recent years, it has provided health insurance coverage for roughly 60 million beneficiaries, including 14.7 percent of beneficiaries who are living with a disability.[1]

Medicaid is a means-tested program that Washington finances jointly with the states. Most of its funding goes for health coverage for children and working-age households. It provides support as well for low-income Medicare beneficiaries, covering the costs for standard services (e.g., premiums, deductibles, and co-payments) and of some services that Medicare does not cover. Medicaid is also an important part of America's retirement landscape because one-third of its funds goes to provide long-term care to eligible beneficiaries, including retirement-age Americans.

Collectively, these programs proved invaluable during COVID-19, when tens of millions of seniors depended on them to provide income, healthcare, and other support in a period of unprecedented insecurity—especially for older Americans who experienced elevated health risks due to the nature of the virus. As painful as the virus was for this cohort, it is hard to imagine the breadth of suffering that would have occurred if these programs did not exist.

Their value notwithstanding, these programs are not cheap. Social Security, Medicare, and Medicaid are the largest federal "entitlement" programs—programs under which people receive benefits or services based on age, income, and other criteria. Entitlements in general comprise a little less than half of all federal spending, and, with budget deficits and debt both rising, the largest of them may prove almost irresistible targets for cuts if policymakers decide to try to reduce federal budget deficits or even slow their growth. At the same time, Social Security and Medicare have their own internal budget challenges, with trust funds that are projected in the coming years to run short of the funds required to finance their benefits. The trust fund shortfalls threaten not only these programs but the retirement of millions of Americans. Even small changes in these programs, however, would have outsized consequences for most older Americans. So, program beneficiaries have much at stake in the budget debates to come.

SOCIAL SECURITY

While Social Security provides a variety of benefits, the most notable is an annuity ("old age benefit") paid to almost all retired Americans. As we noted in Chapter 2, some past studies have suggested that about half of retirees rely on it for all or almost all their retirement income, and another quarter rely on it for about half of their income. Recent research from the Census Bureau, however, found that many families older than age 65 had been underreporting their incomes on the Current Population Survey, which has been a key source in past studies to estimate the incomes of older households. By using other government data sources, the researchers concluded that while Social Security is still a critical source of income, only about one-fifth of retirement-age families rely on it for most of their income.[2] We would not discard the earlier research findings completely, but putting all the research together, our reading is that about a third rely on it for all or almost all of their income, another third relies on it for a sizable portion, and another third relies on it to supplement income from other sources.[3]

Because Social Security covers people with vastly different lifetime earnings and those earnings represent different shares of retirement income, we need to take a closer look at the drivers of benefits received. The size of the benefit is largely a function of three factors: the age at which a retiree begins to claim benefits, the retiree's earning history, and the spouse's lifetime earnings (if the retiree is married or was for at least a decade). Under program rules, Social Security determines a beneficiary's basic benefit in two steps. It first calculates the average monthly wage, indexed to inflation, over one's 35 highest earnings years.[4] It then applies that monthly wage to a formula that replaces a greater share of low-wage work than high-wage work.[5] It also adjusts that amount for a variety of factors, two of which are worth noting:

- The benefit is adjusted up or down depending on the age at which a retiree begins to claim benefits (relative to the full, or "normal," retirement age, when he or she would get 100 percent of the benefit). In the 1983 Social Security Act, policymakers gradually raised the full retirement age from 65 for workers born in 1937 or earlier to 67 for workers born in 1960 or later. So, for instance, a worker who was born in 1955 (and reached 65 in 2020) has a full retirement age of 66 and 2 months. Workers who claim their benefit before their full retirement age receive a smaller benefit every month, while those who delay claiming their benefits beyond the full retirement age receive a larger monthly benefit.

- The benefit is also adjusted by an "earnings test" which applies to workers who have not yet reached the full retirement age and are still working, but who have begun to take their Social Security benefits. Social Security limits their benefits, with $1 in benefits eliminated for every $2 in earnings above a certain threshold.[6] Say, for example, a worker had not reached the full retirement age, claimed an early benefit, and had $20,240 in earnings. This worker would see his or her annual benefit (regardless of the benefit amount) reduced by $1,000—or by half of the $2,000 in earnings over the threshold. Once that person reaches the full retirement age, Social Security adds the foregone earnings back to the benefit, making the retiree whole in terms of the lifetime benefits he or she receives.[7]

While providing benefits for retirees, Social Security also provides spousal, survivor, and disability benefits. The spousal benefit is generally based on the spouse's age and the benefits owed to both members of the couple. Specifically, the maximum spousal benefit equals half the benefits of the main beneficiary (though adjusted if either member claimed benefits before the full retirement age). Consider a worker who claims $2,000 per month at full retirement; the spouse can claim $1,000 at full retirement age as well. The spouse also can claim early (lower) benefits but would not receive a higher benefit for waiting to claim benefits beyond the full retirement age. A spouse can receive benefits after divorce if the marriage lasted at least a decade. Widows and widowers can receive benefits promised to a deceased worker and can receive early (lower) benefits as early as age 60. Minor dependents or dependents with disabilities can claim other benefits.

A separate Social Security benefit goes to workers with a disability. To be eligible, workers must have worked for a decade and for 5 of the 10 years before the disability's onset, though younger workers can qualify after working fewer years. In addition to these Social Security benefits, people 65 and older, or those with a disability, can qualify for Supplemental Security Income (SSI) if their income and resources are low enough. Whereas both old age and disability benefits are delivered through Social Security and are based on work history, SSI is a separate program that is designed to help those who lack sufficient income or assets to qualify for these programs.[8]

Social Security benefits are modest for many households. While, in 2021, the maximum old age benefit was about $47,000 per year for a retiree with a high lifetime income who waits until 70 to start collecting benefits,[9] the average benefit for Social Security's 46 million beneficiaries was just $18,528. Also in 2021, another 8 million workers received an average of $15,360 in disability benefits, 3.8 million widows and widowers received an average survivors' benefit of $17,050,[10] and 8 million people (two-thirds of whom were working-age adults with a disability) received an average SSI benefit of only about $6,600. SSI recipients who do not have a disability must be older than 65 and have minimal alternative income and assets.

Nevertheless, not all older Americans receive Social Security. For most of its history, Social Security let state and local government employees participate, although it did not require that they do so and the rules by which they could participate varied over time. In the most recent significant change, President George H. W. Bush and Congress in 1990 made the program mandatory for public-sector workers unless they were covered by an alternative arrangement. Consequently, Social Security participation for such workers varies greatly by state, from states like Arizona, New York, and Vermont, where more than 90 percent participate, to states like Massachusetts and Ohio, where less than 5 percent do. All told, about three-quarters of public-sector workers are covered by Social Security.

MEDICARE AND MEDICAID

Medicare and Medicaid are broad programs that, together, provide comprehensive health benefits to beneficiaries, although older Americans are expected to pay a significant share of the cost. For example, in 2016, the typical Medicare beneficiary spent about $5,500 on health costs, including around $2,300 on premiums and $3,200 on services such as long-term care facility costs, prescription drugs, and co-pays for medical services.[11] Medicare has four main parts:

- Part A is for inpatient hospital services, including nursing facilities and hospice care. For hospital stays of up to 60 days, beneficiaries pay a flat deductible of about $1,500. In any given year, about a fifth of Medicare beneficiaries will stay in a hospital and tap into Part A.
- Part B covers physician services, including outpatient hospital services and durable medical equipment. Around 90 percent of eligible Americans enroll in Part B, and, of those, about 90 percent use services in any given year. After reaching a low deductible, beneficiaries pay 20 percent of costs, as determined by a pre-set fee schedule. They also pay a monthly premium; the standard was $145 in 2020, although some paid less and high-income beneficiaries pay more.
- Part C, known as Medicare Advantage, is an alternative to Parts A and B. Beneficiaries can voluntarily choose to receive "bundled" services through a private insurance company. Under Medicare Advantage, Medicare pays private health companies a per-beneficiary amount to provide services to beneficiaries, and these companies have discretion in how they deliver the services and whether to charge beneficiaries additional premiums. Sometimes, they deliver these services as a health maintenance organization (HMO); at other times, as fee for service. About one-third of Medicare beneficiaries enroll in Part C.

- Part D provides prescription drug coverage, which is optional and which beneficiaries get through private insurance companies that must offer a minimum level of benefits but have discretion over premiums and certain drug coverage. Generally, beneficiaries have a deductible ($435 in 2020), then pay 25 percent in co-insurance up to a certain level ($4,020 in 2020), after which the cost for the benefit declines until catastrophic coverage kicks in (at $6,350 in 2020). In recent years, around three-fourths of eligible individuals enrolled in Part D.

About one of every five Medicare beneficiaries is also eligible for Medicaid, although the share of these "dual eligibles" in Medicare varies considerably by state. Some 34 percent of Medicare beneficiaries in Maine are also eligible for Medicaid, compared to just 10 percent in Colorado.[12] We have given a rather detailed description here of the Medicare program, which illustrates what a complicated plan it is. The program has been changed many times since its inception, sometimes to expand coverage (the prescription drug provision) and sometimes to control costs. A simpler program would likely be better from a policy viewpoint but may be hard to accomplish in the fractious political environment in which decisions are made. Despite its flaws, it is a lifesaver for older Americans. It is very costly, just as all medical insurance is in the United States.

TRUST FUND WOES

The challenge for Social Security lies mainly in its projected solvency, an oft-misunderstood issue. Social Security's old-age program is funded through a payroll tax on wages. Every worker's earnings are subject to a 12.4 percent payroll tax—with the worker and the employer each paying 6.2 percent of it—up to a cap that rises each year with the rise in average wages across the society. In 2021, the cap was $142,800, meaning that workers and their employers paid the 12.4 percent tax on all earnings up to that level and then no taxes on earnings above it.

The Treasury receives the payroll tax receipts and credits them to the Old-Age Social Insurance (OASI) Trust Fund and the Disability Insurance (DI) Trust Fund. Traditionally, 10.6 percent of the 12.4 percent payroll went to the OASI Trust Fund and the remaining 1.8 percent for the DI Trust Fund, although policymakers have revised those proportions slightly in recent years.

For much of Social Security's history, the trust fund balances grew, meaning they were receiving more in tax revenue than they were paying in benefits. But with the retirement of baby boomers—the huge group of Americans born between 1946 and 1964—coupled with growing life expectancy and a shrinking share of wages subject to the payroll tax,[13] Social Security's trust funds in recent years have been paying more in benefits than they have been receiving in taxes. Under the latest projections, the old age trust fund will be exhausted in 2034. The disability trust fund, which typically has a more volatile exhaustion date, is now projected to be solvent for the whole 75-year projection period—1 year after the fund was projected to run dry in 2057.

Medicare's trust fund finances Part A, the part that covers hospital stays. It receives about 90 percent of its funding through a 2.9 percent payroll tax on all wages that, like the Social Security payroll tax, is split evenly between employers and workers but that, unlike Social Security payroll tax, has no cap and thus applies to all earnings.[14] The remaining trust fund revenues comes from a tax on the Social Security benefits of middle-income families and from interest payments on the trust fund balance. (Medicare Parts B and D are mainly funded through general revenue, like most government programs, while Part C is funded through premiums that beneficiaries pay.[15]) Medicare's trust fund will be exhausted in 2028, according to the most recent program estimates (see Figure 4.1 for the change in reserves as a share of costs over time).[16]

Medicaid has no trust fund; the federal government shares program costs with the states. For each state, the federal share is generally determined by a formula that accounts for state per-capita income, with the federal government paying a higher share of costs for poorer states. (In recent years, the federal "matching rate" has ranged between 50 percent

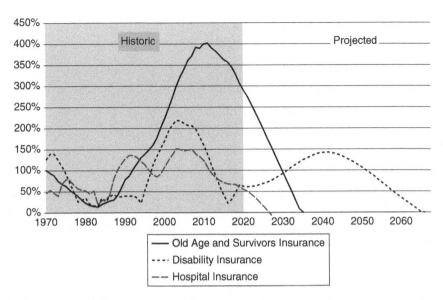

Figure 4.1 Old-age social insurance (OASI), disability insurance (DI), and health insurance (HI) trust fund ratios (asset reserves as a percentage of annual cost). SOURCE: Social Security Administration.

for high-income states to about 75 percent for low-income states.) All told, the federal government covers about 60 percent of Medicaid costs.

So, what happens when the Social Security and Medicare trust funds are exhausted? For Social Security, the impact is unclear. Even if its old age trust fund is exhausted in 2034, the incoming payroll taxes would still be enough to pay roughly 75 percent of the promised benefits of that time— so, in a worse-case scenario, most beneficiaries would get most of their benefits. Whether, under the law, the federal government could pay less than the promised level is unclear. As a Congressional Research Service report notes,

It is unclear what specific actions the Social Security Administration (SSA) would take if a trust fund were insolvent. After depletion, the trust funds would continue to receive tax revenues, from which a majority of scheduled benefits could be paid. One option would be to pay full benefits on a delayed schedule; another would be to make timely but reduced payments. Social Security beneficiaries would remain legally entitled to full, timely benefits and could take legal action to claim the balance of their benefits.[17]

The situation is similar with Medicare's Part A. In the initial years after the trust fund is exhausted, incoming revenues would cover about 90 percent of program costs, so Medicare could still provide much of its hospital services.

Politically, trust fund solvency is likely a sideshow. A future president and Congress almost certainly would never let Social Security benefits go unpaid—and raise the wrath of tens of millions of current and future beneficiaries—and it can transfer funds from the general budget to the trust fund to prevent the problem. The same is true of Medicare Part A. The more relevant issue is whether, at some point, policymakers will seek to slow the growth in Social Security and Medicare costs as part of a broader effort to rein-in rising budget deficits and debt.

ENTITLEMENTS IN THE LARGER BUDGET DISCUSSION

Our country is in the midst of a profound fiscal experiment. In light of the massive health and economic risks posed by COVID-19, the president and Congress appropriated trillions of dollars in relief while tax receipts plummeted—likely driving the steepest increase in debt that our country has seen since World War II. To be clear, this statement is not a critique: one of the federal government's most important roles is to stabilize the economy and backstop state governments in times of crises. Yet this does not change the fact that our fiscal outlook has deteriorated sharply due to COVID-19, exacerbating long-term budget pressures, followed by the war in Ukraine.

The timing of the recovery effort, which will occur throughout 2023 and beyond, means that our statements on the US fiscal standing will be incomplete. As of this writing, the president and Congress are debating relief efforts and contemplating major spending bills—largely financed through tax changes—aimed at addressing long-standing concerns like unaffordable child care and climate change.

Yet, whatever the plans that policymakers ultimately enact, we suffer from the same long-term budget pressures that were present before the pandemic. From the long-term perspective, three trends concerning future debt and deficits stand out:

- First, government debt is rising rapidly. The debt (the sum of all annual deficits, minus surpluses, since the nation's founding) has grown from 33.7 percent of GDP in 2000 to 80.2 percent in the first quarter of 2020. Some of that rise is due to the Great Recession of 2008 and 2009, which reduced tax revenues as businesses made less money and more people were out of work, and to the tax cuts and higher spending that policymakers enacted at the time to revive the economy. But it also reflects a long-standing mismatch between what government spends and what it receives in taxes. Exacerbating the problem, the 2017 tax law sharply cut business tax rates, and the 2018 Bipartisan Budget Act paved the way for more than $320 billion in spending above that year's spending caps that were previously set for non-entitlement programs. Together, those two measures raised the 2020 deficit by about 1 percent of GDP.[18] The decline in the economy and in tax revenues due to COVID-19, plus the additional spending to help families and boost the economy, pushed the debt to almost 100 percent of GDP in the first quarter of 2022.[19]

- Second, even in the pre-COVID "full employment" economy, the gap between spending and revenues was about 5 percent of GDP—one of the highest persistent gaps in the postwar period.[20] In prior decades, the federal government has only run such large deficits during the Great Recession and in the mid-1980s—in the aftermath of recessions earlier in the decade, President Reagan's huge tax cuts of 1981, and his massive defense build-up. Today's deficits are largely due to the COVID response but, over the long

term, they are driven by increased spending on entitlements
and inadequate tax revenue. See Figure 4.2 showing deficits and
surpluses from 1970 through an estimate for 2030.[21]

- Third, and most troubling, virtually every official government
projection for future years shows the gap between spending
and revenues widening, deficits rising, and debt soaring to
unprecedented levels. Under current tax and spending policies,
the Congressional Budget Office (CBO) projects, the debt will
reach 202 percent of GDP by 2051.

The debt build-up is largely attributable to the rising costs of Social
Security and, even more, health-related entitlement programs. In 2020,
Social Security spending equaled 4.9 percent of GDP, and federal
spending on major health programs equaled 5.4 percent. By 2049, those
figures are projected to grow to 6.4 and 9.0 percent, respectively. Over
the next 30 years, rising deficits are projected by the CBO to send interest
payments soaring, from 1.7 percent of GDP today to 5.7 percent of GDP
in 2049. In short, as rising costs for healthcare and Social Security increase
deficits, debt is expected to accumulate and push up interest payments.
After 30 years, the share of GDP devoted to Social Security, federal health
programs, and net interest payments is projected to rise from 12.0 to

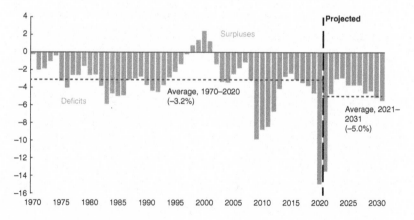

Figure 4.2 Total deficits and surpluses (percentage of gross domestic product [GDP]).
SOURCE: Congressional Budget Office.

21.2 percent. Interest rates have remained low for several years, but spiked up in 2022 with the Federal Reserve's policy response to the surge in inflation. It is hard to predict how this will impact budget pressures—we talk more about this in the next section.

While these projections are sensitive to various factors, the most important is the growth in healthcare costs. One of us (Harris) studied the issue with Alan Auerbach and William Gale and found that, by 2040, the debt would equal about 110 percent of GDP if health costs grow at the same rate as the economy. If, however, health costs grow 2.5 percentage points faster than the economy—a rate that is not out of line with recent experience—the debt would grow to almost 190 percent of GDP by 2040.[22] While projections about how quick the population will age, how much immigration we'll have, and how much incomes will grow all matter in determining the size of future deficits, the elephant in the room is the trajectory of healthcare costs.

Entitlement spending that pushes the debt to well over 100 percent of GDP would raise three big concerns. One is that entitlements will "crowd out" non-entitlement spending so that almost all spending goes to entitlements and interest payments on the debt, leaving little for education, training, criminal justice, defense, energy, and other priorities. Already, this "discretionary" spending—which, unlike entitlements, the president and Congress must fund each year—has shrunk from a peak of 13.1 percent of GDP in 1968 to 6.3 percent today. (Defense, which traditionally comprised about half of discretionary spending, shrunk over this period from 9.2 percent of GDP to 3.2 percent.) Further cuts in this type of spending could severely hamstring the government's ability to provide needed services.

A second concern is that future debt levels will violate notions of "generational fairness." A child born in 2030, for example, could enter adulthood, at least on paper, owing hundreds of thousands of dollars of debt (i.e., that person's share of the total debt) before receiving any substantial benefit from major federal entitlement programs that overwhelmingly benefit elderly Americans. Already, federal spending that is devoted to children has fallen from 11 percent in 2010 to about 9 percent today and is expected to fall to 7 percent by 2030, according to a KidsShare report. Tomorrow's adults, who are paying the payroll taxes to support today's retirees, may, when they retire, be the first generation to see their Social Security and health benefits curtailed.

A final concern is that high government debt will push up interest rates. An increase in the projected deficit of 1 percent of GDP[23] will raise long-term interest rates by 25–35 basis points, says a 2004 study by William Gale and Peter Orszag. These higher interest rates would mean higher borrowing costs for businesses looking to invest, couples looking to buy homes or cars, students seeking loans to pay for their higher education, and anyone using a credit card. A related concern is that excess debt may eventually prompt the government to default on a federal interest payment on government securities, which would send interest rates soaring and could shake global markets.

WORRYING, OR NOT, ABOUT DEFICITS AND DEBT

Unfortunately, we do not fully understand the economic consequences of high public debt. All else being equal, debt, deficits, and projected deficits raise interest rates and can undermine financial stability, according to high-quality academic papers. Recent experience, however, suggests a different relationship. In 2021, 10-year Treasury bonds were trading at around 1.5 percent and the 30-year yield was hovering around 2 percent. That meant that the federal government could borrow money at very low interest rates that were below the rate of inflation, largely because investors desperately want the safety of US government securities.

In a situation when rates are so low: Do deficits and debt even matter? Twenty years ago, the question alone would have raised eyebrows. Today, however, mainstream economists are debating how current debt levels are linked to interest rates and financial stability. In a piece for *Foreign Affairs* in the spring of 2019, influential economists Jason Furman and Lawrence Summers, who both served as White House advisers to Presidents Clinton and Obama, argued that while debt was still a long-term concern, deficits in the short term were not a major concern and their costs and benefits had changed. They noted that, in 2000, the debt as a share of GDP was expected to plummet while interest rates rose, but the exact opposite has occurred over the past two decades.[24] In a follow-up paper, they noted that if the focus were shifted from the level of debt to the costs of servicing the debt, the United States could at least reasonably accommodate a debt-to-GDP level that was roughly 50 percent higher than the current level.[25]

Across the ideological spectrum, concerns about deficits and debt appear to be fading. The recent experience with COVID-19, in which the federal government enacted an unprecedented increase in government spending, is a perfect case in point. Indeed, the question isn't whether to borrow during economic downturns—economists have long supported that idea—but rather whether to run persistently high deficits during times of relative economic strength. If we run deficits of 5 percent or more of GDP indefinitely with a healthy economy, the debt could exceed 150 percent of GDP in a few decades. Pro-deficit economists acknowledge that interest payments on the debt will comprise a growing share of the budget but argue that this won't matter because with low interest rates the federal government can borrow at relatively little cost. The major retirement programs will continue unabated, they reason, and future retirees will receive all the benefits they are expecting.

In 2022, interest rates have increased, with the 10-year Treasury hitting 2.8 percent in July. This is not because of rising debt levels, however; instead, it is the response to a surge in inflation. Inflation cuts both ways in terms of the debt burden. Higher interest rates increase the burden but inflation also reduces the burden by eroding the value of debt relative to GDP. In short, inflation is bad for the economy, but higher interest rates combined with higher inflation do not impact the burden of the debt much either way. What of the future? The dollar remains the world's reserve currency as global conditions continue to make America the preferred risk-free place to invest. Cryptocurrencies are not yet a legitimate contender with the dollar. The world's financial markets remain relatively connected. We expect that low inflation and low interest rates will return in coming years. There is uncertainty, however, and this all could change if debt levels grow too fast for too long.

WHAT'S TO COME FOR ENTITLEMENT PROGRAMS

Asked why he robbed banks, the famed Willie Sutton said, "Because that's where the money is." When it comes to federal spending, entitlements represent the bank. In the coming decades, as we have noted, entitlements and interest payments together will represent roughly three-quarters of all spending, and we have to pay the interest owed to avoid a federal default. So, if we find ourselves concerned again with fiscal prolificacy, entitlements will likely top the list for cuts, and the biggest targets will be the three biggest entitlements: Social Security, Medicare, and Medicaid.

What might Social Security cuts look like? The CBO in 2018 outlined options to close Social Security's shortfall. Pegging the 75-year shortfall at 1.7 percent of GDP, the CBO provided 36 different ways to help eliminate it, including tax increases and benefit cuts.[26] As the options make clear, policymakers can close much or all of the gap with moderate changes on both sides. Raising the full retirement age, for instance, to 70 (from 67, where it is now headed) would reduce the long-term shortfall by 0.4 percentage points of GDP. Letting benefits vary with population-wide longevity so that benefits decrease when Americans start living longer would shave another 0.3 percentage points. Changing the way taxes fund Social Security could close the rest of the shortfall. For instance, raising the cap on earnings subject to the payroll tax so that 90 percent of economy-wide earnings are taxed, as they were decades ago, would slice the shortfall by another 0.3 percentage points.

To be clear, these changes would have a marked impact on those affected, raising their taxes, cutting their benefits, or both throughout their lifetimes. Indexing lifetime benefits to longevity would cut lifetime benefits by about 10 percentage points for those born in 1980. Raising the retirement age would cause big problems for those who have trouble working. While Social Security's disability benefits might be an option for them, program requirements are strict, beneficiaries often wait a half-year to get benefits, and benefits are often inadequate to keep recipients out of poverty.

With Medicare, future cuts are less clear. Letting the federal government fully negotiate Medicare drug prices is a popular option, often with bipartisan support. President Biden, for example, has proposed to let the federal government negotiate prices down to a cap based on international costs. Conservatives occasionally take a different route by backing cuts in reimbursement rates: in his 2021 budget, President Trump proposed $845 billion in cuts to Medicare, mostly by cutting reimbursement payments to hospitals and physicians.

Rather than cut Medicare, conservative policymakers often favor cuts to Medicaid. For example, Trump's budget called for $1.5 trillion in cuts over 10 years, mainly by lowering federal reimbursements to states that expanded their Medicaid programs under the Affordable Care Act (ACA). Similarly, then-House Speaker Paul Ryan called for steep Medicaid cuts, including $800 billion in cuts by repealing the ACA. Rather than backing programmatic cuts, progressive lawmakers often favor approaches that "bend the cost curve" by creating more competition in the healthcare industry. In his first year, President Biden backed policies to control consolidation in the hospital industry and limit surprise medical billing.

As with Social Security, Medicare and Medicaid cuts would have real impacts—in this case on physicians, hospitals, patients, medical device producers, drug companies, health insurers, and beneficiaries. Consider Speaker Ryan's proposal, in his "Better Way" plan, to introduce "premium support" into Medicare. The federal government would give eligible households a voucher with which to buy health insurance either through a private employer or through a traditional Medicare fee-for-service program. Some analysts believe that would drive steep premium increases for many beneficiaries, including low-income beneficiaries who might have to forego care.

Policymakers who want to address rising deficits and debt but, at the same time, avoid or limit cuts to entitlements have one more option: raise taxes. In the context of Social Security, that could mean raising the payroll tax rate or, as we have discussed, the share of wages subject to it. Beyond Social Security, tax increases could include increases in corporate tax rates, individual tax rates, or estate or other taxes, and it could include reductions in tax credits, deductions, and other preferences, including those designed to spur retirement saving and investing. Improving tax administration so that more Americans pay the taxes they owe is another powerful, but often overlooked, option.

For would-be tax raisers, we offer two observations. First, our economic counterparts—namely, other countries of the Organisation for Economic Cooperation and Development (OECD)—have moved in this direction. From 2000 to 2017, 21 of the 35 non-US OECD nations raised their taxes as a share of GDP, with the OECD average rising by 0.4 percent points of GDP.[27] Second, policymakers cannot realistically address the federal fiscal challenge solely on the tax side. In 2010, Roseanne Altshuler, Katharine Lim, and Roberton Williams simulated the tax increases needed to close the budget gap (which has worsened since then) and found that stabilizing deficits at 2 percent of GDP would require a 30 percent increase in the top three income tax rates. As a practical matter, we will probably need to pair tax increases with budget cuts.

Addressing the fiscal challenge does not portend well for economic growth. Tax increases, especially of the magnitude needed to help address the budget shortfall, are typically associated with lower economic growth. Higher taxes on investment income can reduce savings and investment, which tends to depress growth over time. Higher taxes on wages, including payroll taxes or taxes assessed on earnings, tend to reduce the number of hours that people work. (Other tax increases, like eliminating tax incentives for homeownership, are usually more growth-neutral.)

On the other hand, benefit changes can spur more economic growth. If, for instance, policymakers raise the eligibility age for either Social Security or Medicare, workers will spend more years in the labor market, which may burden workers but will spur higher economic growth due to a greater supply of labor. Longer lifespans and the end of company pensions will probably mean longer working lives anyway. Either way, the days of widespread retirement at age 60 or 65 may be long gone.

The nation's fiscal and retirement challenges have been mounting for many years, and they will mean more constraints on any expansion of government programs to help older households. That puts more responsibility on individuals and families, and one way they can face that challenge is by finding ways to work longer. We examine the opportunities and challenges involved in working longer in Chapter 5.

Working Longer

Americans must decide when and how to retire in a new retirement land-scape that includes the shift away from pensions and toward 401(k) plans or similar retirement savings vehicles.

For a worker with a pension, the decision is often dictated by pro-gram rules. When a worker can retire and receive a full pension, con-tinued work often makes little sense from a financial standpoint, given that the worker continues paying into a retirement system but receives no additional benefit on the back end. With a 401(k), however, workers have an added incentive to work beyond the standard retirement date because they can continue contributing to their plans, receive employer contributions, and, as a result, watch their retirement savings grow even larger.

Until COVID-19, Americans were already working longer; that is to say, they were continuing to work more years, until they were older. Whereas labor force participation overall has declined in recent decades, participation by older workers, both men and women, was rising through 2019.[1] Some of the increase was surely due to the shift from the certainty of employer pensions to the insecurity of wondering whether, with a 401(k) and other savings that could shrink in value if the market dropped, one has enough money to retire. But some of the increase was likely driven by positive factors, such as expanded lifespans, employers' trust in older workers, and those workers' ability to offer a lifetime of experience and a willingness to train younger colleagues. The pandemic, of course, has greatly complicated this story of people working longer. We will talk about the impact of the pandemic shortly in this chapter.

One central conclusion to our study of retirement is that workers should consider the option of working longer, employers should give their employees the opportunity to work longer, and policymakers should support longer working lives. We recognize, though, that working longer is not for everyone and will not by itself solve America's retirement challenge.

The contribution of longer working lives is only one part of meeting the retirement challenge, however. The shift to 401(k) type plans has transferred longevity and investment risk to households while providing unequal saving incentives to lower-income workers. Government programs, particularly Social Security, remain the foundation of America's retirement system, but benefits are not especially generous for those in the middle or at the bottom in terms of wages, and Medicare retirees must allocate some of those benefits to cover the premiums and out-of-pocket health costs that they pay. Medicaid provides nursing home care for low-income seniors, but these may not have the same quality as facilities where residents pay for themselves.[2] In addition, long-term budget challenges at some point may prompt lawmakers to cut "entitlement" programs, the largest of which are Social Security, Medicare, and Medicaid. Such cuts could include a rise in the full retirement age in Social Security—the age at which retirees can get full benefits. In short, Americans who are looking ahead to a retirement that may last 20 or 30 years face uncertainty and other formidable challenges.

As we said in Chapter 2, economists have theorized how a rational family should prepare for retirement. Families should look at their income over their working lives, decide when they expect to retire, and assess the uncertainties that they will face in retirement. The family should then save during their working years and invest in a retirement account, home, or other investment vehicle. Another important way in which families face the challenge of retirement planning is by adjusting the age at which they retire, depending on how their circumstances change.

We also noted that some Americans make short-sighted or even irrational decisions, even if they start with good intentions. They know they need to save for retirement but did not do so. Many of them retire with inadequate assets, perhaps because they have lost a job or their health has deteriorated. Behavioral economists have found that people are hard-pressed to visualize what their lives will be like 50 years into the future, or even 20, and make decisions today that they hope will prepare them well for their old age.

In this chapter we focus on one important aspect of retirement planning: When do people retire? We observe that Americans are responding to an altered retirement landscape by working longer, but, unfortunately, they still face barriers and disincentives to staying at work, and sometimes they make decisions they may later regret.

HOW DO PEOPLE DECIDE WHEN TO RETIRE?

The framework for rational saving and retirement decisions that we summarized above (and discussed in more detail in Chapter 2) is called the *life cycle model*.[3] It examines how people choose to work and consume over the cycle of their lives: youth, middle age, and retirement. At the time it was developed, many middle-class families had pensions through their employers, so pension rules strongly affected their decisions about when to retire. Retirement age was usually influenced, and perhaps determined, by their employers. Age 65 was a common retirement benchmark, although under union contracts blue-collar workers often retired earlier, reflecting the physical stress and impact of factory work. Workers with good company pensions did not need to make the most important retirement, saving, and investment decisions themselves; they could rely mainly on their pensions plus Social Security benefits. People with good company pensions probably had less freedom over their working lives but also faced fewer tough retirement planning decisions and less risk than people do today. Employers assumed the responsibility for life cycle saving and retirement planning, and they guaranteed retirement income.

Not all workers had traditional pensions, even in the "good old days" of the 1950s and 1960s. Now, since the introduction of 401(k) plans in the late 1970s, traditional private-sector pensions have largely disappeared. Meanwhile, life expectancy has increased over time, so the number of years for which people need their retirement income has increased. Workers now need to plan their own retirement and decide the age at which they stop working or reduce their hours at work.

Given that people are now making their own retirement decisions, what will they consider when deciding when to quit working? If there are jobs available, workers can weigh the benefit of more months or years of income if they keep working against the loss of time that they could spend with family and friends as retirees. Retirement becomes more attractive as people age because they accumulate enough assets to cover their retirement and because life expectancy shrinks for them, reducing the chance they will grow much older and have low income. That's the answer that the life cycle model gives: people retire when the benefit of more work (i.e., more income) equals the cost of more work (i.e., forgone leisure in retirement). People's choices vary, of course. Some enjoy work and the companionship it brings and never retire voluntarily, while others retire as soon as they find it financially feasible.

The world, of course, is more complex than this simplified description. Some share of people will experience bad health and cannot work or cannot work at a job with heavy physical demands or lots of stress. Some will suffer involuntary layoffs from a late-career job, and some will face discrimination against older workers. Meanwhile, many people do not make an abrupt retirement decision but choose instead to keep working part-time, continuing to generate income but avoiding the stress of full-time employment.

Public policy choices and the state of the economy affect retirement decisions. For those in jobs with health insurance, that benefit encourages people to work until 65, when they can enroll in Medicare. The option to collect Social Security seems to encourage retirement.[4] As recently as 2013, 42 percent of men and 48 percent of women started collecting benefits at age 62, and only about 2 percent of people waited until 70. That is very surprising because, as noted, the structure of Social Security benefits provides a large financial incentive for people to wait to collect them until they reach 70. Each year that they postpone from 62 to the full retirement age adds about 5 percent to the monthly benefit level. Each year after the full retirement age up to age 70 adds 8 percent to what they receive. The percentage of people that start drawing benefits at the earliest possible age is declining as families learn the value of waiting. As of 2020, 23.5 percent of men and 25.7 percent of women started collecting benefits at 62, while the number waiting until 70 has risen (though it remains small at 5.9 percent of men and 7.5 percent of women).[5]

The business cycle affects retirement decisions as well. The Great Recession had two offsetting impacts. Many older workers lost their jobs and had trouble finding new jobs to replace them. This prevented many people from working longer. At the same time, the stock market plunged and home values declined sharply, leaving older families with a smaller pool of assets and a lower net worth. That encouraged those who kept their jobs to postpone retirement in order to rebuild their retirement as-sets. While both effects were at work, the weakness in the labor market and the loss of jobs had the greater impact, and, on net, older workers left the labor force.[6]

As shown by retirement patterns during the pandemic, economists have discovered that public health emergencies can also affect retirement decisions. One unexpected feature of the pandemic was an increase in the share of workers in retirement relative to pre-pandemic expectations, which is perhaps not surprising in light of the pandemic's dispropor-tionate health impact on older workers. A survey by the Pew Research Center reported that 50.3 percent of those older than 55 had retired in the third quarter of 2021 compared with 48.1 percent just two years prior, a big change over such a short period.[7] As the pandemic eases, many older workers have returned to the workforce—over a million between May 2021 and May 2022.[8]

Taxes also affect retirement decisions, and conventional wisdom says that taxes on wages will discourage people from working and encourage them to retire. If people compare their take-home pay against their wish to retire, then taxes will encourage them to retire early (this is called the *substitution effect*, comparing additional cash income to the pleasures of retirement). If, however, people work until they have enough assets to live in retirement, then the taxes they pay while working can, instead, encourage them to work longer and keep saving to achieve a target level of retirement wealth (this is called the *wealth effect* or *income effect*).[9] So, in theory, the effect of taxes on when people choose to retire is ambiguous.

Moreover, the tax system is complex. Income tax rates vary with the amount of income earned. Payroll taxes are substantial, and many households pay more in payroll taxes than other kinds of taxes.[10] Both Social Security benefits and withdrawals from 401(k)-type plans are subject to tax, so people do not escape all taxes after they retire. On balance, taxes probably encourage people to retire earlier, although the impact is not large.

Some workers go directly from full-time work to full retirement, but many scale back gradually. Often, people do not want to—or cannot—keep working full time but do not have enough money to last if they or their spouse lives to a very old age. Perhaps they are concerned about needing part- or full-time nursing care at some point. Some employers welcome part-time work and value the experience that older workers bring to the job, but others use various incentives to encourage older workers to leave. Even if an employer does not allow part-time work, some older workers find part-time work elsewhere. Skilled workers—like carpenters, plumbers, teachers, and nurses—remain in demand for part-time work. Realistically, however, most workers who retire from their main employer find it hard to work part-time except at lower wage rates than they were earning.

ARE PEOPLE MAKING GOOD RETIREMENT DECISIONS?

In Chapter 2, we reviewed saving behavior, pointing to studies suggesting that some families are saving enough on which to retire, and, by implication, they are working long enough to support their retirement without deprivation. Poverty is low among current retirees. At the same time, other studies suggest that many families are not saving enough and have not built up enough retirement wealth. Behavioral economists particularly stress how hard it is to save enough.

One way to overcome a shortfall in retirement saving is to keep working, and some families do indeed follow this path. They would like to retire at age 60 or 65 but they keep working, perhaps part-time. The increase in the number of older workers is one possible sign that some may be reaching normal retirement ages and realizing they must either pinch pennies or keep working.

Many are left short of funds for retirement in part because the retirement landscape has changed enough that even if peoples' retirement decisions were on target in the past, when pensions were common, they may not be now or in the future. Not everyone has adapted to the new reality of a world in which they must manage their own retirement planning.

Many families also rely too heavily on Social Security for their retirement. In 2021, the Social Security Administration reported that the average benefit paid was $1,543 per month for retired workers, $801 per month for spouses of retired workers, and $1,455 for older widows or widowers receiving survivor's benefits. These amounts are often not enough to enable someone to maintain the same standard of living in retirement as during working years. Even if two people in a household collect benefits, the household income from those benefits may be modest. As noted, those recipients must use part of the benefits to pay for Medicare coverage and out-of-pocket health costs. Many, of course, receive higher benefits than the average but, for all those who receive above-average benefits, many others have been low-wage workers, experienced spells of unemployment, or stayed home to care for children, and their benefits are below the average. That is particularly a problem for those who start collecting benefits early, around age 62.

One clear sign that families do not all decide when to retire based on a well-thought-out plan comes from the ages at which most people choose to start collecting Social Security benefits. People generally start collecting at one of two different times. One spike is at age 62, when over a third of people claim benefits even though their benefit level will be low. Their decisions may not be irrational because their financial circumstances and health status may explain them, but, given the financial incentives, it is nevertheless surprising. A second spike comes at the "full retirement age"—the age specified in law, which has risen over time in 2-month increments. For someone born in 1941, the full retirement age was 65 years and 8 months. It rose to 65 years and 10 months for those born in 1942 and to 66 years for those born in 1943 and later years.

When the full retirement age rose from 65 years and 10 months to 66, peoples' behavior changed markedly. The percentage of men first claiming their benefits at 65 fell from 29.4 percent to 13.3 percent. When people visit the Social Security Administration to sign up for benefits and Medicare, they are informed of their full retirement age and many choose to start claiming benefits at that age. The so-called full retirement age, however, has no special significance compared to any other age when people can begin claiming. Between ages 62 and 70, the monthly benefit level rises with each month that a person delays taking benefits. Another possibility is that many households are not well-informed about their best option for taking benefits and, if a government official suggests the full retirement age is appropriate, many make that choice.

Finally, and perhaps most importantly, one sign that many families have trouble planning their retirement needs is that many run out of money in their 80s.[11] Say, for instance, that someone reaches age 65 and is tired of working. They have saved some money, or they own a home and can collect Social Security, so they retire. For several years they do fine, enjoying their retirement and perhaps making a little extra money on the side. Over time, however, they run into health problems, and co-payments and prescriptions mount up. Their home needs repairs, and they can no longer make the repairs themselves. Their savings are gone, and Social Security is not covering their living costs. When the family made their retirement decision, they found it hard to visualize how the future would play out and how expensive it could be. If they had it to do over, they would save more or work longer.

Lots of families, of course, are well-prepared when they choose to retire, but the costs of a mistake are high and that is why we support efforts to encourage people to work longer if they need to do so. How many years are Americans now working, and what may be driving changes in the age at which they are retiring?

HOW MUCH ARE ADULTS WORKING, AND WHY?

The *labor force participation rate* (LFPR) measures the share of Americans who are working or looking for work, and it has assumed a hump-shaped pattern over the past half-century. It grew steadily from the early 1960s to the late 1990s, when it peaked at 67 percent, then fell gradually until it reached 62.7 percent in 2015; it has since risen slowly and reached 63.1 percent in 2019.[12] Understanding these longer-run trends is important, and we discuss them now. The pandemic, however, has derailed these trends at least temporarily, and we will discuss that shortly.

Looking behind this national trend, the LFPR for men aged 25–54 has declined steadily over the past six decades, from 97 percent in 1960 to about 88 percent by 2013 before stabilizing since then. Many adult men chose to leave the workforce in their 50s, and some even earlier. By contrast, the LFPR for women in the same age range rose between 1960 and 1990, stagnated, and then fell modestly before rising over the past several years.[13]

While participation rates for those 25–54 moved in opposite directions for men and women, older Americans of both genders have been working more; for adults 55 and older, the LFPR has been rising since the mid-1990s after falling slowly throughout the 1970s and early '80s.[14] After stabilizing at about 30 percent in the mid-80s, it rose to about 40 percent just before the Great Recession and has remained mostly constant ever since. The decline of the 1970s and early 1980s was driven largely by men, whose LFPR fell roughly 10 percentage points, while older women stayed in the labor force at roughly the same rate. The subsequent increase was driven by both men and women, starting in about 1995. Between the mid-1990s and the Great Recession, participation rates rose by about 13 percentage points for women and about 10 percentage points for men. The increase put the men's rate roughly where it was in 1975, while the rate for women reached its highest level in modern history. (Women, of course, have always worked hard in the home and on farms. Here, we are referring only to women working for pay outside the home.)

For those 55 and older, participation rates fall steadily with age, with an especially stark drop starting at about age 65. By 2017, nearly 60 percent of Americans in their early 60s were in the labor force, compared to just over 30 percent of those in their late 60s. About one in five adults in their early 70s is still in the labor market, including 16 percent of women and 24 percent of men. But participation is extremely uncommon for those in their late 70s, at just 8 percent for those over 75.

Although participation remains uncommon for those over 65, their participation rates have been rising. The run-up in overall labor force participation from the mid-1990s to late 2000s was also witnessed by older Americans, with participation rates for those 55–74 rising by about 10 percentage points for most 5-year age groups. The increase was moderately less for older workers, with participation rising from about 5 percent to about 8 percent over this period.[15]

Older workers who work tend to be those who are in management or professional services. More than 40 percent of them—or roughly 15 million people—work in management, professional, or related services, the Bureau of Labor Statistics reports. Another 8 million work in sales, while fewer than 5 million more work in the remaining occupational categories, including service; production and transportation; and natural resources, construction, and maintenance (see Figure 5.1). Older workers are also self-employed at high rates—about 16 percent of those older than 65, which is higher than the rate of prime-age workers (see Figure 5.2).

Labor force participation among older workers is expected to be higher in the future than previously, once the pandemic's effects are gone. As we noted, the pandemic appears to have driven down the share of retired workers who did not return to the labor market, thereby driving down the LFPR for older workers. For those 65 and older, their LFPR had been above 20 percent for over a year by February 2020, the first time that had occurred since the early 1960s.[16] From February to June of 2020, however, this figure dropped from 20.8 to 18.6 percent due to the pandemic. This

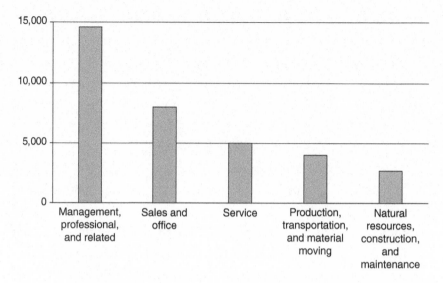

Figure 5.1 Employment of workers ages 55 and older, by occupation group, 2016.
SOURCE: Bureau of Labor Statistics.

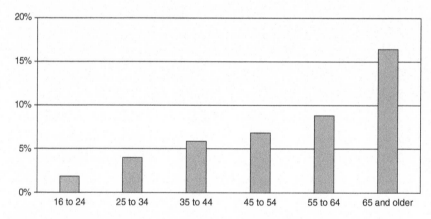

Figure 5.2 Percent self-employment (unincorporated) by age, 2016.
SOURCE: Bureau of Labor Statistics.

trend already shows signs of partially reversing, and we may well see a near-complete reversal after the pandemic ends. As of yet, we simply don't know the long-term impact of COVID-19 on work by older Americans.

Over the next decade, the Bureau of Labor Statistics has projected that, for those 65 to 74, LFPR is expected to rise from 26.6 to 32.0 percent between 2020 and 2030, and for those 75 and older, LFPR is expected to rise from 8.9 to 11.7 percent.[17] Participation would rise slightly more for women than men in the 65 to 74 category. For men 65–74, participation is projected to rise by 4.8 percentage points (from 31.5 to 36.3 percent), compared to 2.6 percentage points (from 11.8 to 14.4 percent) for those 75 and older. For women 65–74, participation is projected to rise by 5.7 percentage points (from 22.4 to 28.1 percent), compared to 1.5 percentage points (from 5.3 to 6.8 percent) for those 75 and older. We do expect that more older workers will remain in the labor market.

Economists do not agree on what is driving these longer-run labor force trends, but a few factors seem clear. One reason that overall labor force participation is falling is that America's population is aging;[18] with people less likely to work as they pass 65, a larger share of Americans in retirement means lower overall labor force participation, all else being equal. One study found that nearly 80 percent of the decline in labor force participation from 2007 to 2017 was simply due to an aging population.[19]

For men, labor force participation also may be falling because they're relying more on their spouse's income, they're receiving more disability benefits, they've served time in prison (which can be a stubborn barrier to future employment), or they're facing a dearth of good jobs due to automation and trade liberalization.[20]

For women, similar factors to some extent also may be driving lower labor force participation, including automation and the decline in manufacturing jobs. But women's job opportunities have improved as jobs and professions that once were exclusively male have opened up to them. Many women work in healthcare, a sector in which employment has steadily expanded. Women's labor force participation is likely limited by a scarcity of family-friendly workplace policies, but, at the same time, it is bolstered by public policies that provide support for working parents— namely, the continued expansion of the federal Earned Income Tax Credit as well as state Earned Income Tax Credits. In addition, some researchers have found that lower fertility rates and marriage rates among prime-age women have helped to increase women's labor force participation.[21]

The pandemic lowered LFPR in meaningful ways, especially for older workers. The aging of the population meant that, even before the pandemic, millions of Americans were expected to retire each year, but the pandemic sharply accelerated the number of workers who were in retirement by more than 2 million.

These unexpected retirements were driven more by a drop in the workers who were expected to come out of retirement, rather than the share of workers who left the workforce. Older workers often cycle between different ways of engaging in the labor market, sometimes jumping back and forth between retirement in their later years. Kansas City Fed economists Jun Nie and Shu-Kuei X. Yang found that workers moving from working to retirement during the pandemic stayed mostly constant, at around 0.6 percent each month. What changed was a sharp drop in the share who went from retirement back into the labor market. Before the pandemic, around 2 percent of retirees rejoined the labor market each month, but this rate was roughly halved during the pandemic. It appears that once older people were out of the labor market, the pandemic was a sufficient disincentive to keep them out.

This increase in retirement accounted for more than half the decline in Americans who are engaged in the labor market during the pandemic. The LFPR fell from 63.4 percent to 60.4 percent over the first few months of the pandemic, a truly stunning drop for a rate that usually only shifts by a tenth of a percent or so each month. The rate climbed in the middle part of 2020, but, as of this writing, only about a third of the drop was recaptured. We simply don't know whether this means that workers are returning to the labor force, and the pandemic has gone on long enough that many speculate that it was sufficient to keep older workers out of the labor market for good.

DO CHANGING INCENTIVES HELP EXPLAIN THE LABOR FORCE TRENDS OF OLDER WORKERS?

Do taxes, pensions, Social Security, and other public policies or private-sector factors help explain rising labor force participation by older workers? As noted, labor force participation seems likely to rise with a strong economy, when the demand for labor is strong and wages are rising. In such a situation, adults in general and prime-age workers in particular seem likelier to join the workforce than engage in other activities, such as raising children or attending college. Also, job seekers are likelier to find suitable jobs, and fewer workers drop out of the labor market altogether.

In practice, however, the impact of the business cycle on labor force participation by workers older than 55 is not strong. We noted earlier that the Great Recession had a negative impact on older workers, but the effect was not huge. Participation was 40.2 percent in May of 2009 and dropped to 39.9 percent in December, as the impact of the Great Recession grew. It peaked at 40.7 percent in December of 2012 and sat at 40.3 percent in January of 2020. The population of Americans over 55 is trending older, with a rising share of them in older age groups (e.g., 75 or older), and that drives down participation for that population group.[22]

As for Social Security, the gradual increase in the full retirement age from 65 to 67 likely has persuaded people to work longer before claiming benefits. As Giovanni Mastrobuoni found, every increase of 2 months per year in the full retirement age raises the average retirement age of affected workers by about a month for that year. Because Social Security benefits are based on a worker's earnings history, an extra year of work can boost one's benefits in retirement.[23] Benefit levels are based on one's 35 years of highest earnings, relative to an earnings maximum, so an extra year of work does not necessarily boost benefits—and it always means an extra year of paying payroll taxes.

Some workers are subject to an earnings test—a complicated set of restrictions that effectively force some working seniors to defer some of their benefits. Because these seniors eventually get their benefits, the deferral is more like a forced saving plan than a tax, but the delay in benefits is often viewed as a high tax on work. Thus, Social Security can dissuade older Americans from working an extra year.

The penalties to working longer have been shrinking over time, however. In 1983, President Reagan and Congress enacted three important reforms as part of an effort to prevent Social Security from going bankrupt in the months to come. First, they boosted the benefit that retirees would get in waiting longer to claim their benefits, giving an extra boost to older Americans who—whether working or not—waited before receiving benefits. (The legislation gradually raised the benefit from each additional year of delay to around 8 percent, from 3 percent.) Second, they raised the full retirement age, so that workers had to wait longer before receiving their entire benefit amount. And third, in the 1983 law and subsequent legislation, they gradually scaled back the earnings test, providing relief for workers who viewed that test as a tax on their earnings.[24]

As we have said, Medicare provides an incentive for workers to work until age 65 if their employer provides health insurance. Most employers take away benefits for those who work part-time, so the incentive to keep working full-time is strong. Once someone reaches 65, Medicare kicks in and enables people who had wanted to retire to do so without losing their health insurance coverage.

Medicare rules affect employers and may influence their hiring decisions. By law, employer health plans must offer the same coverage to all employees regardless of age. That means that an employee who is older than 65 does not have to move onto Medicare but can stay on an employer's health plan, which can prove expensive for employers and discourage them from hiring or retaining older workers.

In the past, workers with strong pension plans often also had retiree health plans. They could retire with health insurance before they were eligible for Medicare, which encouraged them to retire before 65. Some employers viewed these retiree plans as a good way to encourage older workers to retire, and they were not too expensive when health costs were much lower. Some union workers have such plans, and some firms still have them for those employed under old rules. More recently, employers have moved away from health insurance for retirees, however, and that has played a key role in convincing workers in their late 50s and early 60s to keep working.[25]

Another factor in the rising labor force participation of older workers may be greater longevity. Workers seeking to smooth their consumption across their lives must respond to longer lifespans by working longer or consuming less. The link between greater longevity and rising labor force participation by older workers remains unresolved. Though studies have demonstrated the link between more years of life and a greater capacity to work,[26] we don't know the extent to which workers choose to work longer for that reason.[27] As long as workers believe that the benefits of capitalizing on higher longevity by working more years outweigh the dissatisfaction that delayed retirement can bring, one set of researchers found, workers will work longer.[28]

MAKING THE RIGHT RETIREMENT DECISIONS

Some retirement decisions result from job losses. A worker is laid off if a plant closes or a company imposes a reduction in force (RIF). Perhaps the worker looks hard for a new job but cannot find one except at a very low wage. Perhaps employers want younger people or those with technical skills. After several applications and rejections, the worker gives up searching and decides to retire. In the policy section of this book, we will discuss the steps that might be taken to provide older workers who have lost jobs with more options for a second career.

Those who have jobs and can keep working have to decide how much they want to retire, how much they like or dislike their jobs, whether their health is good or bad, and whether their financial resources are adequate. For those who have the option to work, deciding to work a bit longer may be a good choice. And, before the pandemic, there is clear evidence that many older workers were agreeing with that and choosing to keep working longer than their parents did.

Those who work longer may also need to save more. For many Americans, however, that is no easy challenge. The obstacles that they face can seem insurmountable, as we explore in the next chapter.

Why Is Saving So Hard?

In terms of preparing for their own retirement, almost every worker in America pays Social Security's payroll tax, which promises eventual benefits throughout retirement. Millions of Americans also save by contributing to retirement accounts and other investment vehicles, by buying homes and accumulating equity through them, and by growing small businesses that they can then sell to help finance a more prosperous retirement.

Nevertheless, as we have discussed, millions of households do not have the assets to enjoy a comfortable retirement where they can maintain the standard of living they are used to. Too many retirees, especially older women, are poor. Too many people rely on Social Security for all or nearly all their retirement income. Too many are not prepared for the risks they may face in retirement, which include living more years than their financial assets can support and developing health problems that force them to tap their savings to pay for long-term care. The problem has grown worse over the past two decades, with more Americans lacking the assets for an adequate retirement.

How did we get here? The challenges to retirement saving come in many forms. Some Americans are myopic, focused far more on consuming today than saving for tomorrow. Many workers lack access to a workplace retirement program run by their employer. Some may lack the financial literacy to set up and manage a retirement savings account. In this chapter, we look at these and other barriers to saving, and we then analyze our current system of tax breaks for saving, which we find deeply flawed.

BARRIERS TO SAVING

To look at the barriers to saving, we first have to define "saving." Certain behavior, like putting money into a 401(k) or a savings account, clearly qualifies. But what about paying off a mortgage? Or investing in a small business venture?

Economists classify income as either saving or consumption. Consumption is spending on things that don't generate income in the future, and saving is what's left over. Most saving is invested, so a person can reasonably think of saving and investment as anything that leads to more income in the future. For example, buying a car for personal use is consumption, while buying one to operate a ride-sharing service is an investment and would be classified as saving. Paying down debt, too, is a form of saving.

This classification leaves further questions about saving. If a stock increases in value by $5,000, but the investor never sells it, does that constitute saving? If a house increases in value by $10,000, and the homeowner keeps the equity in the home rather than taking out a home equity line of credit, is that saving? In both cases, the answer is yes. These are both examples of income in the form of *unrealized gains*, or income that accrues to an investment that the investor has not "realized" (i.e., sold). While the IRS doesn't count (or tax) that income until the investor sells the asset, we should count the income as saving from an economic perspective.[1] Similarly, other types of increases in net worth, such as gains in the value of an art collection or a small business, also count as saving.

The first barrier to saving lies within human nature. For many, it is easier and more gratifying in the short run to spend than to save. Dining out or shopping on Amazon is very easy, whereas directing money from a paycheck into a retirement savings account on a consistent basis is hard.

The behavioral bias against saving is strong, largely because humans can't seem to help themselves. As one group of behavioralists put it:

> Our preferences for the long run tend to conflict with our short-run behavior. When planning for the long run, we intend to meet our deadlines, exercise regularly, and eat healthfully. But in the short run, we have little interest in revising manuscripts, jogging on the StairMaster, and skipping the chocolate soufflé á la mode. Delay of gratification is a nice long-term goal, but instant gratification is disconcertingly tempting.[2]

The bias is never stronger than in saving for retirement. Workers often know that they *should* save for retirement, but their urge not to do so is too strong. In one survey of workers with access to a workplace saving plan, two-thirds acknowledged that they were not saving enough—no one said they were saving too much—and, while more than a third of the self-described undersavers said that they planned to start saving in the next few months, none of them actually did so.[3]

We will talk more about solutions to encourage saving in the final policy section of this book, but an important development in economics is worth describing here. While many Americans find it very hard to save in certain ways, they find it easier to save in others. For what appear to be psychological reasons, Americans often find it harder to engage in active saving (taking the initiative to move an asset, like cash, into a saving vehicle), but they struggle much less when it comes to passive saving (in which part of their pay is moved into a retirement account every pay period). This development in behavioral economics has encouraged a promising approach to encouraging saving: *automatic enrollment*. This is where companies introduce a system of automatic enrollment for employees in a 401(k)-type retirement plan. The company deducts a percentage of each worker's paycheck each month (say, 3 or 5 percent) and automatically directs the contributions to a designated investment. A worker can change any of that at any stage in the process, but it remains in place if the worker takes no action. Automatic enrollment can dramatically change saving behavior. In one company that switched from voluntary to automatic enrollment, the share of workers participating in the company plan immediately rose from 37.4 to 85.9 percent.[4]

The second barrier to retirement saving is access. Roughly half of the workforce lacks access to a 401(k)-type savings plan. They may be self-employed, for instance, or they may work for a small employer that has not set up such a plan. In principle, workers can set up their own retirement savings program by creating an individual retirement account or IRA, but that requires a real commitment by the worker to contact a financial institution, do the paperwork, and arrange for regular contributions to the account. Automatic enrollment in a company retirement plan makes it much easier to save. Having to set up one's own IRA account and keep contributing regularly makes it hard to save, and lots of workers who do not have access to a company plan also do not have IRAs or do not contribute consistently.

The third barrier to saving is poor financial literacy. Americans often score poorly on financial literacy assessments, according to many studies that typically focus on whether respondents can correctly answer questions on financial-related material—in particular the power of compounding, the role of inflation, and the value of portfolio diversification.[5] Economist Annamaria Lusardi, who has written extensively on this topic, found that only one-third of baby boomers could correctly answer three simple questions about financial literacy.[6]

If workers don't understand the value of saving, they won't save; indeed, Lusardi found a connection between literacy and financial planning. Across the economic literature, however, the link between financial knowledge and behavior is more tenuous, as several studies revealed that financial education in high school has little or no impact on saving behavior as an adult.[7] Discovering ways in which more knowledge can conclusively change financial behavior remains a major challenge for policymakers.

Financial literacy can also include functional literacy, as well as theoretical literacy. In a *Wall Street Journal* op-ed, one of us (Harris) described a situation in which a group of research assistants sought advice on how to establish IRAs. This was not a case of financial illiteracy; these young workers became PhDs in economics and MBAs from some of the nation's top programs and well understood economic theory. They did not, however, know the mechanics of how to set up a retirement account. As with the difference between understanding the principles of how a combustion engine works and knowing how to fix a problem in one's car, so, too, is there a difference between knowing the value of compounding interest and how to set up an Ameritrade account. Proper saving often requires understanding both the value of saving and how to set up an account.

Some economists are skeptical that the behavioral biases we have described are important. Many people have a rational perspective on saving, and their behavior is described by a *neoclassical* approach, which assumes that people act in whatever way enables them to maximize their welfare or well-being over the course of their lifetimes. This approach pinpoints saving incentives and investment returns as factors that will affect saving. Saving incentives can come from the tax code, which we discuss at length below, but programs intended to help poor families can also create savings incentives.

A barrier to saving for those at the lower end in terms of income and wealth comes from asset tests in public programs, which can discourage saving. The tests affect eligibility for programs like Medicaid (the major program that provides health coverage for lower-income families) and Supplemental Security Income (SSI, which provides modest cash to low-income seniors or people with disabilities). Individuals are ineligible for these programs if they have more than a certain amount of saving. With SSI, the limit is $2,000 for individuals and $3,000 for couples, and that limit has been in place since 1989, with no increase since then to account for inflation. While some assets, such as homes, home furniture, and cars, don't count for the test, the low asset limit means that most types of saving disqualify potential beneficiaries from SSI. Assets tests seem to shape how much, and what, low-income households save, but the evidence is not conclusive.[8]

Even the most rational family that realizes the need for retirement saving may struggle to save if they have substantial debts. The debt that people assume early in their lives—mainly student loans and mortgage debt but also credit card balances, medical debt, and auto loans—can also depress saving. This type of debt has been rising for young people who have to devote large shares of their earnings to pay it off rather than save for the future. On the other hand, higher student loan debt is associated with higher levels of education, which drive substantially higher lifetime wages. Bigger mortgages are associated with more home equity, which is a major source of wealth for older Americans. To assess whether debt-financed investment (including borrowing to nourish skills or buy a house) affects lifetime saving, we need to evaluate both the costs and returns to the investment.

Student loan debt is clearly a rising burden for young people; it exploded over the past three decades, rising in inflation-adjusted terms from $64 billion in 1985 to $1.7 trillion in 2021 (and tripling since just 2007).[9] A complex combination of factors is driving the increase, including rising tuition (both before and after accounting for student loans and grants), the changing composition of education that includes higher attendance at for-profit schools and in graduate programs, and the changing composition of student borrowers.[10] The student debt increase is hampering retirement saving, some studies suggest. One found that, among graduates with a bachelor's degree, those with student loans had accumulated roughly half the retirement assets by age 30 as their counterparts without loans.[11] Another found that holders of student debt were about 10 percentage points likelier to be at risk for inadequate saving, although this study did not control for differences between groups.[12]

Student loan debt may influence decisions about home buying. That is, student debt could "crowd out" mortgage debt by reducing the income available for mortgage payments, reducing the assets available for down payments, or lowering credit scores, which in turn would raise borrowing costs associated with a mortgage. Experts have not reached a consensus on these issues. We, the authors, suspect that college attendance raises homeownership rates over time because college graduates tend to make more money than non-graduates, but that student loan debt tends to delay homeownership as people may choose to pay off their loans before assuming a mortgage.

Even those who try to make rational saving decisions can struggle with how to invest, especially in an environment in which the rate of return on safe investments is so low. Another barrier to saving may be persistently low returns to investment. Theoretically, as we have said, the relationship between investment returns and saving rates could move in either direction. That is, low expected returns could depress saving because saving a dollar today buys less tomorrow, but low returns could boost saving if workers decide they need to save more today to reach a given level of saving down the road. We think the evidence supports the view that higher interest rates encourage saving, but the responsiveness of saving is not great. The path of investment returns is, of course, uncertain. Currently, the "equity premium"—the additional expected return on stocks relative to bonds—is high (it compensates for the additional risk in holding equities). It may get lower in the future due to increased ease of diversification, lower trading costs, and a wider pool of capital.[13]

Choosing the "optimal" mix of investments is a further challenge, especially as savers increasingly must decide how to invest. While workers have improved upon past mistakes, such as overinvesting in the stock of their employer, other opportunities for missteps have arisen, such as investing in complex exchange-traded funds intended for professionals. And while the ongoing cost of owning funds ("expense ratios") has fallen with the advent of low-cost index funds and trading fees have plummeted, many investors also may not recognize the costs in terms of bid-ask spreads (i.e., the difference between the price at which an investor can sell or buy a stock). These complex decisions can both dissuade workers from investing at all and make it increasingly difficult for them to pinpoint the most appropriate portfolio given their age, wealth, and taste for risk. Employers are now required to make sure their employees have access to advice in their 401(k)-type plans.

Social Security may also be a barrier to saving as workers must pay the payroll tax that finances the program but only benefit upon retirement. Social Security offers a lifetime annuity, with a progressive benefit formula that provides more benefits per dollar of saving to lower-income workers. With this program in place, households can save much less, whether in retirement accounts or elsewhere, to achieve a given standard of living, and some don't need to save at all. Households have far less need to stock-pile a large share of assets in case retirees live to advanced ages, so they have more income to spend during their working lives.

In the 1970s and '80s, economists worried much more that Social Security's impact on saving, along with program restrictions that pro-hibited Social Security from investing its trust funds in anything but Treasury securities, would hurt economic growth. By reducing the need for households to save as much in private accounts, economists reasoned, Social Security would reduce the amount of capital available for invest-ment, which ultimately would mean a smaller economy because available capital is a major factor in determining the pace of economic growth. The large global "glut" of capital that developed in subsequent years has largely assuaged those fears, as we discussed in Chapter 3.

Ironically, efforts to force people to save more can become a barrier to saving. Consider what happens with "leakage," which occurs when working-age savers dip into their retirement accounts, including 401(k)-type accounts and IRAs. Outside of a few unique circumstances, those younger than 59-and-a-half can only access their retirement assets if they pay taxes and a 10 percent penalty on their withdrawals. Policymakers enacted this provision to discourage savers from using their retirement accounts for other purposes.

Savers have ways to avoid the tax and penalty, however. At the employer's discretion, some plans let savers take out loans against their assets, though the amount is limited, the loan must be tied to a financial need, and the account holder typically must repay the loans over 5 years with interest. Plans also can allow for hardship withdrawals—penalty-free withdrawals in the event of "immediate and heavy financial need"—and savers must pay only the income taxes due and don't need to repay the withdrawals. (Not all plans offer the option of loans or hardship withdrawals.)

Leakage can occur in other ways. Roughly 10 million workers with re-tirement accounts each year change employers and, at that point, can "roll over" their balances into a new plan, keep their assets with their old em-ployer, or—in an example of leakage—"cash out" their balances, paying taxes and penalties. In 2013, the Government Accountability Office found that retirement accounts lost $69 billion from leakage[14]: $40 billion from early withdrawals, $19 billion from hardship withdrawals, $10 billion from cash-outs upon leaving a job, and less than $1 billion from unpaid loans from 401(k)s.

The combination of leakage options and tax penalties represents an attempt to balance incentives to keep retirement funds in accounts against steps that would discourage saving in the first place. The taxes and penalties make it less likely that people will succumb to the temptation to keep up with the Joneses at the expense of their retirement security, reduce dependence on Social Security, and help ensure that tax breaks for retirement saving do not become loopholes for well-informed savers. On the flipside, if people can never dip into their 401(k)s, even as their home is foreclosed or they face steep medical bills, such restrictions would impose undue costs on them and perhaps prove a disincentive to retirement saving in the first place.

A complicating factor for saving, which is too complex to qualify as a "barrier," is *wealth transfers*: either as inheritances or as gifts while the giver is alive. Wealth transfers between individuals are massive and widespread.[15] An estimated 51 percent of wealth accumulation occurred through intergenerational transfers, one study found, while another found that 30 percent of households expect to receive a gift or inheritance and that the transfer will comprise about 40 percent of the household's wealth at the end of their lives.[16]

Wealth transfers seem to influence saving in only limited ways, however, for three reasons. First, uncertainty surrounds the timing and amount of inheritances, and risk-adverse people choose to save in the face of such uncertainty. Second, transfers typically happen later in life, most often around age 60, and people likely have accumulated nest eggs by then. And third, the desire to leave an inheritance is a strong incentive to save, offsetting the disincentive among those who have received inheritances or gifts themselves. And while expected wealth transfers may reduce saving for some, the transfer of wealth can be an important contribution to retirement assets for others.

For low- and middle-income workers, the last major obstacle to saving is the inadequate and unequal set of tax incentives to encourage it. That's an important and complicated enough subject to deserve its own section, which follows.

UNEQUAL TAX BREAKS FOR SAVING

The tax code promotes saving through a series of tax preferences. The largest relate to contributions to retirement accounts, but they also include lower tax rates on investments in stocks, tax breaks for owning a home (which is a form of saving), and tax breaks for holding investments until death. Collectively, these tax breaks are hugely expensive, exceeding $300 billion a year in lost federal revenue.

Workers and employers generally pay no income or payroll taxes on the income they use to contribute to retirement accounts. The contributions also can grow tax-free in these accounts, and the money is taxed only when account holders withdraw it. Workers benefit because they don't have to pay tax as their retirement accounts grow and because they pay tax only in retirement, when they will likely pay a lower tax rate than during their working years.

If, for example, a 35-year-old puts $1,000 into a 401(k), he pays no tax on that $1,000. Then, assume that the $1,000 grows by 7 percent a year. In the first year, it would have generated $70 in returns, and a taxpayer in the 20 percent bracket would have otherwise owed $14. As the returns on that initial contribution grow each year, so does the value of the tax benefit.[17] After the worker retires and begins withdrawing funds, the distributions are taxed at income tax rates that, for most people, are lower in retirement than in their working years.

An alternative, but less popular vehicle for retirement saving is a "Roth" type account, including Roth 401(k)s or Roth IRAs. Contributions to them are not tax free, but the funds in them can grow tax free and account holders do not pay tax on their withdrawals. Whether the benefits of a Roth-type account are greater or less than those of a traditional retirement account depends heavily on the account holders' tax rates during their working years as compared to their retirement.

Both traditional and Roth-type retirement accounts are highly regressive, with their tax benefits flowing overwhelmingly to those at the top.[18] As shown in Table 6.1, just 2.0 percent of households in the lowest fifth in

Table 6.1 TAX BENEFITS OF DEFINED-CONTRIBUTION PLANS AND IRAS BY CASH INCOME PERCENTILE, 2004.[A,B]

Cash income percentile[c]	Percent of tax units with benefit[d]	Benefit as percent of after-tax income[e]	Share of total benefits	Average benefit ($)
Lowest quintile	2.0	0.1	0.2	−6
Second quintile	12.7	0.4	2.9	−77
Middle quintile	24.9	0.7	7.9	−208
Fourth quintile	43.0	1.1	19.3	−509
Top quintile	61.0	1.4	69.7	−1838
All	28.7	1.2	100.0	−528
Addendum				
Top 10 percent	63.8	1.4	48.6	−2566
Top 5 percent	61.9	1.2	30.4	−3211
Top 1 percent	53.3	0.6	7.8	−4111
Top 0.5 percent	51.6	0.4	4.0	−4252
Top 0.1 percent	51.4	0.2	0.9	−4645

[a] Source: Urban-Brookings Tax Policy Center Microsimulation Model.

[b] Distribution of the present value of lifetime tax benefits for new contributions made in 2004.

[c] Tax units with negative cash income are excluded from the lowest income class but are included in the totals.

See http://www.taxpolicycenter.org/TaxModel/income.cfm for a description of cash income.

[d] Both filing and non-filing units are included. Filers who can be claimed as dependents by other filers are excluded from the analysis.

[e] After-tax income is cash income less individual income tax net of refundable credits, payroll and estate tax liability, and imputed burden from corporate taxes.

terms of income benefit in any given year, compared to 24.9 percent of households in the middle fifth and 61.0 percent in the top fifth. The distribution of benefits is even more skewed, with 69.7 percent going to the top fifth, 7.9 percent to the middle fifth, and just 0.2 percent to the bottom fifth.[19]

President George W. Bush and Congress created the Saver's Credit in 2001 to incentivize lower-income households to save. It provides a tax credit for contributions to retirement accounts, with larger credits offered to those with the lowest incomes. A worker with very low income, for instance, might receive a $500 credit for investing $1,000 in a retirement account. Unfortunately, the credit has done little to boost saving probably because it is complicated, it does little for those with the greatest means to save, and it provides no benefit to those who make too little to owe any income taxes.[20]

Retirement saving incentives are far from the only tax subsidies for saving. Taxpayers pay substantially lower tax rates on investment income (capital gains and dividends) than on ordinary income, such as wages. Tax rates on ordinary income range from 12 to 37 percent, while rates on long-term capital gains and dividends (investments held for at least a year) range from 0 to 20 percent (though investors with especially high incomes pay a 3.8 percent surcharge on their investment income to help fund Medicare). With respect to capital gains, investors also can choose when to sell an asset and realize a gain, which lets them do so when tax rates are low.

Whether these lower rates boost investment is among the most contentious issues in public finance. Some economists believe that lower rates incentivize substantially more investment, driving higher rates of capital, more economic growth, and, some believe, greater benefits to workers in the form of higher wages. Other are skeptical, finding limited benefits for anyone other than the wealthiest taxpayers. Several studies have found that every $100 in tax-based saving incentives only raises saving by about $1.[21]

When it comes to capital gains, investors benefit from more than low tax rates. When someone holds an asset until death, the heir pays no tax on its increase in value over the years. That produces a massive tax benefit to the heirs of investors with the means to invest large sums of money and the flexibility to hold assets until death. Some economists criticize this provision on equity grounds, arguing that it preserves wealth across generations and limits economic mobility, while others say that by incentivizing investors to hold assets to escape capital gains taxes, it starves the economy of capital needed for more productive investments.

The tax code also provides savings incentives to spur home ownership. Homeowners who itemize their deductions can deduct their mortgage interest and property taxes. They don't pay capital gains tax on the first $250,000 (per person) in gains on the value of their homes or on any gains if they hold their homes until death.[22] Overall, however, economic research has shown that these incentives for home ownership have not boosted home ownership rates.[23] At best, these tax incentives prompt people to buy more expensive homes and assume more mortgage debt, rather than pay off their homes and invest more in financial vehicles.[24]

Having said that, tax incentives for home ownership have been shrinking. In particular, the 2017 Tax Cuts and Jobs Act sharply reduced deductions for home ownership by greatly increasing the standard deduction (thus discouraging itemized deductions), limiting deductions for state and local taxes to $10,000 (thus limiting the amount of deductible property taxes), lowering tax rates (thus reducing the value of every dollar of deduction), and limiting the size of mortgages from which interest is deducted (to $750,000). These limits reduced the share of taxpayers who claim the mortgage interest deduction from 20 to 8 percent—with almost no one earning less than $50,000 claiming the benefit.[25]

Aside from the meager Saver's Credit, then, tax incentives to spur saving are worth far more to upper-income taxpayers. So, while the federal government allocates hundreds of billions of dollars to subsidize retirement saving and home ownership each year, these tax breaks are largely wasteful, are worth little to anyone but the wealthiest families, and reward investors for holding on to poorly performing investments and assuming more mortgage debt than they otherwise would.

While those who want to prepare for retirement face barriers to savings as well as savings incentives through the tax code that overwhelmingly favors upper-income taxpayers, they must navigate a changing labor market that presents both new challenges and new opportunities. That is where we turn next.

Transitioning to Retirement in a Changing Labor Market

As we discussed in Chapter 5, one way for families to prepare for retirement is to work longer and not retire until they have a secure base of financial assets. That does not necessarily mean working full time up to the day of retirement. By phasing down work over a period of years, individuals can enjoy less stress and more opportunity to develop retirement hobbies and activities while still earning income. Workers can choose part-time work and a phased retirement.

The labor market is changing, and that presents both challenges and opportunities to those approaching retirement. Change is hardly new, and, as the economy evolves, the plentiful jobs of one era often disappear a few years or decades later. Still, change today seems bewilderingly rapid. For some older employees, the skills that were valued when they started working are no longer prized, or they must supplement those skills with new technological savvy. If we expect workers to keep working, they must be able to remain qualified for good jobs. As a result, retooling skills can be an important part of phased retirement.

Self-employment is one way for older workers to keep working. In many cases, that occurs when a worker retires from a company but does contract work for that same company after retirement. Alternative approaches to self-employment are open to those with professions—such as lawyers, carpenters, or healthcare workers—who can often work freelance after they retire from their regular jobs. Self-employment is an important avenue for older workers to keep working, perhaps part-time.

Have online work platforms provided opportunities for older people to work in new ways? Those with technical expertise can offer their services through internet platforms that are designed to support "gig" work (where people work on a single job or gig rather than in regular employment). Rather than work for a taxi company, for instance, they can work for Uber or Lyft. Realistically, however, most older workers should not expect to make steady income from these platforms, although they can serve as a supplement to other forms of income.

Older workers are often at the mercy of changing workforce trends that raise the demand for some jobs over others, while macroeconomic trends can affect the demand for work more generally. The shock that COVID-19 inflicted on the labor market is one prime example, for the pandemic made it much harder for all workers to keep working and it accelerated some technological trends already under way.

The pandemic was especially hard on service workers, such as those in restaurants and bars, retail, tourism, and customer-facing services where people could easily postpone their purchases or find an online alternative. Companies that had been looking at automating positions over several years found ways to accelerate the technology and reduce the number of workers they needed. Workers in stable higher-paying jobs were protected and could often work from home, but the young and old were very hard hit. Young people starting out on the job ladder initially found that few companies were hiring. Older workers who were laid off found it hard or impossible to get their jobs back or find a good alternative position. And, of course, older workers were much more vulnerable to the disease and often decided to forgo employment rather than face exposure to COVID. As of this writing, it remains unsettled whether these trends will become permanent.

Phased retirement can help offset the social and cognitive challenges that older Americans face, and it can extend their lifespans. Theoretically, the social aspect of work can partially mitigate the loneliness epidemic that has gripped so many older individuals. Similarly, the intellectual stimulation that part-time work offers can forestall the cognitive decline of many in old age. These benefits are helpful reminders that the gains from work can extend beyond a paycheck. Similarly, while retirement does not always drive unhealthy habits, staying in the workforce may be the "nudge" that some people need to remain physically active or eat healthier foods.

All told, phased retirement in all its forms offers many potential benefits for older Americans. A strengthened system of phased retirement is an important part of any modern retirement landscape.

PART-TIME WORK AMONG OLDER WORKERS

To assess the merits of phased retirement, an important consideration is the share of older workers who choose part-time work. As Figure 7.1 shows, around 10 percent of employees in their 50s are working part-time, but the share rises to about 30 percent for those in their 60s and to about

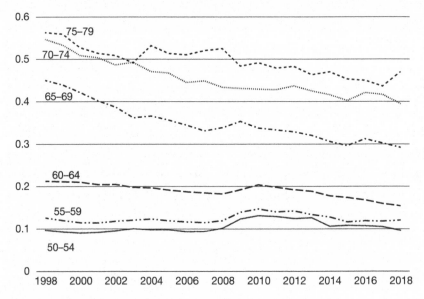

Figure 7.1 Shares of older employees working part-time.
SOURCE: Bureau of Labor Statistics.

40–45 percent for those in their 70s. Part-time workers as a share of all workers have remained mostly constant among those in their 50s and fell for the older groups.[1] In short, working part-time is common among older workers, but it has become less common over time.

Do the many older workers who are working part time do so because they cannot find full-time work? When the Bureau of Labor Statistics surveys a sample of Americans each month about whether they are working full or part time, it asks part-time workers why they are working part time. Overwhelmingly, the reason is that they wanted to do so. In 2019, only 8.8 percent of part-time workers older than 55 said they wanted to work full time but could find only part-time work.[2] Since then, the COVID-19 pandemic has resulted in enormous disruptions to the labor market, disruptions that will likely take several years to work through. Some older workers who lost their jobs as a result of the pandemic may never return to full-time employment with the wages and seniority that they achieved beforehand. And, as we discussed earlier, the share of workers exiting retirement to rejoin the labor market fell sharply.

It is worth putting the long-term trends that emerged before the pandemic into perspective. The older workforce doubled in size from around 19 million in 2000 to 38 million in 2019 as both the number of older people and their labor force participation rose. The labor market absorbed a massive influx of older workers and did so while the unemployment rate was low (before COVID-19 struck in 2020) and while the great majority of workers could choose whether to work part or full time. Among those who kept working into their 60s and 70s, many chose to work part time and have a phased retirement. Thus, working part time seems an important option for those approaching retirement and who want to keep making money but also scale back from full-time work.[3]

PATHS TO RETIREMENT

Based on a survey that followed workers over time, the path to retirement is quite complicated.[4] One might have expected workers to go from full-time work straight into full retirement or to work part time for a while before retiring. As it turns out, people retire and then un-retire, or they shift to part-time work and then back to full-time work. That's an important consideration for policymakers as they develop retirement policies and for individuals and families that are considering their options. On the way to a secure retirement, people change their minds or their circumstances may change, giving them new choices. Recognizing this may be especially important as the economy emerges from the pandemic.

How many people take an unconventional route to retirement? The following results came from a survey in which respondents from a sample of those born between 1931 and 1941 were followed for 6 years, with interviews that extended through 2002:[5]

- Just over half (52.2 percent) left a full-time job, completely retired, and stayed retired. This is what we call the "traditional view of retirement," and most respondents followed that path.
- Nearly a fifth (19.2 percent) retired and stopped working completely but returned to work later. Some returned to full-time work, while others worked part time. They later said they had retired but then changed their minds. (Perhaps they had lost a job or left a job they did not like and then looked for a new job, either full or part time.) Apparently, their decision was not driven by economic necessity. More than 80 percent said they chose to return to work; they were not forced to do so.
- The rest (28.6 percent) transitioned from full- to part-time work or reduced their hours of work substantially in their existing job. Most of this group transitioned to complete retirement, but a small portion moved from partial retirement back to full-time work.

All told, nearly half of the respondents followed a nontraditional retirement path, with some even retiring and then un-retiring. Partial or phased retirement is an option that many people take, letting them earn money for a longer time. With phased retirement, people move in and out of retirement. Those crafting retirement policy and those advising retirees must recognize that the path to retirement often involves part-time work and that the decision to retire is not irrevocable. We cannot know as this is written how the labor market recovery from COVID-19 will ultimately play out, but we think it likely that even more older workers will take non-traditional paths to retirement, especially as telework has become more common and more established. This involves less commuting and less physical strain and perhaps a greater willingness among employers to accommodate more flexible work schedules. Ultimately, this will lead to an improved outlook for workers overall, as older Americans will have more agency to tailor their work effort to their specific preferences and circumstances.

SELF-EMPLOYMENT AT OLDER AGES

If we expect people to work longer, what jobs do we think they will fill in those additional years of work? One recent study, based on an extensive Gallup telephone survey, provided a very helpful picture.[6] The survey covered those aged 18–79 and included detailed questions to determine whether people worked for an employer or for themselves. What did it reveal?

First, more people work for themselves than previous surveys estimated. Lots of people, especially older workers, are independent contractors who take assignments (providing services directly to customers or, often, to companies). When older workers retire from their regular jobs, they may continue to work—even for the same company—but on assignment, under which they are paid for a specific task. Independent contractors have more freedom to control their work hours, but they don't receive fringe benefits, such as health insurance and contributions to a retirement fund.[7] For Medicare-eligible workers who are 65 or older, however, the absence of health insurance benefits may be a less important factor than for younger workers.

Second, self-employment of all kinds comprises a much greater share of work as people grow older. Among those 18–79, 67 percent said they have done some paid work. Of that group, 23.6 percent are self-employed. Self-employment rises steadily with age, reaching 45.5 percent for those 65–69 and 67.5 percent for those 75–79.[8] *So, about a half to two-thirds of those who work into their 60s and 70s are self-employed.* Some retire and then do contract work for their old employer, while others find clients that are willing to pay them for their services.

Not everyone has the qualifications or skills for self-employment. People's level of education has a big impact on the jobs they secure. Workers with higher education are likelier to be in career positions in which they like their jobs and are well paid. The Gallup survey confirmed a pattern from previous studies: workers with a college degree remain in the workforce much longer than those with a high school education or less. Nevertheless, among those who keep working at older ages, self-employment is common among those without a college degree. Just as a lawyer can keep practicing law as she gets older, so, too, can a carpenter or painter.

CAN INTERNET PLATFORMS HELP OLDER PEOPLE FIND WORK?

New platforms on the internet enable people to offer their services and may help older people who want to be self-employed and work part time but are unable to find clients.

Two of the best-known mobile apps are Lyft and Uber, which let people provide what are known as *peer-to-peer services*, in this case taxi service. Another important example of peer-to-peer services is Airbnb, through which people offer "hotel" services, renting out rooms or homes. Upwork and TaskRabbit let individuals select or bid for one-off tasks. Marketplaces such as Etsy allow for the sale of art or craft-made products. Amazon, of course, provides a market for millions of retailers, small and large, to sell their products, even though these retailers often do not have retail premises.

Given media coverage of the gig economy, one could expect the emerging new economy to provide an important source of jobs and revenue for older people looking for part- or even full-time work. That is not the case, however. From the Gallup survey cited above, just 3.1 percent of employment by all ages (based on a person's main job) was work performed using internet platforms. As Figure 7.2 shows, for those older than 60, it's more like 2 percent.

Similarly, the JP Morgan Chase Institute mined its enormous dataset of millions of checking account and credit card customers to identify income generated from work conducted through online platforms. In 2017–2018, the Institute reported that just 4.5 percent of its sample of bank customers had income from online platforms over a 12-month period. That figure had risen from less than 2 percent in 2012–2013. On the other hand, the percent of customers reporting income in any given month was much lower, at 1.6 percent in 2017–2018, indicating that most people using these platforms did so sporadically rather than consistently.

Moreover, the money collected through online work platforms was low and fell over the 5-year period. Monthly earnings averaged $762 for all users in the months of 2017–2018 when they were working. Transportation (think Uber and Lyft) was the most frequent area of work, while Airbnb

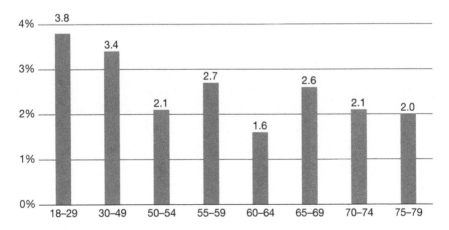

Figure 7.2 Share of workers participating in online platform work, by age group (percent of group).
SOURCE: Authors, using data from Abraham, Hershbein, and Houseman (2020).

had the greatest monthly earnings. Among those 65 and older, only 0.5 percent used online platforms for work.

While the labor market is changing in important ways, online platforms have not significantly changed opportunities for older workers. Perhaps that will change in the future. Through 2018, however, online platforms did not represent a sizable share of the work of older workers, and we are almost certain this remains true to the present.

OLDER WORKERS MUST UNDERSTAND THE CHANGING LABOR MARKET

For older workers to work long enough to support themselves in retirement, they must understand how a changing labor market affects them. Three main forces are driving labor market change and shaping the job prospects of older workers: demographics, trade, and technology.

Demographics

After World War II, the combination of a baby boom and greater labor market participation by women drove a young, rapidly growing workforce. Today, the opposite is occurring.

The birth rate has slowed sharply. In 2020, America's fertility rate was just 1.64 births per woman, well-below the 2.1 rate required to keep the population stable in the absence of immigration, and the lowest level in US history.[9,10,11] Historically, the combination of steady immigration and a fertility rate above 2.1—the rate was 3.7 in the post-war baby boom— has meant a steadily rising population. Meanwhile, America's population is aging and will continue to do so, women's labor force participation is peaking, and life expectancy has increased. Due to all these factors, the rate of labor force growth has fallen considerably, while the average age of the population has risen. With the labor force of older workers (55 and older) doubling in size since 2000 and the labor force of younger workers (25–54) remaining flat, the ratio of older to younger workers has increased dramatically, as has the number of baby boomers moving into retirement.

What do these changing demographics mean for today's older workers? In modern labor markets, older workers who seek to keep working often face stiff competition for jobs. Recessions, including the most recent one in 2020, often devastate the job market for everyone, but rebuilding a career is much harder for older workers who have lost their jobs. This is particularly bad for low-income workers who may have preexisting financial retirement challenges that compound in downturns. We hope to see policymakers launch a major initiative to help older and disadvantaged workers navigate the impact of changing demographics. But workers also will need to make a major effort themselves to remain productive if they have not saved enough to retire early.

The Decline in Manufacturing Jobs

The number of manufacturing jobs peaked in 1979 at about 19.5 million. After the Great Recession, it reached a low in early 2010 of just under 11.5 million and then rose modestly to around 12.9 million before COVID-19. Blue-collar jobs declined as a share of all manufacturing jobs, with only 9 million production worker jobs in manufacturing in 2019.[12] In April of 2020, manufacturing employment fell to 11.4 million; it has been gradually recovering since then, but, as of this writing, employment remains well below its 2019 peak.

Liberals and conservatives alike blame international trade, and trade with China in particular, for the decline. Trade with China surely has played a role, but manufacturing output and employment have been *declining steadily as a share of the economy for more than 50 years*. Trade is not the only, or even the main, reason for this long-term trend, which is common to all industrial countries and driven heavily by technology. It took 10.1 worker-hours to produce 1 ton of steel in 1980, but just 1.5 hours in 2017.[13] Manufacturing jobs are only about a tenth of all jobs today, and that share will likely remain flat or keep declining, regardless of whether politicians keep promising to reverse the trend.

In the past, manufacturing played an outsized role in the labor market, providing well-paid jobs to millions of workers who lacked a college degree. Many of the jobs were unionized, with good benefits and pension programs.[14] Although the wages of men without advanced degrees have stagnated for several reasons, the loss of manufacturing jobs has been an important factor. Exacerbating the problem has been the decline in unionization because unions were instrumental in protecting worker interests. Facing the competitive pressure of imports, US companies resisted union demands and often built new factories in states that make it hard for workers to unionize.

What does this mean for older workers? Many workers reached their 40s and 50s as part of a unionized workforce, making good wages and expecting a pension, but they later lost their jobs, perhaps because the plant or company that employed them closed or went bankrupt. These workers face a tough road ahead in the job market because, while they have skills and experience, their skills are now less economically valuable. They may find new jobs, but they will not likely regain their previous salaries and benefits.

Blue-collar workers who have lost their jobs in manufacturing or related fields face a particularly tough road. In the last section of this book, we propose ways to help older Americans who want to remain in the labor market, but the specific problems of blue-collar workers demand proposals that are tailored to them.

- Retraining can help blue-collar workers fill jobs as plumbers, carpenters, auto mechanics, and welders, for which the pay is good and positions are available.
- We should follow the example of countries such as Denmark, France, Germany, and Sweden, which have committed relatively larger shares of the economy to retraining while also embracing data-oriented approaches to job matching and identifying labor shortages.

- Policymakers and the courts must protect pension benefits even when companies go through bankruptcy or when pension liabilities fall short of their promised benefits.

Technology and Tomorrow's Labor Market

Manufacturing jobs shrank so much in part because manufacturing adopted automation more than other economic sectors. With promised advances in robots, self-driving vehicles, and artificial intelligence, many more types of jobs beyond manufacturing may disappear as well. In addition, the need for digital skills will only increase, especially if workers incorporate working from home as a strategy for phasing into retirement. (One recent Urban Institute study[15] showed that roughly one-third of workers older than 65 lacked any digital skills, compared to less than 10 percent for younger workers.) These inevitable advances in technology will increase the challenges for Americans as they plan retirement and consider working longer.

Some fears about the job market of the future—specifically, that it will offer too few jobs for tomorrow's workforce—are generally not justified. While some jobs disappear, others will remain in demand and the economy will create new ones as well. These fears may be exacerbated when the economy slows, but we expect the historical trend of strong job growth during economic recoveries to continue. Over the past 30 years, in fact, recoveries have been stronger than in the prior 30 years. While the economy of the 1970s and early '80s was plagued by high inflation and persistent unemployment, unemployment fell below 4 percent in 2000, to about 4 percent in 2007, and to below 4 percent again in 2019. Technological advances are not limiting the availability of jobs.

The problem, instead, is a shortage of *good jobs*. As we have seen, good manufacturing jobs are in short supply. Beyond manufacturing, jobs that once paid well have been "deskilled"—that is, they require less skill and training to accomplish the tasks in question—and, as a result, they pay less. Meanwhile, income inequality has grown wider; those at the top enjoyed sizable income gains in recent decades, while most workers experienced only modest gains or even declines in inflation-adjusted wages.[16]

A shortage of good jobs emerged as technology evolved. Some of the same forces that eliminated many blue-collar jobs in manufacturing emerged in the service sector. Banks, for example, programmed their computers so they can hire low-skill workers as bank tellers and pay them low wages. Experts on emerging digital technologies worry that this technology trend will continue, if not accelerate.

Nevertheless, technology futurists foresee faster productivity and economic growth down the road, and they believe that new digital technologies will make things better overall, enabling more healthcare, more education, and more entertainment. Not everyone will enjoy the benefits, however. Mid-level jobs will shrink, and wages will stagnate for many workers. Compared to technological change historically, the new digital technologies will likelier create winner-take-all markets, with some growing rich, others falling behind, and many jobs eliminated. Those with special technological skills or education will prosper, while those with only ordinary skills may not. The most successful of all will be entrepreneurs and senior executives, as well as those who work in the financial sector.[17]

As we discuss in later chapters, policymakers will need to address the shortage of good jobs and stagnant incomes for all-too-many workers by strengthening core social insurance programs like Social Security and Medicare. They should make the tax system more progressive so that it takes less and offers more to those in the middle and at the bottom. They should make sure that giant companies do not exploit their size to squeeze workers or crush unions. At the same time, workers will need to make sure they have the right skills and acquire new skills as they get older.

Fears that the pandemic would initiate widespread changes in the labor market appear to be generally unfounded. Instead, long-term trends in the labor force will persist. Even before the pandemic, "brick and mortar" retailers were losing ground to online shopping—and that trend will likely continue. Businesses providing certain services, like dry cleaning and nursing home care, closed at rapid rates during the pandemic and have been slow to recover—which is bad news for workers employed in those industries. Not all these developments will be bad for jobs, however. The pandemic exposed the dangers created by value chains that are spread across the world. Some goods became unavailable and others took weeks to get. As a result, companies are rethinking where to locate production and where to source parts. That will not mean iPhones will be assembled in America, but we may see some increase in manufacturing jobs at home, spurred in part by policies to encourage companies to keep vital activities in the United States.

CAN PHASED RETIREMENT IMPROVE HEALTH?

By working longer, older workers will do more than earn more money. They also may forestall their cognitive decline and increase their social interaction.

"[I]n our rush to leave the office," retirement expert Richard Johnson wrote in a *Wall Street Journal* op-ed of April 2019, "we don't realize that retirement also has a downside, especially over the long term. Many retirees indulge in unhealthy behaviors. They become sedentary and watch too much television. They eat too much. They drink too much. They smoke too much. Without the purpose of fulfilling work, retirees can feel adrift and become depressed. Without the camaraderie of their co-workers, retirees risk becoming socially isolated. Without the intellectual stimulation that work can provide, retirement can accelerate cognitive decline."[18]

Johnson cited a paper by Maria Fitzpatrick and Timothy Moore, who studied the impact on mortality of people beginning to take their Social Security benefits at age 62, which is the first year of eligibility. They found a link between Social Security eligibility and a 2 percent increase in mortality for men and much larger increases for men who retire at that age. This study builds on a growing literature suggesting that retirement can lead to greater mortality, especially for male blue-collar workers.[19]

We don't know why retirement can boost mortality, but loneliness and the lack of a strong social network may play a role. Over a quarter of retirement-age Americans are considered "socially isolated," and several studies show a connection between social isolation and health.[20] The Centers for Disease Control (CDC) notes a link between social isolation and such indicators of poor health as higher rates of hospitalization, heart disease, and stroke. The CDC characterized the health impacts of loneliness as similar to those of obesity, smoking, and inactivity.[21]

A related concern is the impact of retirement on cognitive decline. A handful of studies suggest that cognition falls more for individuals who have been retired longer.[22] That is consistent with other research showing a link between intellectual challenges and higher levels of cognition. On average, staying in the workforce probably improves cognition over time, although the impacts vary for different populations, occupations, and dates of retirement.

The challenge of convincing people to keep working to maintain their health and cognitive abilities is, of course, that many people enjoy retirement. After all, there is more to retirement than staying healthy and being intellectually stimulated. Many workers report post-retirement improvements in "subjective well-being"—a fancy term for happiness. Also, if leaving work means less healthy and engaged lifestyles, then finding strategies to improve retiree health is an alternative to recommending that they keep working.

Nevertheless, phased retirement offers workers real promise—at least for some years—to remain engaged while retaining substantially more time for whatever activity makes them happy. While we do not know of any research that links numbers of hours worked to changes in health and cognition, it appears likely that the positive impacts decelerate with each additional hour worked. That is, the 1st hour spent at a job each week is probably more important to one's health than the 40th hour.

All told, phased retirement offers the triple benefit of higher wages, improved health, and more social interaction. For people with sufficient retirement income, with the discipline to avoid unhealthy habits, and with plenty of friends and family to enjoy, the benefits of phased retirement may not be worth the costs of less time for other pursuits. But for those who need the income or who suspect that retirement means a descent into a less healthy lifestyle, phased retirement may offer the best of both worlds.

As Americans consider how much to work in their later years and when to retire, they need the savings vehicles through which they can ensure themselves a comfortable retirement. One vehicle that gets far too little attention and that holds particular promise is a *longevity annuity*—the subject of our next chapter.

How Annuities Can Mitigate Uncertainty and Improve Retirement

In its purest form, an annuity is a contract between an individual and a life insurance company in which the individual pays a premium in exchange for guaranteed payments from the insurance company until the individual dies. With these guaranteed payments, annuities reduce the financial risk associated with unknown lifespans. In essence, the risk shifts from the individual to the insurer because the insurer pays the individual no matter how long the person lives. For the individual, "de-risking" the longevity risk in retirement brings important benefits, such as reducing the need to stockpile savings to protect against an especially long lifespan.

De-risked retirement products were once popular. Under the retirement paradigm of decades ago, many workers had company pensions, received guaranteed income for life, and enjoyed comfortable retirements free of financial anxiety. Today, workers who still have pensions, such as union members and public-sector workers, value them highly and fight efforts to end or cut their benefits.

The new de facto paradigm, however, has shifted to one characterized by risk. As we have emphasized throughout this book, many workers reach retirement with little or no financial assets, while even those with sizable savings rarely have protection against long lifespans. Middle-class families that reach retirement with ample retirement nest eggs rarely buy annuities to ensure lifetime income. Few employer retirement plans offer annuities, and annuities that an individual would buy remain unpopular. In fact, *longevity annuities*—a product (as we explain later) that specifically targets longevity risk and that, according to economists, should provide substantial value to retirees—have not yet achieved even modest acceptance by households. Retirees are largely choosing to weather retirement with more risk and uncertainty than they need to face.

Tax accountants, asset managers, and even some researchers note problems with the annuity market as it now operates: the market often features confusing products that are labeled as annuities but do little to "de-risk" retirement, those who put too much money in an annuity can find themselves without enough cash, and fees can be extraordinarily high. These problems, however, do not apply equally to all annuities—especially the types of annuities that economists favor and that we describe in this chapter.

Financial advisors are often reluctant to recommend annuities to their clients for many reasons: advisers may see better value in financial investments, they are often not licensed to sell annuities, and they traditionally have not been able to accept the commission that insurance companies pay when an annuity is sold. Also, since financial advisors' compensation is often directly tied to the size of their clients' investment portfolios, allocating retirement funds to annuities can reduce the share of stocks and bonds in portfolios and thus siphon fees from the advisers who manage them.

Expanding the market for annuities is critical for the retirement landscape for two reasons. To start, if more life insurance companies offered annuity products, that would mean more competition among these companies, which can then lower fees for the products. More importantly, in a landscape without pensions, there is practically no way, other than annuities, for retirees to reduce longevity risk in their portfolio.

The most promising way to expand the annuity market is to involve employers. Encouraging employers to make annuities available to employees as part of their retirement plans would enable employers to negotiate fees downward and help alleviate the confusion that their employees may have. Under this system, employers would not only help workers build up their nest eggs, but they also would help workers settle on a strategy for turning their nest eggs into streams of income payments. Employers can also establish strategies for providing employees unbiased information about the benefits of annuities (and other retirement products).

The market for annuities depends in part on the state of the economy. All else equal, low interest rates make annuities more expensive for consumers, because lower interest rates mean a lower return for the annuity and life insurance companies that buy bonds with the premiums used to purchase annuities. Because annuity providers earn a lower interest return, they will charge higher fees or offer lower payouts to customers in order to maintain their profitability.

We expect low interest rates to be a common feature of the economy moving forward. As of this writing, rates have moved higher but are likely to return to low levels once inflation subsides, although this trend might reverse if the rise in government indebtedness we described earlier continues and boosts interest rates in the future. To offer protection against interest rate risk, some, but not all, annuities adjust their payouts depending on changes in interest rates. That can be helpful when retirees benefit from higher rates, but adds risk if interest rates decline.

ANNUITY PRODUCTS

Annuities are complicated products, with a perplexing array of features and add-ons—all obscured further by complex industry jargon. All told, individuals have a dizzying array of options from which to choose as they compare products, making it hard if not impossible to sort through them. In fact, one annuity sales and education website, *annuityguys.org*, recently listed thirty-seven different types of annuity products. In this section, we boil down the main features of annuities and discuss their relative merits.

In broad strokes, annuities can be either *variable annuities* or *income annuities*. (*Indexed annuities* are a third category but share many of the characteristics of variable annuities.) Income annuities are products that do not have a built-in investment component and simply involve a consumer paying a set amount—called a *premium*—in exchange for a stream of payments in the future. These types of annuities can pay benefits on different schedules, with some starting immediately (within a year of purchase) and others (called *deferred annuities*) starting after a deferral period that lasts years or even decades; a *longevity annuity* is one with a deferral period of roughly two decades. Purchasers can pay the premiums for income annuities either in a lump sum or over time.

A popular example of an income annuity is a *single-premium income annuity*, or SPIA. A buyer of a SPIA will pay a one-time premium in exchange for a series of payments, usually beginning shortly after the premium is paid and often only ending when the policyholder dies. Similarly, Social Security can be considered an income annuity for which workers pay by paying payroll taxes throughout their working careers.

From an economic perspective, income annuities are similar to an insurance product. With other insurance policies, like auto or home insurance, consumers pay into the same pot of money, and some collect if they face some type of event—like a car crash or house fire. The key feature of insurance is that everyone pays premiums into the same pool of money, and some collect more than others based on life events. In short, the essence of insurance is sharing risk among a pool of policyholders.

Likewise with income annuities, everyone pays into the same pool—but the amount they collect generally depends on how long the policyholder lives. Two policyholders might buy an identical product, but one could die after 5 years and the other could live for another 30. The longer-living individual collects more, just as the person who gets into a car crash collects more from auto insurance.

Variable annuities are the alternative to income annuities. (Indexed annuities are usually a special class of variable annuities, in which the investment component is tied to a stock market index like the S&P 500.) These products function like a supplemental 401(k) account, in which contributions are invested in stocks or bonds and receive preferential tax treatment. High-income individuals buy variable annuities with their after-tax income (i.e., they do not exclude their contribution from taxes), but their earnings on investments are not subject to tax until the individuals withdraw the money from them. Individuals can buy variable annuities within the account without paying capital gains taxes on each transaction. In practice, variable annuities mainly help high-income individuals shield more of that income from taxation once they have exhausted the contribution limit on their 401(k)s. For this reason, variable annuities are different from income annuities and are more like a financial product (such as a mutual fund) than an insurance product.

Unlike a standard 401(k), the individual may buy an insurance guarantee to protect against low investment returns. Also unlike a 401(k), the individual may leave all the accumulated earnings in the account past age 72 without having to make withdrawals. Individuals can withdraw funds through a lump-sum payout, periodic distributions (likely monthly), or a lifetime income stream—with policyholders rarely choosing to annuitize their investments by selecting a regular distribution option. For most owners who never annuitize their investments, the annuity serves a similar purpose as a 401(k), but with no contribution limit or required minimum distribution rules.

Annuities can offer different options that guarantee various levels of income and returns on investments. Many annuities with an investment component, for instance, offer minimum guaranteed returns on part of the premiums and caps on how much the investments can earn. Many annuities offer other guarantees and options that can reduce the link between longevity risk and annuity payouts. For example, some annuities guarantee the return of principal (i.e., a "cash refund") to beneficiaries if an owner dies before receiving the full principal. Other annuities guarantee payouts over a set period, such as 10 or 15 years, regardless of whether an annuitant dies during that period, with beneficiaries receiving the payouts if the annuitant dies.[1] Naturally, the consumer ultimately pays for the benefit of these guarantees in the form of lower payout rates or higher fees.

One of the risks people face as they retire is inflation risk. In the 1970s and early 1980s, inflation rates were very high, and fear of inflation was very common. Since then, inflation has been much less of a problem, with consumer prices growing only slowly for many years. Still, for someone looking at 20 or 30 years of future retirement, inflation is a concern. Even a 2 percent rate of increase over 20 years will cumulate to a nearly 50 percent increase in the price level. Further, as we have said, inflation has suddenly become more of a problem in 2022 and it may persist for a while. Annuities can provide inflation protection. Some annuity products have explicit inflation protection, adjusting the payout each year based on the increase in the consumer price index. Annuities that adjust with the rate of interest also can provide protection because interest rates will rise if inflation increases.

Individuals can also buy *riders*, such as for long-term care insurance, that supplement basic benefits. These riders, not surprisingly, add to the cost. Importantly, too, consumers can elect varying frequencies for receiving their benefits, ranging from a one-time payment to monthly checks for life. Since annuities offer an insurance component and a contract to make payments for many years into the future, the creditworthiness of the company selling the annuity is an important issue for the purchaser.

Annuities of all stripes can carry high commissions, although that depends very much on the product. Determining the typical fees for various types of annuities is exceptionally difficult. Our best guess is that fees are trending lower but are still substantially higher than for comparable products: the weighted commission on annuities has fallen over the past decade, from around 8 percent before the Great Recession to less than 6 percent today, according to the market research firm Wink. But commissions vary substantially among sellers and types of annuities, with "plain vanilla" immediate annuities (such as SPIAs) carrying sales commissions of just 1–3 percent and deferred income annuities or longevity annuities carrying commissions of 2–4 percent. Variable annuities appear to have commissions of 5 percent or higher.[2]

ECONOMISTS VALUE ANNUITIES; CONSUMERS DO NOT

If it were up to economists, annuities would be widely popular. Economic models of rational behavior predict that households that are planning their retirement will buy annuities to protect themselves against the risk of running out of money. In practice, relatively few households do so. Economists dub this conundrum the "annuity puzzle."

Running out of money can have severe consequences, forcing a sharp drop in consumption that typically causes a substantial decline in welfare or well-being. Although individuals vary in how well they adjust to less income and consumption, people tend to value consumption more at lower income levels. A hundred dollars, for instance, can boost a person's happiness more if they are poor than if they are wealthy. Similarly, declines in consumption are more painful for those with lower income.

Falling into poverty, or suffering a precipitous drop in income, can be particularly disastrous for older individuals. A 40-year-old person who runs out of money can look for a job, but someone at 75 or 80 would find it very hard (and in many cases impossible) to secure a job that gives them continued financial support. That is especially true for those with health problems. Most retirees have Social Security and Medicare to support them, and those programs provide some protection against poverty, but Social Security is not very generous for the average recipient and is even less generous after accounting for the Medicare premiums and other health costs that retirees pay. Older people who exhaust their assets have other options, such as living with relatives or securing a slot in a Medicaid-funded nursing home, but these options do not eliminate their potential hardship. In short, running out of money in old age is a bad idea.

The human desire to avoid steep declines in income is why economic models typically assume that people are risk averse. People will pay an insurance premium each year to avoid the loss if their house burned down or thieves ransacked it. While people also buy lottery tickets that offer a miniscule chance of winning and go to casinos where the odds favor the house, they view these risky behaviors as entertainment for which they will happily pay small amounts. When it comes to insuring against a severe hardship, we expect sensible people to avoid assuming the risk of a costly event when they can avoid it. In the context of retirement, we would expect rational consumers to mitigate longevity risk—the risk posed by living longer than expected and exhausting one's savings.

As previously discussed, lifespans are inherently uncertain. While averages across different groups of individuals based on age are well known, averages tell us little about the distribution of possible lifespans. Vanguard's life expectancy tool, for instance, indicates that a 65-year-old man has an 80 percent chance of living at least another decade, a 41 percent chance of living two more decades, and a 6 percent chance of living three more decades. For a woman of the same age, the probabilities are 85 percent for one more decade, 53 percent for two more, and 13 percent for three more.[3] That 65-year-olds have a good chance of living for many more years is unequivocally a good thing, but the longevity uncertainty brings significant risk when people retire at a given age with a fixed amount of assets.

We have discussed the role that company pensions used to have in mitigating various types of risk for workers, and how this lower risk made the products a popular benefit for many workers. While workers regret their demise, and some labor leaders would like to restore widespread coverage, a significant comeback for pensions is unlikely. Even the federal government is moving its employees away from its traditional pension plan (the Federal Employees Retirement System) and toward a defined-contribution plan (the Thrift Savings Plan). Given the popularity of defined-benefit pensions, one might expect their decline to spur a widespread demand for income annuities since the latter offer similar benefits in the form of life-long payments.

That has not occurred, perhaps because people do not see the connection between annuities and pensions.[4] Annual sales of income annuities—which are most akin to the products that economists favor—are low and falling. In the first quarter of 2020, sales of SPIAs were just $1.9 billion and had fallen by nearly one-third relative to 1 year earlier. Sales of deferred-income annuities were just $470 million in the same quarter, a decrease of more than one-quarter over the year.[5]

Annuities also have yet to gain traction within employer-sponsored retirement accounts.[6] Of the $1.6 trillion in variable annuities reserves, just 17 percent is in employer-sponsored retirement accounts and 12 percent is in IRAs. That may be due in part to the limited benefit to individuals of holding variable annuities in tax-preferred accounts, but it also may be due to the low availability of annuity products in employer-based accounts and the little interest from those eligible for them. In a Deloitte 2017 survey of 148 plan sponsors, just 6 percent said they offered annuities as part of their retirement plans. Meanwhile, the Labor Department found that, in 2002, only 6.1 percent of defined-contribution plans were directly converted to annuities within a year of the account holders' retirement, and the figure fell to just 4.1 percent by 2008 (though some savers likely converted their accounts after more than a year of retirement).[7]

Ultimately, the current market for income annuities—including those that pay out immediately and those that pay out with a lag—has yet to fulfill the promise that economists envisioned. Given the historical experience, we suspect that until annuities are widely available in workplace retirement accounts, and until the products can overcome their reputation as high-fee endeavors, savers will continue to avoid them.

BEHAVIORAL BIASES AGAINST ANNUITIES

In economic models of rational decision-making, people assess their well-being under possible future scenarios, weighing alternatives by the probability that each will occur (which is called the *expected utility framework*). Needless to say, what actually ensues often does not match predictions. People find it hard to assess the likelihood of events they do not understand well and cannot control, and they may overestimate how well they can influence events. People, for instance, hear news stories, on the one hand, that the risk of floods and hurricanes has risen or, on the other hand, that global warming is a hoax. How do they make rational judgments about the value of flood or hurricane insurance? A large majority of people judge themselves above average in driving skills (which, mathematically at least, cannot be true), so they likely underestimate the chances that they will crash their vehicles, which is one reason why most states make liability insurance compulsory.

Behavioral economists are exploring the ways in which people make decisions that do not reflect the economic model of expected utility. Behavioral economics pioneers Amos Tversky and Daniel Kahneman developed "prospect theory" as a formal model that differs from expected utility theory,[8] and their work has opened the door to alternative ways of thinking about retirement decisions.[9] People have trouble making retirement decisions because they cannot visualize their lives in the future and see how the decisions they make today will alter that future. That is particularly true if they are forced to think about unpleasant options, such as being unable to care for themselves. By contrast, people like to visualize their lives under happier scenarios, such as winning the lottery.

Workers seem to feel differently about a benefit from an employer than about a benefit they buy for themselves. That is important because retirees view the funds in their 401(k) plan as their own money, and they want to control it. Retirees who put all their retirement funds into an annuity would surrender access to it and lose control over it. An employer-provided pension feels different from an annuity: the employer provides it for its workers, rather than the worker buying it. In addition, people may overestimate their ability to invest wisely, making them more likely to want to control their assets.[10]

Similarly, people may worry that if they buy an annuity, they will receive benefits only for a limited time or not receive any benefits at all. Those nearing retirement commonly say that they eschew annuities out of concern that they will die before the annuity has paid enough in benefits to make the investment worthwhile. These near-retirees are—wrongly, in our opinion—comparing annuities, which are insurance products, to financial products that offer a rate of return. If, instead, people view annuities as the insurance products that they are, they will see that their value lies in the financial stability they offer. Insurance companies have tried to address the concern about dying before the annuity has paid off by offering ways to provide a guaranteed minimum "payout." That raises the cost of the annuity, however, which can reduce the effectiveness of the insurance provided.

As behavioral economics has found, and as we noted earlier in this book, small changes in the way decisions are structured can make a big difference to how people behave. In *Nudge*, their book of 2009, Richard Thaler and Cass Sunstein show that if workers are automatically enrolled in a contributory retirement plan, they will very likely continue contributing. If, however, they must choose to enroll, a smaller share of them do so. These findings suggest an important reason why few people buy annuities. Most employer retirement plans (such as 401(k) plans) do not provide any option to contribute to an annuity, and almost no plans include the automatic purchase of an annuity as the default option within the plan—that is, as a provision that takes effect unless workers take steps to change it.

In essence, behavioral economics suggests that it is worth nudging people toward decisions that lead to greater retirement security but not forcing people to behave in any particular way.

LONGEVITY ANNUITIES

Economists increasingly favor one type of annuity—a longevity annuity—because it can address a person's risk of outliving assets. As noted, a longevity annuity is a kind of deferred annuity—an annuity with a lag time between when an individual pays a premium and starts receiving benefits. (Longevity annuities go by several names, including *deferred-income annuities* and *advanced life deferred annuities*. In this chapter, we refer to them all as longevity annuities.) While most deferred annuities function as investment products, longevity annuities are more like standard annuities with a lag of several decades between the premium and the first benefit.

A person might buy a longevity annuity at, say, age 60 and receive nothing until reaching 75 or 80, at which point the person begins to receive a fixed amount each month or quarter. That means that individuals in their 60s or 70s can plan their spending knowing that if they live into their 80s or 90s, they will be covered financially by the checks from their longevity annuity and their continuing Social Security benefits.

It has proven hard to explain to people why they should buy a longevity annuity, which is perhaps why such annuities remain a niche product. Nevertheless, consider how a family with money in a retirement account could benefit from the lifetime protection that a longevity annuity, in particular, would offer.

- The family could draw money from their retirement account to supplement their Social Security benefits, hoping they can manage their investments and withdrawals so they have enough to live comfortably and not run out of money.
- Or, they could use all or most of their assets to buy a regular annuity that provides payments every month or quarter until they die. Unless they have a large nest egg at retirement, however, the payment from a regular annuity will not be very large and they will have only a small cash reserve to finance unexpected expenses.
- Or, they could buy a longevity annuity. The family maintains control over most of their retirement assets, investing as they want and drawing money as they need. They use part of their retirement assets to buy a longevity annuity that pays benefits to either partner in the family if they live into their 80s and beyond. If neither family member lives that long, of course, they get nothing. If, however, one or both live a long time, they are protected to the end of their lives and will receive a substantial supplement to their Social Security benefits.

The longevity annuity is a much cheaper way for individuals to secure a guaranteed income supplement late in life. The insurance company can profitably provide it because (1) the up-front money it receives when individuals pay their premiums will earn interest for, say, 20 years before the company must begin making payments to the individuals, and (2) some people will die before receiving any benefits, which enables the insurance company to provide a more generous benefit to those who live.[11] Thus, like other types of income annuities, longevity annuities are insurance policies, not investments. Not everyone gets a payout, but the annuity is worthwhile for the insurance it provides.

We can see the insurance value of a longevity annuity from an example with actual sample quotes. In 2020, a 65-year-old man seeking $3,000 a month in benefits, beginning immediately and without inflation protection, would pay a one-time premium of $619,016 for the annuity. The same benefit ($3,000 per month without inflation protection) that begins at age 80 would cost just $191,358. For a woman seeking the same benefits, the immediate annuity would cost $653,680, while the deferred annuity would cost $222,723.[12]

THE TAX IMPLICATIONS

The federal tax code provided about $250 billion in tax benefits for saving, typically through the concept of deferral. We discussed the details of these accounts in Chapter 6 and elsewhere, but briefly recount them here. Retirement savers (and their employers) can deduct contributions to retirement plans, up to a limit, from their taxable income. The plans then invest these contributions, and they can grow tax free until the plan holder withdraws money from the plan, at which time that "distribution" is taxed at ordinary income tax rates. The tax benefit derives from two factors: (1) the investments grow tax free and (2) one's income tax rate in retirement is typically lower than in one's working years. Unfortunately, the vast majority of tax benefits for saving go to those with both the means to contribute to retirement accounts and with tax rates that are high during their working years and lower during retirement—in other words, overwhelmingly upper-income households.

Tax laws limit how much workers can contribute each year to these types of accounts. In 2021, the limit on employee contributions was $19,500 and the limit on total contributions (employee plus employer) was $58,000. Deductions for contributions to IRAs, which are similar to employer-sponsored accounts but are not sponsored by a company, were limited to

$6,000 in 2021. Workers older than 50 can make "catch up" contributions of an additional $6,500 to employer-sponsored accounts and $1,000 to IRAs. Individuals can start withdrawing money from their tax-preferred retirement savings accounts starting at age 59-and-a-half without facing a tax penalty. Starting at age 72, they must withdraw minimum amounts each year to avoid a tax penalty.[13] Annuities held in these tax-preferred accounts face the same tax treatment as other investments, except for certain types of qualified annuities that are exempt from standard minimum distribution rules.[14]

Accumulation annuities that are held outside of retirement accounts offer tax advantages as well. Individuals who hold annuities with an investment component can defer taxes on investment earnings until they take a distribution from them—that is, they pay no tax on the "inside build-up" within the account. And, while individuals face penalties for early withdrawals, as with 401(k)s, they typically can keep their funds in an annuity without penalty until age 90. A 40-year-old, for example, can contribute to an annuity and let it grow for 50 years without paying any taxes. Unlike with retirement accounts, individuals can contribute to annuities without limit, providing a substantial advantage for high-income households that want to shield substantial funds from taxes.

Another difference between annuities inside employment-sponsored accounts and annuities outside of them are the rules on pricing based on gender. In 1983, the Supreme Court ruled that all employer-sponsored retirement accounts must use unisex pricing.[15] Now, pension payments have to be equal in nominal terms for men and women, providing a higher lifetime benefit for women overall due to longer life expectancy. But the Supreme Court ruling also affected annuities in employer-sponsored saving accounts, giving female workers a roughly 3 percent cost saving relative to purchases outside employer accounts, which can (and usually do) offer gender-specific pricing.

A handful of factors may be driving down demand for annuities. As we have noted, the low interest rates environment drives up the cost of annuities because insurance companies earn less on premium payments. (Interest rates have risen in 2022 but so has inflation and the combination of the two will not make annuities necessarily more attractive—returns are higher in dollar amounts but not in inflation-adjusted terms.) We also speculate that the pandemic could hurt demand for longevity annuities as people may increasingly adopt a "life is short" approach, choosing to spend their retirement savings rather than devote their assets to an annuity premium.

Conversely, the demand for annuities may be rising for other reasons. First, to the extent that annuities are a form of insurance, people may seek the stability of annuity payments to address their uncertainty about the future and the uncertainty of the stock market. Second, to the extent that people buy long-term care insurance as a rider to an annuity policy, higher demand for long-term care may also drive up the demand for annuities. Third, some older Americans may increasingly view living with their offspring as an untenable backup option, perhaps increasing interest in the guaranteed income associated with annuities.

To think correctly about annuities, we should recall the days when defined-benefit pension plans were common. Employers promised their workers lifetime income through pension plans after enough years of service. People loved having these pensions even though the workers themselves financed them, with employers passing along the costs to workers in the form of lower wages than otherwise.[16] In short, we think that annuities were tried and they worked.

Unfortunately, fewer companies in recent years offered defined-benefit plans and workers—left with the responsibility to save for their own retirement—wanted to control their own money and were unwilling to convert it to annuities. If workers once again see guaranteed lifetime income as an important part of their retirement strategy, then annuities will become a vital part of the retirement toolkit.

Finances, of course, are not the only issue that Americans must consider as they plan for retirement. They also must think hard about the chances that their health will fail, and how they might cover the costs of end-of-life care. It is a big issue, and one that we explore in the next chapter.

How Are Families Planning for End-of-Life Care?

Most families are not preparing adequately for the care they may need at the end of their lives.[1] Some think that relatives will care for them or that they can go on Medicaid, which pays for nursing home care and some in-home care. People often do not know that Medicaid requires that people exhaust almost all of their assets and turn over their incomes to contribute to the cost of care and that the quality of care in some Medicaid nursing homes is not very good. Many families may also think, incorrectly, that Medicare covers long-term care starting at age 65; in fact, it only covers post-acute care for up to 90 days after hospitalization.

Families can buy private insurance for private nursing home care or in-home support, but these policies are expensive, have coverage limits, and may not always cover the types of care that people want. Typically, insurance does not pay the full cost and will run out after a few years. Perhaps as a result, the market for private long-term care insurance has waned over the past decade.

COVID-19 and cost increases for long-term care have raised the urgency of solving the problem. Tragic and widespread COVID-related fatalities in nursing homes—which numbered about 135,000 through the fall of 2021, according to the Center for Medicare and Medicaid services—have exposed the health threat that older Americans face in institutional settings. That threat may accelerate the shift away from nursing homes and toward in-home care.

A longer-term increase in the number of older Americans also makes the long-term care challenge more urgent than ever. The number of elderly people in America is rapidly growing: between 2010 and 2019, the number of Americans who were 65 or older increased by 34 percent. The share of Americans who were 65 and older rose from 13 percent in 2010 to 17 percent in 2019, and will continue to rise.[2] That increase will drive an explosion in projected government funding for care, coupled with ever-increasing costs for private facilities and in-home care.

Solutions to the long-term care challenge are not obvious. For the most part, neither families nor policymakers want to deal with the challenge—the former because their possible need for long-term care is a hard reality to face, the latter because such care is already straining federal and state budgets. Americans should plan better for the possibility that they will need long-term care as they age. In addition, because, realistically, many families will not plan adequately, and because the private market does not work very well in this area, policymakers should consider creating incentives to grow the private long-term care market and perhaps expand Medicaid so that it provides such care to a broader cross-section of families.

LONG-TERM CARE AND THE POPULATION THAT NEEDS IT

Who needs long-term care? People of any age may require long-term care, either from family members if their illness or health impairment is mild, or in an institution if the impairment is serious or personal circumstances dictate it. Individuals may require assistance with everyday functions such as eating and bathing, medical help including physiotherapy or administering injections, and emotional support. Though impairments can occur at any age, the need for care rises precipitously at older ages.

In 2018, about 14 million people required long-term care, and, of them, 56 percent were older than 65.[3] This older population may require long-term care for, say, arthritis, heart conditions, diabetes, or strokes. The length of care tends to be short, with one study finding that only about a quarter of older adults will receive more than 2 years of paid care and only 15 percent will spend more than 2 years in a nursing home.[4]

Some 53 percent of those who turn 65 will require long-term care at some point, as shown in Figure 9.1, and more than one-quarter will require long-term services and support (LTSS) for at least 2 years. The probability of needing care is higher for women than men, with 58 percent of women needing care at some point compared to 47 percent of men. Compared to men, nearly twice as many women will require care for 5 years or more.

These probabilities translate into large populations of people needing care. Among those over 65 in 2018, 7.9 million people required some form of long-term care. Of these, 1.2 million received such care in nursing homes, while the remaining 6.7 million received care in their communities, usually by family members.[5] Women are likelier to need care than men

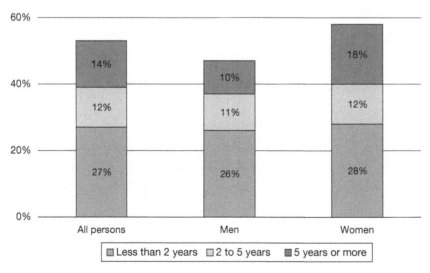

Figure 9.1 Projected lifetime long-term services and support (LTSS) need for persons turning 65 in 2015, by duration of need.
SOURCE: AARP Public Policy Institute (2017).

because they live longer and have higher rates of disability; as such, they made up 58.2 percent of all long-term care recipients in 2016. Given the rapid rise in the number of elderly people as baby boomers age, the demand for long-term care will also rise rapidly, posing a significant challenge to policymakers and families.[6] The private market is also responding to the increased need for long-term care, such as the growth of assisted-living and guaranteed-care communities. Policymakers can look for ways to push the private market forward.

Dementia is a major source of impairment, and its rising prevalence has increased the need for long-term care. Severe dementia requires very intensive care. Some 11 percent of Americans aged 65 and over have some form of dementia, according to one major study.[7] Alzheimer's disease is the most common form of dementia, accounting for 60–80 percent of all cases, and it almost always requires long-term care. By 2050, the number of people with Alzheimer's age 65 and over is projected to be 12.7 million.[8] Alzheimer's disease can require many years of care. Those 65 and older live an average of 4–8 years after an Alzheimer's diagnosis, but as long as 20 years for some patients. On average, lifetime care for someone with Alzheimer's dementia costs an estimated $387,442 in 2021 dollars.[9]

Options for Long-Term Care

Most long-term care is provided at home rather than in an institution. At any given time, 53 million Americans are serving as long-term caregivers, a number that has risen dramatically over the past decade.[10] Half of unpaid caregivers of adults provided care for a parent, while 12 percent provided care for a spouse or partner, 14 percent for another relative, and 10 percent for a non-relative.[11]

Unpaid caregivers are obviously a cheaper option for patients, but the care that they provide can carry steep and lasting consequences for caregivers. They suffer diminished wages, financial instability, worsened physical and mental health outcomes, and even worsened preparation for retirement, studies find. While providing unpaid care may bring intrinsic rewards, its financial and health costs can be overwhelming for the millions, mainly women, who provide it.

Nursing homes and other assisted-living facilities offer other options.[12] Only 1 in 10 Americans who received care in 2018 lived in a nursing home, and, among those living in the community, the vast majority received some unpaid assistance from family or friends.[13] As per Figure 9.2, 34 percent of those receiving care hire paid assistance but, of this group, only 5 percent relied solely on paid assistance.[14]

Many individuals prefer to receive care at home. The AARP found that about 76 percent of Americans over the age of 50 preferred to remain in their homes as they grew older (a concept dubbed "aging in place").[15] And, in fact, individuals increasingly receive long-term services at home, although the trend is much stronger for younger people than those of retirement age. Among Americans who receive long-term care from Medicaid,

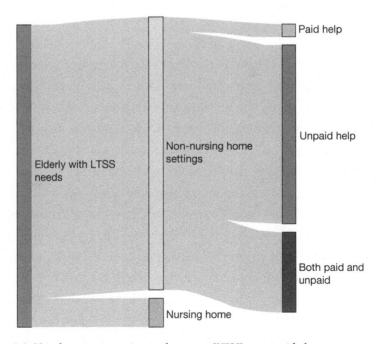

Figure 9.2 How long-term services and support (LTSS) are provided.
SOURCE: Authors, using information reported in Freedman and Spillman (2014).

roughly 80 percent of those people under 65 get their care at home, compared to less than half of seniors.[16]

Providing long-term care in the home is not without its downsides. Some individuals require more intensive care than caregivers can reasonably provide outside of an institution, and there is at least some evidence that at-home care leads to higher rates of hospitalization and can lead to greater burdens on unpaid caregivers.[17] And the labor market for in-home care has traditionally been characterized by low-wage jobs with high turnover rates,[18] which can lead to subpar outcomes for both the providers and recipients of care.

Despite these shortfalls, developing better ways to provide care to seniors in their homes is a promising strategy for improving long-term care. That could come in part by changing rules for public programs and in part through higher subsidies for private long-term care insurance, which often provides for in-home care.

LONG-TERM CARE: ITS COSTS AND FINANCING

Health insurance covers most of the cost for acute illnesses, and even those who lack insurance can get hospital care if their need is urgent and serious. Health insurance, however, does not pay for long-term care beyond 90 days after hospitalization. Hospitals are not set up to provide long-term care, and they require patients with chronic health issues to go a nursing home or other medical facility or they will return patients to their families. Long-term care costs in 2017 totaled an estimated $235 billion, an amount that includes only the dollars spent on *formal* care. Private long-term care insurance only covered 4 percent of these expenses.[19] The cost of *informal* care that family and friends provide totaled an estimated $470 billion in 2017.[20]

In 2021, the median annual cost of nursing home care with a private room was $108,405 according to the Genworth 2022 Cost of Care Survey. Assisted-living cost $54,000, and a home health aid cost $61,776 for 44 hours a week of care.[21] Prices vary substantially by region, with Oklahoma having the lowest cost and Connecticut the highest.

Long-Term Care Insurance

The cost of long-term care would seem to make insurance a compelling need, and, from 1998 until 2005, the number of people buying long-term care insurance policies grew 12 percent a year. Growth slowed after that, however, and, from 2005 to 2011, growth was not much higher than growth in the population at large. Among seniors receiving long-term care in 2010, 11 percent had private insurance, down from 14 percent in 2008.[22] Only 7.2 million Americans had long-term care insurance in 2018, a number that has been trending downward.[23]

Insurance policies also are very unevenly distributed among different groups. About a quarter of the wealthiest 20 percent of Americans are insured, while very few in the bottom 20 percent are. Women are a bit likelier to be insured than men, and married people more than singles.[24] Although most private health insurance policies are sold as group policies, generally through an employer, most long-term care policies are sold as individual policies.[25]

Long-term care policies often cover in-home care as well as nursing home care, but they come with limits or restrictions. A person must be receiving care for 30–90 days before insurance payments begin, and policies usually limit the duration of benefits to between 1 and 8 years (though about a quarter of policies are not limited). Typically, policies set maximum daily reimbursements that do not cover the full cost of a nursing home. The maximum rate is often fixed in dollar terms or rises over time at a low fixed rate. Thus, coverage is usually incomplete. A typical policy that someone buys at age 65 on average would cover about two-thirds of the cost of care.

Even with limits and deductibles, policies are expensive. The 2020 average cost of a policy for a 55-year-old male was $1,700 a year, according to the American Association for Long-Term Care Insurance. The equivalent for a female was $2,675 because women live longer and are more likely to go into long-term care. A combined policy for a couple cost $4,826 a year. The policy benefit amount (the maximum that is paid under the policy) was $164,000, the amount payable for care was $150 a day, and the policy would pay out for a maximum of 3 years. The annual premiums will rise with the age of the policyholder and can be substantially more expensive for individuals seeking more expansive coverage. And, due to underwriting, a large fraction of individuals—between 20 and 40 percent—can expect to see their applications for insurance rejected.[26]

Taxpayers can get a range of tax breaks for buying long-term care insurance, thus mitigating its cost. Employers that offer policies to their employees can deduct their full cost as a business expense, and employees do not pay income or payroll taxes on the value of the policy. People who buy policies on their own can theoretically include part of the cost of premiums as a medical expense, which they can then count as an itemized deduction to the extent that their combined medical expenses exceed 7.5 percent of their income. These limitations, coupled with the 2017 tax law which reduced itemization, means that almost no taxpayers claim this benefit.[27] For both employer-provided and individual policies, the benefits are not taxable. Overall, the tax benefits from employer-provided insurance are substantially more generous than those from policies that people buy on their own. As with all tax deductions, the effective subsidy for buying insurance policies is greater for those who pay higher income tax rates.[28]

President Reagan and Congress created the Partnership for Long-Term Care as a demonstration project to encourage more people to buy long-term care insurance policies, and President George W. Bush and Congress later expanded the program. Under it, policyholders could qualify for Medicaid nursing home coverage once their private insurance reached its maximum payout, and they could retain more of their assets than Medicaid normally allows. In 2011, private long-term care policies under this program accounted for 10 percent of all policies issued. Whether the program helped to increase long-term care insurance coverage coverall or merely prompted people to shift their existing policies to the program, however, is an open question.

Concerned about the rising costs of care and uncertain about the liability they will incur, insurance companies are leaving the long-term care market. The market was thin to begin with; most people do not buy policies, costs rise, and insurers leave. Whether the private market will survive is an open question.

Medicare and Medicaid Costs for Long-Term Care

Medicare and Medicaid pay a much higher share of long-term care costs than does private insurance. Medicare is not intended to pay for long-term care, but, as we have said, it covers some post-acute care (care outside of a hospital), providing skilled nursing facility care and home health care visits for a limited time. Medicare provided about $80 billion in post-acute care in 2019.[29]

State and federal Medicaid spending covers institutional care for those older than 65, such as nursing homes, residences with supportive services, and other facility-based care, and it also provides some community-based long-term care, including in private homes. Such Medicaid spending also comprised $80 billion in 2019. Both Medicare and Medicaid spending for such purposes are expected to rise rapidly in the years ahead, at about 5.5 percent a year for Medicare and 8 percent a year for Medicaid for those over 65.

The Cost of Informal Care

The most important source of long-term care for seniors is from relatives and friends. The estimated dollar value of long-term care from such unpaid caregivers was $470 billion in 2013.[30] The average number of hours that these unpaid caregivers, many of whom have paying jobs in addition to caregiving, worked each week was 24.[31] Surprisingly, those who provide long-term care are almost as likely to work in other jobs as those not providing it. Some 59 percent of women who provided care to their parents work, compared to 61 percent of a comparable group who did not provide care.[32]

Not surprisingly, providing long-term care takes a toll on the providers whether they continue to work or not. Those who work are absent from work more often and may have to take more days off. Some may choose less demanding, lower paid jobs to manage their combination of work and care. Those providing care are likelier to fall into poverty and require public assistance, while the mental and emotional strains of providing care are considerable.[33]

Paying Long-Term Care's Out-of-Pocket Costs

Out-of-pocket spending on formal long-term care is substantial. In 2017, out-of-pocket spending comprised 23 percent, or $54 billion, of the $235 billion spent in total on long-term care.[34]

The cost of long-term care provides a very compelling reason why many families hoard their retirement savings rather than spend more of it in retirement. If one spouse is healthy but the other requires long-term care, the care often occurs within the family. Caring for a spouse with dementia is very hard, requiring special skills and round-the-clock care. If a spouse dies, the remaining spouse has a greater need for formal care. Upper-middle-income families with a retirement nest egg of $300,000–400,000 may decide that they cannot afford to spend it down because they may need all of it to pay for a nursing home. They could spend their money and then opt for a spot in a Medicaid nursing home, but many will prefer to finance a higher quality option. Parents may decide to keep enough to pay for a nursing home or extensive in-home care and then, if they do not need the money, leave it to their children.

With data from the asset management company Vanguard, researchers from the Vanguard Research Initiative studied 1,241 individuals, 55 and older, with average assets of $808,000 but ranging from $101,000 to $1,602,000. After asking them about such factors as their risk preferences and their views on their healthcare needs, researchers concluded that an important reason why people hold their wealth into retirement is that they are taking precautions against the need for more healthcare spending late in life.

Many families hedge against future healthcare spending needs by building equity in their homes. Although, as we have seen, many families do not invest much of their income in 401(k)-type accounts, many accumulate substantial net worth by paying off their mortgages, making their homes a valuable asset. In 2018, roughly 78 percent of households over the age of 65 owned their home, and the median homeowner household had accumulated home equity of $143,500.[35] Home ownership gives retirees another way to finance end-of-life care and avoid a Medicaid nursing home. If need be, they can sell their house and use the proceeds to finance their health needs. And, as with cash retirement accounts, if they do not need expensive long-term care, they can leave their house to their heirs.

How COVID-19 Changed the Long-Term Care Environment

By the fall of 2021, there had been 686,000 cases of COVID-19 among residents of nursing home facilities and an additional 630,000 cases among staff. As we noted earlier, there had been 135,000 deaths among residents and an additional 2,000 staff deaths at this time.[36] Even before COVID-19, Americans did not want to go into a nursing home unless there was no choice, and the additional threat of a disease sweeping through a facility made that prospect even less attractive.

The experience of the pandemic will likely increase the demands on Medicaid to provide additional in-home care, but the average waiting time to gain approval is around 3 years.

MARKET FAILURES AND DISTORTIONS

The market for long-term care has several sources of failure. Here are the most important ones.

Medicaid's incentive effect. In the economics classroom, a market failure occurs when a market price does not reflect the true social cost of a product—if there is pollution as a result of its manufacture, for example. In practice, market failures often occur when a government program changes human incentives and behavior. In some cases, the policy is badly designed, while in others, the policy responds to an important social need but then has the side effect of distorting market incentives. Medicaid provides long-term care to older people who cannot afford their own care, but this has the side effect of reducing the incentive for young people to buy a long-term care policy to pay for private care when they age. And it may reduce the incentive to save and accumulate enough assets to pay for long-term care if it is needed. Medicaid is an "entitlement program," and those wishing to cut the cost of entitlements look at the adverse incentives that the Medicaid long-term care program created as a reason to eliminate it or scale it back. Certainly, if there were no Medicaid nursing homes, more people would buy long-term care insurance. Given Medicaid's incentive effects, one could argue, that with more people buying insurance, the market *could* be healthier and more competitive, and the insurance *could* become a better deal that more companies offer in their employee benefit packages.

We are skeptical of this argument. We certainly do not think long-term care insurance would become universal or even widespread without further changes in the long-term care insurance market.[37] And even with a much more developed market in this area, we doubt everyone or even most people would buy policies. After all, even with the option of Medicaid nursing homes, relatives are the largest source of long-term care, so people are relying much more on intergenerational support for their needed care than on Medicaid. Middle-class families are holding assets in retirement to avoid winding up in a Medicaid nursing home. And low-income families would find it impossible to pay the premiums for long-term care insurance even if Medicaid nursing homes were unavailable. Furthermore, Medicaid is designed to reduce adverse incentives by limiting its funding of Medicaid facilities and requiring families to exhaust their assets before they can secure a place in a Medicaid nursing home.

In short, while Medicaid does discourage some families from buying long-term care insurance, even if Medicaid nursing homes were eliminated millions of Americans still would reach an advanced age no longer able to care for themselves and unable to afford a private nursing facility or adequate in-home care. Some have relatives to care for them, but many do not. A humane society cannot leave seniors alone trying to look after themselves if they cannot do so. There must be a program to step in and help. Church or community groups can provide some support, but charity alone cannot address the large number of seniors who need full-time care.

Medicaid's long-term care plan for services like nursing homes was designed to provide end-of-life care for seniors who lack the necessary financial resources. It has grown to about a $130 billion-a-year commitment.[38] It is an expensive program and it has an adverse impact on the private market for care, but it is an essential program. As one way to offset its impact on market solutions, policymakers should look for ways to revive and expand the private insurance market, even in the presence of Medicaid nursing homes, as we discuss in the next section.

Inadequate planning for old-age care. One reason why few young families plan for long-term care once they get older is that many, perhaps most, people have more than enough present-day issues to worry about and are reluctant to worry too much about what happens 30 years in the future. Median household income in 2019 was $68,703, a level at which a household would struggle to pay all its old-age care expenses.[39] Long-term care policies demand substantial premiums, and most families would need to plan seriously and make a financial sacrifice today to secure the necessary funds for the premiums.

Behavioral economists doubt that individuals and families can plan rationally for their needs at age 80 or 90. Their inability to do so creates a major market failure. Nobel Prize winner Richard Thaler considers himself a "libertarian paternalist," meaning that he does not want to force people to save more or buy insurance, but he sees the need to nudge people toward better decisions about retirement and long-term care. Another leading behavioral economist, David Laibson, takes a much stronger position that is more pessimistic about people's ability to plan, arguing that the siren call of today's consumption will overwhelm rational plans to provide for the distant future.

Planning for long-term care raises many of the same issues as the decision to save for retirement, with the additional concern that some are reluctant to imagine a future when they are frail and need full-time care. The market for long-term care policies is in danger of disappearing because not enough policies are purchased.

Care by family members. Another reason why people do not plan for long-term care is that they expect to live with their children or other family member rather than in a nursing home. And, as we have said, that is in fact the most common way that long-term care is provided. For many families, however, it is far from an ideal solution.

Though caring for children is very time-consuming and costly, our society assumes that people who bear children choose to do so and will care for them. Caring for older relatives is more problematic. Some children, usually daughters, find it satisfying to care for their parents, sustaining fulfilling relationships with them as they age. For others, the care is burdensome, especially for those seniors who can no longer manage basic functions or recognize those around them. It is a tough challenge for a 60-year-old to care for a 90-year-old parent who may be incontinent or unable to feed themselves. Caring for those with Alzheimer's disease is even harder and requires specialized training. Some patients' behaviors change, making them difficult to care for or even violent.

Some who care for spouses or older relatives have trouble paying their bills. Due to the many hours required to care for someone else, the caregiver may find it hard to hold a job or to keep a demanding and well-paid one. Working full-time and caring for a relative can impose stress on a family.

This nation's system of old-age care, and that of many other countries, expects younger people to volunteer to provide care. This is fine for some, but a big problem for others. Providing paid care to replace all the care that relatives are providing would put a severe strain on household or government budgets. Policymakers must look for ways to help families when elder care is an excessive burden.

Wealth and home equity hoarding. Although, as we have said, many people are reluctant to plan for their old age, that is not true for everyone. Many middle- and upper-income families think ahead and plan for a possible stay in a nursing home. As noted earlier, the Vanguard Research Initiative found that such families often hoard their retirement assets rather than spend them down. They want to make sure they have enough in financial assets or home equity to pay for a private nursing home if they need one. Given the weak state of the long-term care insurance market, that is a rational approach. An unfortunate cycle has emerged in which few people buy insurance policies, and it becomes a thin market with little competition and high prices. As the market thins, even fewer people buy policies, and the available insurance policies become even more expensive and restricted.

There is a different possible market outcome in which long-term care policies are included in employee benefit packages, more people opt to buy them, prices are lower, and coverage is better. Only a small percentage of people will need expensive long-term care, and a well-functioning insurance market would cover that eventuality and enable families to use the assets they have saved to live more comfortably in retirement, plan what they want to leave to their heirs, and protect themselves against the huge costs of institutional care.[40] That many families hoard their assets, whether financial assets or home equity, rather than tapping the long-term care insurance market is a sign of market failure. A better outcome would be possible if the insurance market worked better.

Adverse selection in the individual market. Another market failure that is often found in insurance markets is called *adverse selection.* Suppose someone goes to a life insurance company and wants to buy a policy. Perhaps that person has a family background that makes them more likely than the average person to die at an early age. If the company knows that, they would refuse to insure the person or charge a high premium. If they do not know, they charge insurance premiums to everyone to cover the high-risk policies, factoring into their calculation of insurance premiums the fact that high-risk people are more likely to buy insurance policies. This is adverse selection.

The people who buy insurance policies are more likely to collect on the policy than the average person. This pushes up the cost of insurance policies and will discourage people without unusually high risks from buying policies. While adverse selection is a concern for virtually all insurance markets, the problem appears to be especially acute for long-term care.[41] To take one example, a study found that people with Huntington's disease—a degenerative genetic disorder that typically leads to disability—were five times more likely to purchase long-term care insurance.[42] More generally, the insurance premiums for long-term care insurance policies are increased by the fact that the people who buy the policies anticipate that they are likely to need long-term care.

Insurers push back against adverse selection not just by raising prices, but also by imposing stringent underwriting standards that disqualify large swaths of people. One study found that only 60 percent of people aged 50–71 would qualify for life insurance at all and that applicants who were African American, older, or less wealthy would all see significantly lower approval rates.[43]

Group insurance, such as that purchased through an employer, helps to mitigate this problem. These programs offer either less stringent underwriting or "guaranteed-issue" plans with no underwriting at all. Because these programs offer larger applicant pools with risks that average out over time, insurers feel less need to select who they insure. Unfortunately, the group insurance market has shrunk over time.

TOWARD SOLUTIONS

In Chapter 13, which focuses on reforming insurance markets, we provide a deeper look at the options for improving long-term care. In this chapter, we conclude with a brief outline of how to mitigate the problems.[44] Our approach is to promote private long-term care insurance while maintaining Medicaid as a backstop. Policymakers could encourage or require employers to offer insurance as an option in their retirement packages and perhaps even include it as a default option that employees would have to choose to overturn. Employers also would need to educate employees about the value of such insurance.

More people buying long-term care insurance would mean fewer people in Medicaid nursing home care, helping federal and state budgets. So, taxpayers have an incentive to improve this insurance market. Also, if many more people bought insurance and employers negotiated with insurance companies, costs would fall substantially. Policymakers should consider creating a program of catastrophic insurance coverage that kicks in once people have spent more than a fixed sum or percent of their assets or income on long-term care, and it could include financial protections for low-income households.

Medicaid's funding of nursing home and in-home care does discourage people from buying private insurance, but that is a side effect well worth accepting. Medicaid provides an enormous value to those elderly who might otherwise have no viable alternative way to get care. If anything, policymakers should expand Medicaid eligibility to more Americans while upgrading the quality of care. We do not expect that to happen, however, due to concerns about federal and state budget costs.

While boosting their saving and preparing for their long-term care needs, Americans often accumulate wealth in the form of home ownership. In many cases, they would be wise to tap that wealth to help them address their retirement challenges. One way is through reverse mortgages, as we explore next.

Reverse Mortgages

Reverse mortgages are complex products that are often poorly understood. At their essence, reverse mortgages are simply consumer loans that homeowners take out against the value of their home. Unlike home equity loans, homeowners do not have to pay back the loans as long as they maintain and live in their home. They only repay them when they sell or vacate their home (often when the homeowner dies), and the amount they must pay back is capped by the value of the equity in the home. Combined, these two characteristics would seem to make the product uniquely suitable for many retirement-age households, enabling them to access the equity in their homes while still living there. Nevertheless, less than 1 percent of eligible households take out reverse mortgages,[1] and some financial advisors and consumer advocates consider them a dangerous way to exploit older people.

Many older households own substantial equity in their homes but have very few financial assets, suggesting that accessing housing wealth could materially improve their standards of living. Moreover, reverse mortgages reflect the idea that households should accumulate wealth during their working years and spend it down in retirement. Reverse mortgages are pretty much the only way for households to access home equity without paying it back while still living in the home.

Economic recessions enhance the need for homeowners to access their housing wealth, and the pandemic-driven recession in 2020 was no different. For a short period, the recession drove unemployment sharply higher, especially for older workers, while housing prices remained mostly stable and mortgage forbearance programs provided broad support for homeowners. Older workers lost incomes but maintained their housing wealth, suggesting that better opportunities to access home equity would have been useful to older families coping with income shortfalls.

Reverse mortgages could prove very useful for homeowners as part of a retirement strategy, but barriers are preventing most older households from choosing them. Reforms could expand the market considerably, and while reverse mortgages will remain the choice of a minority of older households, they are a valuable addition to the financial market instruments that contribute to retirement security—especially if policymakers improved the regulatory framework for them.

THE REVERSE MORTGAGE MARKET

With a reverse mortgage, homeowners borrow a fixed amount from a bank or take out a line of credit they can draw down if they choose. They must remain in the home as their main residence, maintain it, and pay their homeowner's insurance and property taxes. They pay fees upon taking out the loan, and interest on the loan balance accumulates at a rate to which the homeowner agrees at the start. Banks charge higher interest rates on reverse mortgages than on regular mortgages because the risks are greater. At the same time, reverse mortgages enable homeowners to avoid the fees and costs that come from selling a home and that—depending on the location of the home and the amount that a realtor receives—can approach 10 percent of its value.[2]

Homeowners can access the equity in the family home, of course, by selling it and using the proceeds to cover day-to-day expenses in retirement, pay off a regular mortgage loan and non-mortgage debt (such as credit card debt), or create a fund for health costs or other major expenses.[3] Many families, however, strongly prefer to keep living in their family homes, near family and friends. Another alternative is a home equity line of credit, but, with this financial vehicle, homeowners must immediately begin making regular repayments from what could be their limited retirement income.

The biggest difference between a reverse mortgage and a traditional mortgage is that, with the former, borrowers do not make out-of-pocket payments during the life of the loan. Instead, they take periodic distributions (or often a single lump-sum distribution) that add to the loan, which then grows with interest.[4] When the loan is due (after the borrower dies or sells the home), borrowers or their heirs can pay off the balance and keep the home, sell the home to settle the balance, or let the lender sell the home. Reverse mortgages are usually created as "non-recourse" loans, meaning that neither borrowers nor heirs are responsible for shortfalls if the loan balance exceeds the sale of the property.

Figure 10.1 illustrates the potential appeal of reverse mortgages. It takes a large sample of households aged 55–64 from the Survey of Consumer Finances and looks at their financial assets and home equity. As we can see, many households have substantial home equity (the vertical axis) and few financial assets (the horizontal axis). Indeed, some families have $200,000

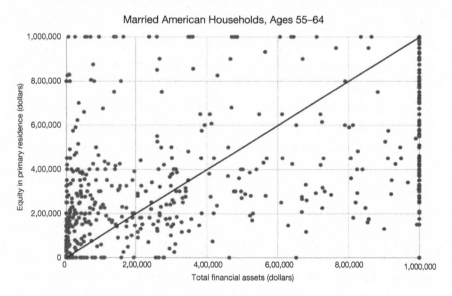

Figure 10.1 Total financial assets versus housing equity.
Source: Survey of Consumer Finances.

to $1 million of home equity but much less than $200,000 in financial assets. The home equity that a reverse mortgage could tap is less than the
amounts shown in this figure and is subject to regulatory limits. Still, the
figure shows the potential benefit of reverse mortgages and explains why
successive presidents and Congresses saw home equity as a possible way
for older families to live more comfortably in retirement.

Reverse mortgages are also a form of insurance in two ways. First, they
provide longevity insurance—that is, protection against outliving one's
assets. Someone who takes out a reverse mortgage at age 65 and stays
in their home to, say, age 90 will likely accumulate interest costs to the
point that the loan balance exceeds the value of the home. The lender (or,
in the case of federally backed mortgage insurance, the federal government) then must cover the loss when the person dies and the home is sold.
Second, if home prices fall enough that the value of the home is less than
the amount of the loan plus interest, the borrower can walk away and leave
the lender with a loss.[5] Such borrowers would not be violating the terms of
their loans, and they would pay no penalty.

Reverse mortgages will not work for everyone, as we discuss in the pages
to come. Homeowners must pay taxes and insurance premiums, and they
face foreclosure if they fail to do so. Those who take out reverse mortgages
tend to be retirement-age, low- to moderate-income homeowners for
whom their residential property is their major source of wealth. Many are
women; in fact, reverse mortgages were created to help widows remain
in their homes. Today, more older households carry balances on traditional mortgages or credit cards into retirement, and many of them find
it hard to make monthly payments on debts when they no longer have
wage or salary income. They use the proceeds of a reverse mortgage to pay
off these debts. Those who had considered whether to take out a reverse
mortgage but decided against it said they wanted to preserve the equity in
their homes in case they needed the money later or to pass the home on
to their heirs.

The federal government wanted to help the reverse mortgage market
get started and gave lenders access to mortgage insurance. As the market
developed, policymakers raised concerns about whether it was operating

smoothly and about fraud and abuse that were hurting consumers. As a result, the federal government extensively regulated the reverse mortgage market through the Home Equity Conversion Mortgage (HECM) program.

THE HECM PROGRAM

For years, the most popular reverse mortgages have been HECM loans that the Federal Housing Administration (FHA)—within the Department of Housing and Urban Development (HUD)—has administered. With its FHA-backed loans representing more than 90 percent of reverse mortgages,[6] the HECM program dominates the market. The most common non-HECM reverse mortgages are those that state or local agencies and nonprofits provide or proprietary reverse mortgages that companies develop and back.

Borrowers can use HECM loans for any purpose, but the borrowers must meet certain criteria. They must be 62 or older, live in the home, and own the property or have paid a considerable share of the mortgage. In addition, borrowers must verify their income, assets, and monthly living expenses and show they have the money to make timely payments of homeowner's insurance and taxes.

The allowable mortgage amount typically depends on the borrower's age (or the age of the younger spouse in the case of a joint loan), the interest rate, and the value of the property. The borrowed amount, known as the *principal limit*, is the product of the *maximum claim amount* and the *principal limit factor*. The maximum claim amount is the home's appraised value, capped by the FHA's maximum lending limit. The principal limit is the share of the maximum claim amount that one can borrow, which rises with the borrower's age and shrinks with higher interest rates.[7] Borrowers are also limited by what they can borrow during the first year of the loan.

Borrowers may draw on available funds with different payment plans, including those with fixed- or variable-rate mortgages. Currently, fixed-rate mortgages, which are the mortgages borrowers usually choose so they

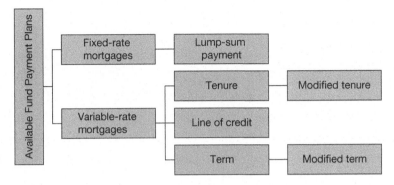

Figure 10.2 Alternative payment plans for reverse mortgages.
Source: Authors.

can lock in low interest rates, provide only one payment option: a lump-sum payment. For adjustable rate mortgages, borrowers may choose tenure, term, or line of credit payment options (see Figure 10.2).

- The *tenure option* pays equal monthly amounts as long as the borrower or spouse continues to live in the property.
- The *term option* makes monthly payments for a fixed period of time that the borrower chooses.
- The *line of credit option* makes unscheduled payments or in installments, at times and in an amount that the borrower chooses until the line of credit is exhausted.

Borrowers can also choose a *modified tenure* option, which combines the line of credit and tenure option plans, or a *modified term* option, which combines the line of credit and term option plans.

In 2018, 91 percent of borrowers took out variable-rate distributions, with just 9 percent taking fixed-rate distributions. Roughly half of borrowers took between 60 and 100 percent of their principal limit in the first month's distribution.[8] The frequency of different distribution options is driven in large part by recent changes to the HECM program, which, in 2013, disallowed the popular full-draw, fixed-rate products and limited the share of available funds that borrowers could withdraw in the first year.[9]

Once the FHA approves an HECM loan, homeowners stay in their homes and tap into their housing equity until the loan is due. As noted above, a HECM loan becomes due under a number of circumstances, such as when the borrower dies, moves to a different primary residence, or fails to make required property tax and insurance payments. When the loan becomes payable, the borrower or heirs can repay the outstanding balance (including the total principal that the homeowner borrowed and any interest and fees that accrued), sell the home, or sign it over to the lender.

The FHA serves as a backstop against both borrower longevity and falling home prices by buying loans from lenders when the outstanding balance reaches the approximate value of the home. Typically, lenders can sell HECM loans to the FHA once the outstanding balance reaches at least 98 percent of the maximum claim amount. In that sale process—known as *assignment*—the lender receives either the outstanding loan balance or the maximum claim amount, whichever is less. In practice, nearly all non-delinquent loans are assigned once the required threshold is reached. (Delinquent loans are those on which the borrower has not paid property taxes or insurance bills.) After assignment, the FHA earns the interest that accrues on the loan, along with the annual mortgage insurance premiums, and it continues to face the risk for any shortfall when the loan is repaid.

The fees associated with HECM loans can be substantial, and they include the mortgage insurance premium (MIP), origination fee, servicing fee, interest on the loan, and third-party charges. The MIP includes an initial insurance premium equal to 2 percent of the loan amount and an annual insurance premium equal to 0.5 percent of the loan balance. The origination fee is the greater of $2,500, or 2 percent of the first $200,000 of the home's value plus 1 percent of the amount over $200,000; the FHA caps these fees at $6,000. Lenders assess servicing fees throughout the life of the loan, with such monthly fees capped at $30 to $35, depending on the type of loan.

Because they are designed to help older consumers, HECM loans carry a particularly high risk of fraud, discrimination, and uninformed consumer decisions that potentially arise from misleading advertising, aggressive sales tactics, and discriminatory practices. Due to those factors, consumers may not fully understand the consequences of their decisions.[10] Other major concerns include the risks that non-borrowing spouses face (e.g., when only one spouse takes out a reverse mortgage), cross-selling (when a lender requires or convinces a borrower to buy a product, like an annuity or insurance policy, when applying for a loan), and foreclosure after the borrower's failure to pay property charges. HECM reforms have addressed many of these issues in recent years.

To address some of these concerns, the HECM program requires mandatory counseling for applicants. They must meet with a HECM counselor to discuss program eligibility requirements, financial implications, and alternatives to an HECM loan, and they receive a certificate upon completing the counseling process. Policymakers also directed HUD to work with consumer groups to improve consumer education, and they gave HUD the discretion to impose restrictions to ensure that consumers do not pay unnecessary or excessive costs for taking out the loans. A survey of borrowers found that close to 90 percent felt they had enough information about the terms of their reverse mortgage loan.[11] After taking out loans, 85 percent said they were satisfied or very satisfied with their decision.

Recent changes to the HECM program have mitigated the risks that non-borrowing spouses face. In 2011, HUD issued guidance stating that, in addition to borrowers, all spouses of prospective borrowers and all co-owners of the property must receive reverse mortgage counseling. And, in 2014, HUD issued guidance clarifying that, for new HECMs, non-borrowing spouses can remain in the home after the death of the reverse-mortgage holder.

The 2008 Housing and Economic Recovery Act mitigated concerns over cross-selling by generally prohibiting lenders from either requiring that borrowers buy a particular product when they apply for a loan or attempting to influence consumers' decisions around these loans. State regulators, too, imposed regulations to protect consumers from cross-selling, including regulations that apply to both HECM and non-HECM products.[12]

Perhaps the largest remaining concern is over consumers' understanding of and ability to pay property taxes and home insurance bills.
Substantial shares of borrowers struggle to make these payments, and
their failure can lead to default. In 2012, 9.4 percent of HECM borrowers
(about 54,000 homeowners) were in default on tax or insurance payments,
marking an increase of more than 1 percentage point from the year before.[13] However, while this is a valid concern, it is probably unfair to blame
reverse mortgage defaults on the products themselves. If a borrower is
going to default on property taxes while under a reverse mortgage, they
will almost certainly default on property taxes without one.

All reverse mortgage borrowers are older homeowners. The average
maximum claim amount (effectively the loan amount) is about $275,000,
and the borrower's average age is 73. Married couples make up roughly
40 percent of borrowers, with single women comprising about another
40 percent and single men about 20 percent. That marks a sizable change
from earlier years, when single women much more frequently took out
reverse mortgages.[14]

THE REVERSE MORTGAGE MARKET OVER TIME

The reverse mortgage market is complex, likely due to heavy regulation
and the desire of lenders to meet different consumer preferences. It has
changed markedly in the past two decades, reflecting efforts to address
its problems and respond to losses during the 2008 financial crisis. Today,
the market is shaped by regulations to limit the losses that federal agencies
suffer rather than to make it an attractive market to consumers.

Reverse mortgages were initially offered in the early 1960s to help
widows keep their homes, and they were written exclusively by local banks
and included no federal insurance. In the late 1970s and early 1980s, reverse mortgages began attracting the attention of federal policymakers as
a way to enable older homeowners to access their home equity. In the late
1970s, the Administration on Aging funded a study on reverse mortgage
pilot programs, and the 1980 White House Conference on Aging issued

a report recommending reverse mortgages as a possible strategy to help older Americans convert home equity to income and still remain in their homes.[15]

Throughout the 1980s, lawmakers proposed legislation to establish a home equity conversion program, but it was not established until 1988, when President Reagan and Congress authorized HECMs as a demonstration project. HECMs remained in that status for a little over a decade, with policymakers periodically raising the total number of loans that HUD could insure. Initially, HUD could insure just 2,500 homes, but the number gradually rose to 50,000 loans. In that period, loans were required to have several features: they had to include counseling for borrowers, and they had to free the borrower from any repayment requirement until death or the sale of the home. In 1999, President Clinton and Congress changed the HECM initiative from a demonstration project to a permanent program, and they raised the maximum number of insured homes to 150,000, maintaining the counseling and non-recourse provisions (the latter of which let borrowers stay in their homes even if the value of the loan exceeds the value of the home).

With the HECM program now permanent, lawmakers and regulators enacted several incremental reforms to increase its scope. Lawmakers, for example, reformed HECM's total loan limit from a county-specific to a nationwide standard of $417,000 in 2006, boosting it to $625,500 in 2009 and $726,525 in 2019. In addition, they raised the maximum number of HECM loans to 250,000 in 2005 and 275,000 in 2006. In 2009, President Obama and Congress allowed owners of FHA-approved multifamily homes to participate in the HECM Purchase program.

During the housing crash of the late 2000s, lawmakers and regulators changed the program in several ways to make it more appealing to consumers (see Figure 10.3). In 2008, President George W. Bush and Congress allowed HECM loans to offer fixed-rate mortgages on lump-sum distributions, which helped nourish the popularity of fixed-rate products. From 2010 to 2014, the share of fixed rate mortgages rose from 31 to 89 percent, with most of them designated for maximum distribution.[16] Hoping, in 2009, to offer low-fee products to low-risk borrowers,

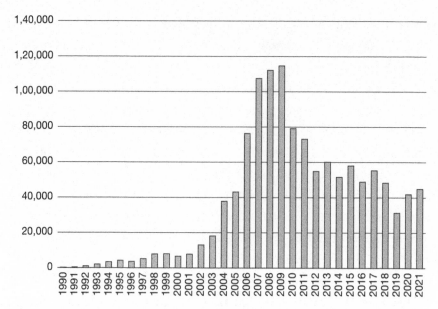

Figure 10.3 Number of Home Equity Conversion Mortgages (HECM) per fiscal year (1990–2021).
SOURCE: Department of Housing and Urban Development, HECM program.

President Obama and Congress introduced the "HECM Saver" program, which offered loans with substantially lower up-front premiums (just 0.01 percent compared to 2.0 percent on standard HECMs) in exchange for lower maximum borrowing amounts.

The risks to lenders and to the federal insurance program occurs when the loan balance exceeds the value of the home (known as *crossover risk*). When home prices were rising rapidly, that risk seemed low but, with housing market changes in the mid-2000s, the risks grew substantially. With the Great Recession and housing crisis, the Obama administration and Congress implemented several changes to control the cost of the program—which was intended to be self-financing but, at times, ran large deficits.[17] In 2013, policymakers enacted the Reverse Mortgage Stabilization Act to help address the financial pressures that the program faced; importantly, it gave HUD more unilateral discretion to impose reforms through regulation without following the normal process of public notice and public comments. HUD subsequently imposed important changes, such as ending the HECM Saver program, limiting the amount that borrowers could withdraw in the first year, and establishing a higher mortgage insurance premium for loans with initial distributions that exceeded 60 percent of the principal loan.[18] More recently, HUD required that lenders consider the loan histories of borrowers before issuing loans, and it gave the FHA's commissioner the authority to design incentives for voluntary set-asides by borrowers (through which part of the proceeds of a loan are kept in a separate account to pay part or all of future taxes and insurance premiums and avoid defaulting on the terms of the loan).

Throughout the program's history, policymakers enacted multiple reforms to increase transparency and help borrowers make financial decisions in their best interest. The 1994 Home Ownership Equity Protection Act required lenders to tell borrowers about total annual loan costs at the start of the application process. In 2001, HUD and AARP partnered to establish HECM counseling policies and procedures, which later became mandatory.[19] The 2008 Secure and Fair Enforcement for Mortgage Licensing Act required states to implement consistent procedures when licensing and registering HECM loan originators. The Housing and Economic Recovery Act, also of 2008, limited origination fees, prohibited lenders from overselling additional services to borrowers, and strengthened the independence of consumer counseling. Over time, as we have noted, consumer reasons for borrowing changed, with reverse mortgages evolving from a source of emergency funding and general consumption to a strategy to pay off a regular mortgage or reduce other consumer debt.

Recent reforms seem to be affecting the volume of reverse mortgages, especially the 2017 reform that lowered the principal loan limit and raised up-front mortgage insurance premiums. Since the housing market fell in 2007, HECM demand stabilized at 50,000–60,000 originations, which is about half of the peak in 2011 (see Figure 10.3), although 2019 witnessed a further decline.[20]

Other recent reforms are affecting the application process and the characteristics of new loans. After HUD rule changes in 2018, roughly a fifth of reverse mortgage applications were required to obtain a second appraisal of the value of the home if it looked as if the original appraisal had been inflated above the true value of the property. The 2014 rule requiring set-asides for borrowers facing the risk of tax and insurance default has proved influential as well: 13.7 percent of loans now have a fully funded set-aside and another 1 percent have a voluntary set-aside. The market also has changed in the proportion of loans with variable interest rates versus fixed rates. In large part due to program changes allowing fixed-rate, full-draw loans, fixed-rate reverse mortgages dominated the market from 2010 through 2013. Since 2014, however, HUD's elimination of fixed-rate, full-draw loans means that lenders are issuing mainly variable-rate mortgages. These provide for a lower interest rate but with somewhat greater risk to the borrower (see Figure 10.4).

The HECM program remains controversial. Media reports of widespread failures, with especially acute rates in Chicago, Baltimore, Miami,

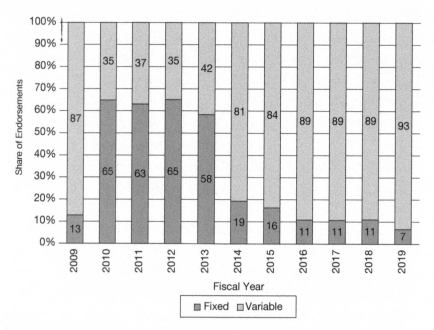

Figure 10.4 Home Equity Conversion Mortgages (HECM) (percentage of each type) issued by interest rate type.
SOURCE: Department of Housing and Urban Development, 2019 FHA report to Congress.

Detroit, Philadelphia, and Jacksonville, paint HECM loans as perilous financial products that can bankrupt consumers. Ongoing attention to the program's fiscal drain may prompt additional reforms that would likely further depress volume. Consumer groups remain on vigilant guard against high fees and the potential for predatory lending by private actors.

REVERSE MORTGAGES: PROS AND CONS

The demand for reverse mortgages is affected by local housing prices. Homeowners were significantly likelier to take out reverse mortgages when home values were rising, according to one study of the explosion in reverse mortgage activity between 2001 and 2006, with the run-up in housing prices in that period explaining roughly half of the increase in reverse mortgages.[21] Examining the housing boom, bust, and recovery of that period, another study found higher take-up rates in states with high house price volatility and higher prices than the historical average, suggesting that some homeowners use reverse mortgages to lock in home equity and insure against price declines.[22]

Recent reforms, in response to financial losses by the federal backstop insurance program, slowed the growth in demand for reverse mortgages. For instance, several studies show that HECM reforms after the housing crisis, which were designed to improve the program's fiscal position, dampened demand over the past decade. The 2013 reforms likely reduced demand by tightening borrowing limits for most retirees, even though they also lowered mortgage insurance premiums, according to one set of simulations.[23] The 2017 reforms significantly changed the qualification criteria for loans, altered upfront and closing costs, and further reduced the borrowing limit. All of that likely further depressed demand, although we do not yet have the evidence to prove it. Borrowers who expected to stay in their homes only for a short time could not justify the higher up-front costs. Mortgage demand drops when up-front costs rise.[24]

The demand for reverse mortgages is low also because many older homeowners want to leave a bequest for others. Absent that motive, the take-up rate for reverse mortgages would jump—to 17 percent, according to one study—and borrowers would increasingly use the proceeds of their loans to pay for their general consumption rather than to cover the costs of unexpected housing shocks, researchers estimate.[25] Older families often do not want to take out reverse mortgages because they want to preserve their home equity in case they need nursing home care.[26] If they do not, they can pass on the value of the house to their children.

For older households, reverse mortgages also can prove a backstop for unforeseen declines in income. COVID-19 showed how quickly the economy in general, and the labor market in particular, can fall deeply. Under these circumstances, older households who were relying on earnings to make ends meet may find themselves with an income deficit and limited recourse to earn more money. In these circumstances, emergency access to capital—as a reverse mortgage would offer—may be a rational way to fill the gap in their incomes, despite its high fees.

Are Consumers Evaluating Reverse Mortgages Correctly?

Given the complexity of reverse mortgages, we should not be surprised that consumers find it hard to evaluate them. Older people undoubtedly see the equity in their homes as an asset to fund long-term care if they need it, discouraging them from taking out reverse mortgages. Under this thinking, older households plan to remain in their home unless they require care—in which case they will sell their home and transfer to a facility. This approach, however, leaves the homeowner with an elevated level of risk and also dictates that they leave their home, which many people hope to avoid.

Reverse mortgages can facilitate a better outcome. In particular, reverse mortgages can support in-home long-term care. With a reverse mortgage, older homeowners in need of care can take a reverse mortgage to help pay long-term care costs but remain in their home while simultaneously transferring the risk of outliving the value of their home equity to the lender. The cost for this transfer of risk is the mortgage fees and associated interest.

Households also may not consider reverse mortgages correctly when it comes to upfront costs. Lenders face crossover risk when the value of the loan exceeds the value of the home. A reverse mortgage's upfront costs in part compensate lenders and federal insurers for that risk; borrowers pay for the fact that neither they nor their heirs will have to make payments if the value of the house does not cover their mortgage balance when the house is sold. The mortgage terms must include that feature because lenders do not want to ask older people to start making payments or face eviction because their loan balance became too high, and they cannot collect recompense from the borrowers' children. This feature of a reverse mortgage is quite valuable to borrowers[27] since it protects them from defaulting on their loans when they are at the end of their lives. Borrowers, however, do not value this feature of the loan very much. They merely see the upfront costs.[28]

Moral Hazard and Adverse Selection in the Reverse Mortgage Market

Moral hazard and adverse selection are important concepts. If prevalent, they can disrupt the smooth working of a market to the detriment of consumers. *Moral hazard* occurs when people change their behavior because they do not bear the financial costs of their actions. (Doctors and patients, for instance, may choose more expensive procedures if an insurance company is paying for them than if they were paying for themselves.) *Adverse selection* occurs when sellers know much more about the problems with a product than potential buyers. (A car salesman, for instance, knows that a car is a "lemon," but the buyer does not.)

Lenders and the government agencies that insure reverse mortgages recognize moral hazard. They respond either by imposing regulations that restrict the amount of allowable borrowing (to avoid crossover) or higher fees or interest rate premiums.[29] That raises costs and reduces the number of people taking out loans. Lenders can reduce moral hazard by taking simple steps. Sending quarterly letters and providing a refrigerator magnet to remind borrowers of their property taxes and due dates for home insurance premiums reduced defaults by roughly a third, according to one study, and the figures could be higher for borrowing-constrained households who may need advance planning to find the funds to make the payments.[30] That suggests that default rates could shrink and the reverse mortgage market could work better if all lenders were willing to help their elderly borrowers.

Adverse selection can occur when homeowners have little or no financial incentive to maintain their property once their loan balance exceeds the market value of the house. Far more than their lenders, borrowers know how many years they will likely live and stay in their homes.[31] They may stop paying property taxes because foreclosure and eviction will not occur for a long time; banks and local tax jurisdictions do not like to attract scorn by evicting older homeowners.[32]

Adverse selection of this type does not seem a significant problem. Indeed, many borrowers end up selling their homes soon after taking out the reverse mortgage, which benefits lenders and is costly for borrowers.[33] As we have said, cash-poor households tend to sell quickly even though they would benefit from staying longer in their homes. That is because, real estate experts Thomas Davidoff and Gerd Welke argue, families that take out reverse mortgages are predisposed to consume their housing equity and are thus prone to sell their home soon after taking out a reverse mortgage.[34]

Should More People Take Out Reverse Mortgages?

Public misperceptions about the market and the negative media coverage that it often attracts largely explain why few people take out this type of loan. Some experts who study the market, however, say that a sizable share of retirement-age households could benefit from it, but they do not perceive this benefit.[35] Estimates range widely, from one that says about 9 percent of homeowners older than the age of 69 could benefit to another that says as much as 80 percent of elderly women homeowners could benefit.[36]

Simulating the benefits of reverse mortgages for different types of households, economists Makoto Nakajima and Irina Telyukova found that low-income households without much retirement saving could use reverse mortgages to support a modest increase in their regular consumption spending or cover a large medical expense. Families that do not wish to pass on bequests to their heirs are particularly suited for them.

Reverse mortgages offer another important benefit that is hard to quantify: they enable older homeowners to remain in their current homes, which many retirees say they value. Elderly homeowners have a strong attachment to their homes, and they typically sell them only if they need to enter a nursing home, several studies conclude.[37] A survey sponsored by AARP found that 95 percent of those 75 or older agreed with the statement, "What I'd really like to do is to stay in my current residence as long as possible."[38] Older people also frequently find reverse mortgage debt less stressful than regular mortgage debt.[39]

Others argue that reverse mortgages are a bad choice for older households. After studying the issue, economist Valentina Michelangeli says that households with equity in their homes but very few financial assets are worse off after taking out a reverse mortgage,[40] while cash-rich households (those with more than $40,000 in liquid assets) are likely better off. That is surprising because one would think that house-rich, cash-poor households are just the ones that might benefit. Michelangeli's findings derive from the high up-front charges and high interest rates on accumulated debt that come with reverse mortgages. They prove problematic for cash-poor households because those households often move and sell their homes, the fees and interest costs diminish what they receive after the sale, and, as a result, they wind up worse off. Cash-rich households are less likely to sell and are, hence, better positioned to benefit by staying in their homes longer. Michelangeli's study highlights an important issue: borrowers do not benefit by taking out a reverse mort-gage and then selling the home after a short period.

As we have noted, reverse mortgages often attract negative media cov-erage that stresses the dangers of foreclosure. These stories can be decep-tive, however. The 18 percent foreclosure rate on reverse mortgage loans of recent years is high, but 75 percent of these cases are because the home-owner had already left the home and was living elsewhere.[41] With a reverse mortgage, borrowers must reside in their home or repay the loan if they move. Some borrowers try to avoid this provision by leaving their homes without repaying. Homeowners also must pay property taxes and home-owner insurance, and some do not. Local authorities may initiate foreclo-sure proceedings for the persistent non-payment of taxes. The remaining 25 percent of foreclosures came because the borrowers did not pay their property taxes.[42] Often, lenders lose money with a foreclosure, so they have a financial incentive to work with homeowners to remedy their non-payment of taxes.

All told, the reverse mortgage market can be an important retirement security vehicle for households that have not saved enough, and the reforms that we discuss later in this book could make it more attractive to consumers.

Home ownership is one way in which families save and support their retirement. Owning a home provides a stable place where retirees can live at low financial cost. Selling a home can provide funds for living expenses or a nursing home if the seller needs additional cash. Thus, being able to access the equity in the family home while still living in it is an important option for retirees, and that makes reverse mortgages an important part of the retirement security portfolio.

In the years to come, Americans will increasingly save for the future through 401(k)s and other retirement accounts—with workers and their employers making contributions and account holders investing the funds in stocks and bonds. As we explain in the next chapter, policymakers could take important steps to make these accounts more understandable, more accessible, and more profitable to would-be savers.

Another area of needed reform is the workplace for older Americans. By working longer, as we have said, Americans can boost economic growth and strengthen their own retirements. To incentivize Americans to work longer, however, we need to strengthen the financial rewards they will reap and address the discrimination that older workers sometimes face as they try to stay in the workforce.

How to Improve Retirement Accounts

The traditional "three-legged stool" of retirement consisted of employer-provided pensions, Social Security, and personal saving. With traditional private pensions disappearing, this puts more emphasis on personal retirement accounts to which workers themselves contribute, with their employers also sometimes contributing a percentage of a worker's income to the account.

Retirement accounts (or *defined-contribution pension plans*) come in various forms: 401(k)s, 403(b)s, Individual Retirement Accounts or Arrangements (IRAs), Roth IRAs, Simplified Employee Pension (SEP) IRAs, Savings Incentive Match Plans for Individual Retirement Account (SIMPLE) plans, and so on. They share the same fundamental structure: owned by workers, grown through employer and employee contributions, and typically invested in stocks or bonds. These accounts offer substantial tax benefits for their owners, but they have complicated rules for withdrawing money based on age and economic circumstances.

These accounts now dominate the retirement landscape. Not everyone has an account, but almost every current private-sector worker who expects to get retirement benefits will receive them through such an account rather than a pension. In the first quarter of 2021, $12.6 trillion was in IRA accounts and $9.9 trillion was in defined-contribution retirement accounts.[1] The total of these figures greatly exceeded the amounts in defined-benefit plans (traditional pensions in the private sector) or in state and local or federal pension accounts. In fact, retirement accounts that individuals control have become a force not only in retirement but in the financial system as a whole.

These accounts are the way that workers will save in the years ahead; only union or government workers will likely have traditional defined-benefit pensions. Policymakers should focus on retirement accounts in their efforts to strengthen retirement in general. Workers should have access to retirement plans and be able to contribute to them easily. Policymakers could require that all but the smallest employers create retirement plans for their workers, or states or the federal government could create accounts for workers who do not have access to them through their employers.

In addition, policymakers should reform the current retirement system that provides about $250 billion a year in tax incentives for saving, a disproportionate share of which goes to those at the top in terms of income. Optimally, they would convert current tax deductions for plan contributions into a credit, which would make the tax benefits far more equal across income levels. A more modest approach would be to retain the existing deductions and expand the existing Saver's Credit (as we discuss below).

While reforming tax incentives, policymakers should also take steps to help would-be savers better understand how much they should be saving to meet their needs when they retire. Savers need more information about how best to invest their savings, particularly information about the fees that financial advisers and managers impose, which can force advisers and managers to offer conflicted advice to clients. State experimentation with forcing more industry transparency about them could help guide future efforts.

A RETIREMENT ACCOUNT VISION

As we have discussed, flawed retirement accounts are a big reason why saving is so hard for America's families. The tax code provides generous tax benefits for retirement saving, but these benefits are complicated and are distributed unfairly. Only around half of workers in any given year have access to an account, and the participation rates are lower for small business, low-wage, part-time, African American, and Hispanic workers. Retirement saving can make some low-income Americans ineligible for certain public programs. Retirees and workers may lack the information and financial knowledge to make prudent decisions about saving and investment. And savers have limited opportunities to transfer retirement wealth into a reliable stream of income or health benefits.

Virtually every worker should have access to a saving plan at work and be automatically placed on a path to sound saving and investing. Making this ambitious vision a reality would require either a mandate on employers or a public option for a savings plan that the government would offer. With a mandate, the law would require employers to set up 401(k)-type retirement savings plans for their workers. With a public option, government—likely at the state level—would create accounts for workers in cases in which their employers did not offer them. We do not favor the mandate; instead, we think that government should provide a retirement savings option to all those who need it.

Retirement accounts should enable workers to contribute and invest with ease. Because saving is hard for many workers, retirement accounts would ideally include features that have an automatic opt-in provision that directs savers to sound planning practices and enables them to choose among different saving and investment options (unless they choose to opt-out of the suggested savings program).

These accounts should be *equitable*, meaning that the value of their tax subsidies should not vary widely based on a person's income tax rate. As research shows, the current structure of tax benefits results in an extremely limited overall increase in saving.[2] In effect, 401(k)-type plans are mainly ways for individuals to transfer their funds into accounts with tax advantages, rather than to encourage them to save more. Policymakers should redesign the system so that it encourages more saving by lower- and middle-income savers, those who will depend on it the most to enjoy a secure retirement.

At the very least, the rules that govern these accounts should not discourage people from saving by unduly penalizing them for using their saving when they really need to or for having savings at all. That means eliminating overly restrictive asset tests that make people ineligible for public benefits programs and enabling savers to tap their accounts in times of hardship during their working years—as some account owners can now do by taking a loan or an outright distribution from their retirement account if they experience a downturn in their finances.

The accounts also should be transparent, enabling their owners to understand the fees that they pay while also protecting savers from receiving biased advice from financial advisers and managers. They should offer investments that individuals can easily understand and reasonable options to convert liquid wealth into insurance products, such as annuities or long-term care insurance. The retirement system should give individuals easy access to unbiased information that can help them make wise saving and investment decisions.

People's retirement circumstances vary greatly, and better information and more options can help savers tailor their retirement accounts to meet their individual needs.

REFORMS TO IMPROVE RETIREMENT ACCOUNTS

With incremental, commonsense reforms, retirement accounts can become far more of a widespread vehicle for middle-class families to build wealth and can help all retirees to better manage their risk. And while these incremental reforms would preserve the general nature of the retirement system, they would generate meaningful increases in retirement assets for millions of families each year.

Make 401(k)-Type Plans More Accessible

To help create a system in which everyone has access to a workplace saving plan, policymakers need to incentivize more employers to offer them. Currently, large employers are far more inclined to offer plans than small ones. Some 74 percent of workers at companies with at least 500 employees had access to a plan compared to just 22 percent of workers at businesses with fewer than 10 workers, a Pew Charitable Trusts study found.[3]

Small businesses have several reasons for not offering plans, including the costs of starting them. Under current law, small businesses are eligible for a credit equal to 50 percent of the startup costs of setting up the program, up to a maximum of $500 for 3 years. Startup costs for small businesses, however, are likely much higher. Consequently, policymakers should create additional modest tax credits to offset these costs.

President Obama, and then-presidential candidate Biden both proposed to increase the credit to $1,000 per year and offer another $25 per enrolled employee.[4] That would have proved helpful, but it would not likely have substantially increased workers' access to workplace saving plans. To expand coverage more dramatically, policymakers could (1) mandate that employers offer plans or (2) offer state-administered plans to uncovered workers. Both options would include "automatic" features—such as automatic enrollment (putting workers automatically into retirement plans and leaving it to the workers to reverse that decision if they wanted to do so) and automatic investment (putting savers' contributions automatically into recommended investments that are often tailored to their age)—that put individuals on a recommended path to saving.

Let's take these one at a time.

- Policymakers could require established small businesses with at least 10 employees to offer a plan, but not require them to contribute on behalf of their workers. The impact of that requirement could be massive (depending in part on whether policymakers also reform the tax-based incentives for saving).

Even without such tax reforms, making workplace saving plans nearly universal would boost contributions by about $1,500 per affected taxpayer, raising national saving by about 0.14 percent of GDP.[5] About 24 million to 36 million workers, or roughly a fifth to a fourth of the labor market, would benefit.[6]

- Or, state lawmakers could offer public plans to uncovered workers. More than a dozen states and one city (Seattle) now offer saving programs for private-sector workers. The programs come in various forms, including mandatory participation by employers who do not offer retirement plans as well as voluntary automatic IRA plans (through which employers can choose to enroll their workers in an automatic plan) and state exchanges that offer options for retirement saving (through which businesses and workers can choose from a preapproved menu of low-cost options).[7] In about 45 other states, lawmakers have introduced legislation to create a public retirement option of some sort.

The benefit of mandating that small businesses create plans is, of course, the expanded coverage that it would generate; many if not most small- and medium-sized businesses would likely not create plans unless they were required. Given the remarkable promise of automatic enrollment, requiring near-universal enrollment in automatic saving plans surely would raise retirement saving rates and boost national saving. The draw-back is the burden on business owners. A mandate would force businesses to devote time and resources to creating and maintaining a plan. Tax credits would offset some of the cost, but the mandate still may prove an administrative burden for businesses. At the same time, the diversity of state options provides an opportunity to evaluate what has worked best. Ultimately, a nationwide requirement for businesses might prove the best option, but, for now, the right approach is to let the states experiment before setting a national strategy.

Another complementary approach is to help savers more easily track and access the contributions in their accounts. One problem with 401(k)-type plans is that low- and moderate-income households can end up with several low-value accounts scattered among several employers. Small accounts can be eroded by fees, and they are hard for workers to track. Some workers can even forget where they have their retirement funds if they left an employer many years earlier.

Economists David John, Grace Enda, William Gale, and Mark Iwry proposed to tackle this problem by calling on the federal government to create a "retirement dashboard." Specifically, this dashboard would be a website that Americans could access giving them information about all their retirement accounts as well as their future benefits from Social Security. This information would help people who wanted to consolidate all their retirement accounts.[8]

Make Saving Incentives More Equitable

The value of tax incentives for retirement saving, based largely on people's tax rates, is ineffective and unfair. Policymakers can deliver the hundreds of billions in annual tax breaks more effectively and equitably.

They can choose from two prominent options. The first, which we enthusiastically support, is to convert the current tax deductions for contributions into a credit. The second, which would provide only modest change, is to expand the existing Saver's Credit.

A retirement contribution credit would represent a sweeping change that would equalize the upfront benefit for contributions. Currently, most contributions are excluded from income tax, they grow tax free in the accounts, and they are then taxed at ordinary income tax rates when individuals withdraw money. That system provides massive tax benefits for upper-income taxpayers who tend to be in higher tax brackets in their working years than in retirement and who also pay higher rates on capital gains and dividend income. It offers little or no benefit to workers in the lowest tax brackets.

Under this reform, all workers, regardless of their tax bracket, would get a credit that equals 30 percent of their contribution every time they make one. That means a middle-class family earning $60,000 a year would likely get a $900 credit for putting $3,000 into an IRA or 401(k), rather than a $360 tax break under the current system. It also means that a person with $1 million in income who puts $40,000 in a 401(k) would get $12,000 in up-front tax breaks rather than $14,800.

Economist William Gale showed that policymakers could enact such a reform in a revenue-neutral way with a 30 percent credit. The reform would create winners and losers, but more of the former than the latter. Some 26 percent of families would get a bigger tax break than under current law, Gale estimates, while just 6 percent would get a smaller one. Middle-class families would be especially big winners. For example, about half of families with $60,000 to $100,000 in income would gain and only 2 percent would lose. At the same time, upper-income families on the whole would lose. Among families earning more than roughly $500,000, only 13 percent would get more in tax benefits while about half would get less.[9]

The biggest opposition to this reform comes from the retirement industry, which warns that it would prompt employers to abandon their plans for two reasons. First, the industry says, upper-income taxpayers would not want to contribute to a 401(k)-type plan if the up-front subsidy is only 30 percent, rather than the current 37 (because they pay tax at a 37 percent tax rate and can deduct their contributions). That seems unlikely, however. Upper-income taxpayers would receive a 30 percent tax credit, and, until they withdraw funds, they still would pay no tax as their accounts grow in value.

Second, the industry says, employers that now do not pay payroll taxes on retirement contributions would abandon their plans because they would no longer receive that benefit. This claim seems more credible than the previous one. An employer contributing to a 401(k) pays no payroll tax on those contributions. If, say, an employer contributes $3,000 to an account on behalf of a worker making $95,000 in wages, the employer foregoes the $230 payroll tax liability that it would have owed if it had paid the $3,000 in wages. So, employers would pay a bit more under a flat-rate credit. While we do not know how employers would react, our judgment is that such a change would not cause them to abandon their plans. After all, employers probably offer savings plans mainly as a recruiting and retention tool, not to save money on payroll taxes. To help incentivize employers to either keep the plans they have or offer them for the first time, policymakers could extend a payroll-like deduction for employers that maintain or create plans or they could expand the new credit to more permanently cover the costs of administering a plan.

If policymakers lacked the appetite for such sweeping change, they could keep the current deductions and reform the Saver's Credit, which seeks to make it easier for lower-income workers to save. Depending on their income, it gives savers a credit of 10, 20, or 50 percent of their contributions to retirement accounts. Taxpayers are eligible for annual credits up to $2,000 per individual (or $4,000 per couple).

In theory, the Saver's Credit is ideally suited to reverse the regressive nature of current tax incentives for savings. The credit, however, suffers from two main flaws that greatly diminish its impact. First, it is *non-refundable*, meaning that a taxpayer receives a credit only until it reduces the taxpayer's federal income tax liability to $0 (as opposed to providing the full credit even if that gives a taxpayer a refund from the government). As a result, many low-income families cannot receive the credit's full benefit because they pay little or no income taxes. The credit is also hard to understand and hard to access. Lower-income workers often do not have access to a workplace saving plan, so they would need to set up an IRA to access the credit.[10]

Policymakers could make the Saver's Credit more valuable to low- and middle-income families. They should first make it fully refundable. An estimated 43.3 percent of families, or 75.5 million in total, have little or no income tax liability, so they cannot receive additional tax benefits from the Saver's Credit by contributing more to their retirement accounts.[11] Policymakers also could expand the credit to make it available to more middle-income households, and they could "index" it to inflation so that its benefits do not lose value from year to year.[12]

These changes would increase the number of people eligible for the credit and make it worth more for those who are eligible. The best way to expand its reach, however, is to make retirement saving automatic, so that workers get the benefit of the Saver's Credit when they are automatically enrolled in saving plans. While automatic IRAs alone would boost contributions by $27 billion a year, automatic IRAs in conjunction with the Saver's Credit would boost contributions by $35 billion.

Other targeted reforms that can supplement either of the two reforms discussed above would also make the retirement system more equal. Currently, for instance, only workers earning wages can claim a tax break for contributions to a retirement account, so unpaid caregivers get no tax break for contributing to an IRA. Representatives Jackie Walorski and Harley Rouda have proposed to enable unpaid caregivers who spend at least a year outside the labor market to make "catch-up contributions" to IRAs. (In 2020, catch-up contributions let workers older than 50 put an extra $6,500 in a 401(k) account and an extra $1,000 in an IRA.) This modest reform would help caregivers, who disproportionately tend to be women in their prime earning years, contribute to their nest egg—and it would be worth the most to caregivers with higher-earning spouses who put them in higher tax brackets.[13]

To make the retirement system more fair, policymakers also could index to inflation the asset limits that restrict eligibility to public programs. The Supplemental Security Income (SSI) program prohibits benefits to those with more than $2,000 ($3,000 for married couples) in assets like retirement saving and checking accounts. SSI benefits for seniors are already modest, averaging just $466 a month, and the requirement that people exhaust all of their liquid assets means that some must choose between receiving these crucial payments and maintaining an emergency fund. Policymakers should retroactively index the asset limits to inflation, which would immediately double the asset limits to $4,000 for single taxpayers and $6,000 for married ones.

Fix Informational Problems

In a complementary, though more modest, reform to those discussed above, policymakers could help savers better understand the need for and impacts of saving in retirement accounts.

Proposals to boost saving through more financial literacy are appealing because evidence links literacy to improved behavior (although, as we noted in Chapter 7, the evidence is mixed). Improved financial literacy also requires little new public spending or tax benefits, and it imposes limited burdens on employers.

One option would be to give employers tax incentives to provide financial education to their employees. Employers are already a trusted source of information (some, for instance, provide wellness information for their workers) and are often implicitly involved with their workers' financial decision-making when workers decide, for instance, whether to buy health insurance or how much to contribute to a retirement account. Many employers are increasingly assuming this role; roughly half of them offered financial advice of some sort in 2016, compared to 37 percent in 2014.[14]

Economists Annamaria Lusardi and Peter Tufano propose that employers include guidance on debt literacy in employee assistance programs.[15] They suggest that workers, particularly those in traditionally vulnerable populations or with little financial literacy, receive education on the benefits of debt reduction during their employee orientations. While such a strategy might benefit the companies themselves by making their workers more financially stable and, in turn, perhaps more productive, policymakers could also incentivize them by offering modest tax credits.

Making Good Decisions on Investing Retirement Assets

To reach their preferred retirement age with the money to maintain their standard of living, Americans need not only to save enough but also to make prudent decisions about how to invest their savings. They need a well-diversified portfolio of assets that includes an equity fund and a bond fund. Equity funds generally yield higher returns, but they are volatile and can plunge in an economic downturn. Bond funds provide a steadier return but at a lower rate. Most employer retirement plans offer both equity and bond funds, and some provide guidance to employees about which to choose. At the same time, as we have said, many workers lack access to a 401(k) at work and must choose investment funds themselves.

Savers face a serious challenge in deciding how to invest their retirement funds and how to manage the funds as they draw them down in retirement. Many families feel insecure about meeting this challenge and lack the knowledge to do it themselves. Some families overestimate their own skills and are prone to bad choices. The challenge is particularly tough for young and middle-aged workers because interest rates have been low and will probably remain low once the current inflation surge has passed. That means that savers either choose to invest in secure bonds and accept a very low return or that they invest in the stock market and accept higher risk in the hope of receiving higher returns.

A bond portfolio that offers a secure return today may yield only enough to cover the cost of inflation, or perhaps even less. Thus, the dollar saved today and invested at this rate will be worth just a dollar or less in purchasing power 30 years from now, leaving investors with no real gains over that period.[16] The stock market grew steadily after the financial crisis of 2008 and weathered COVID-19 and the accompanying downturn surprisingly well, until 2022, when another dip or "correction" occurred. Many retirement savers moved more of their assets into equity funds, but there is no guarantee of what the future will bring. At times, equity prices have been depressed for years (such as in the 1970s), and market crashes occur from time to time as we have seen all too well.

Not surprisingly, many savers seek advice. Some just talk to friends, but many seek professional advice. Professional advice can undoubtedly prove valuable, helping people understand how much they need to save, how much they can draw down each year, how they can protect themselves against fraud, and how much they should allocate to different types of assets. Some savers panic when the stock market crashes and take much or all of their money out of the market at that point. That, however, merely leaves them with losses, rather than if they stayed patient and waited for the market to recover. Good advisers can discourage this counterproductive behavior.

Problems arise, however, if financial advisers steer savers or retirees toward funds that are unsuitable for them or that charge high fees, particularly if the advisor gets paid more for recommending high-fee products. High fees can sharply undermine a saver's retirement assets. Suppose an equity fund is expected to earn a return of 5 percent a year on average. Each dollar invested in the fund will be worth $4.32 after 30 years. If the fund keeps 2 percent a year in fees, the return drops to 3 percent and each dollar invested will be worth only $2.43 after 30 years, which represents a sizable difference.[17] The returns on an equity fund are uncertain but the fees are not, and they will always reduce the final value of the fund. The problem grows when advisers do not reveal the full extent of fees. An adviser may report that fees on a particular fund are only 0.5 percent, but the fund in question may include other funds, each charging its own fees.

Are these fees justified? Financial managers say that the fees they receive provide good value because, with them, managers can do the financial analysis that enables them to pick stocks or bonds that will earn higher returns rather than simply picking a broad portfolio. If, for example, a skilled fund manager picks stocks that earn 7.5 percent instead of 5, then the return to the saver is higher, at 5.5 percent, even after paying fees of 2 percent a year. Many financial advisers and managers believe that "managed funds" are a good deal for savers and justify the fees. A growing number of finance experts disagree, however, concluding that managed funds do not generate higher returns than funds that simply invest in the broad market or in an S&P 500 index, so the payoff to the saver after paying fees is actually lower.

President Obama's Council of Economic Advisers argued that financial advisers encourage retirement savers to invest in high-fee managed funds, costing them 1 percent a year in excess fees, or an estimated $17 billion a year. They argued that advisers were giving conflicted advice, putting their own interests above those of their clients. When workers retire and transfer their 401(k) savings into IRAs, financial experts can legally select a high-commission product from a range of generally suitable possibilities. Conflicted advice reduces the value of such savings by 12 percent over the course of a worker's retirement, the Council concluded.[18]

In response, President Obama's Labor Department proposed a "fiduciary rule" to require all financial advisors to act only in the best interest of their clients. The financial industry strongly opposed it, arguing that the rule represented excessive regulation, did not recognize the value of the services that the industry provides, and would make it harder for the industry to provide financial advice to low- and middle-income savers. The Trump administration subsequently shelved the rule.

The attention that the rule garnered, however, raised public awareness of excessive fees, and several fund firms now advertise low-fee investments for retirement savers. Morningstar, which provides investment research, reported in August 2021 that average investment fees have dropped dramatically—both for passive funds (such as an index fund geared to the S&P 500) and funds that professionals actively manage and choose which assets to hold. Passive funds, Morningstar reported, charged less than 50 basis points (i.e., one half of a percentage point), with some charging just around 20 basis points. Actively managed funds are typically charging 60–100 basis points in fees. Morningstar also says that inflows to funds now tend to be invested in low-fee accounts.[19] Furthermore, the Securities and Exchange Commission (SEC) implemented its own Best Interest Standard that, while weaker than the Obama fiduciary rule, goes partway toward outlawing conflicted advice. Looking ahead, the US Labor Department and SEC should make sure that the fees remain low and that all retirement savers have access to low-cost investments.

States also have a role to play in reducing investment fees. In September 2020, Massachusetts enacted the first state fiduciary standard for investment advice, and it applies not only to firms headquartered in the state but also to out-of-state firms operating in Massachusetts. That state's standard provides another opportunity to study the issue and the effectiveness of state action. If biased advice costs savers 1 percent a year in returns, as the Obama administration argued, then researchers should soon see it appear in the data. If a strict standard pushes advisers out of the market or raises the cost of the advice they provide, as the financial industry claims, we should see that in the data as well. The Massachusetts experiment can help guide future efforts.

THE NEED FOR ACTION

America's system of retirement accounts is not perfect, though it works well enough to supplement the retirement income of roughly half of all seniors. While the system is not fundamentally flawed, its shortcomings are big enough that policymakers should act quickly and effectively. In perhaps its greatest flaw, the system does not work well for low-income savers, who receive only modest benefits for saving. The lack of access to workplace accounts, penalties for saving, and biased information all compound the problem.

We suggest targeted remedies to improve the system for savers overall. These include equalizing the tax benefits for plan contributions, making access to workplace saving universal, harnessing the power of automatic enrollment, improving literacy, and addressing the tough issue of conflicted advice. The policies we have proposed could go a long way toward making retirement savings more accessible, increasing savings incentives, and ensuring that investors get a fair deal on their investment returns.

Another area of needed reform is the workplace for older Americans, as we explore in the next chapter. By working longer, as we have said, Americans can boost economic growth and strengthen their own retirement. To incentivize Americans to work longer, however, we need to strengthen the financial rewards they will reap while addressing the discrimination that older workers sometimes face as they try to stay in the workforce.

Improving Opportunities for Older Workers

There are good reasons to inform people of the benefits of working longer and not retiring too early. Life expectancy is much higher today than in the past (especially life expectancy after someone reaches age 65), and work now is generally less physically demanding than it used to be. As we have noted, Americans who reach age 65 can expect to live about 20 years longer and a substantial share of them will live into their 90s. Working longer provides three advantages: (1) it lets people postpone the day when they start collecting Social Security benefits, which substantially increases the monthly benefits they will receive; (2) it enables people to spend more years saving for retirement; and (3) it allows retirees to draw down their retirement assets over fewer years.[1]

From the outset, however, we—the authors—make the important distinction between *enabling* workers to remain the labor market longer and changes to public programs that might *force* people to continue working. People should not be required to work longer, especially those who have performed jobs that are very physically demanding or mentally stressful. Still, it is important that workers have the opportunity to work longer if they are willing and able to do so.

What would encourage older workers to keep working? One option is to provide financial incentives to older workers or their employers. Another is to change attitudes, since many people do not believe they can work when they reach 65 or 70, and many employers believe that older workers are unproductive,[2] lack technical skills, or bring expensive health costs. While seeking to change entrenched attitudes, policymakers and the courts should aggressively enforce anti-discrimination laws to ensure that older workers have a fair shot at retaining their jobs or securing new ones. Finally, policymakers must find effective ways to retrain older workers, and employers must encourage them to join training programs and use teaching methods in their facilities that are effective for older workers, although this can be hard to accomplish.

Some people appreciate the challenge of work and thus do not mind working longer. Others dislike their jobs or perform heavy manual work that exhausts them or leaves them in physical pain at the end of the day. As they age, many workers suffer health problems that make it hard for them to keep working. Finally, some workers cannot keep working even if they want to; their employers may have pushed them out of their jobs, and, now in their 60s, they cannot easily secure new ones.

The pandemic created new challenges for older workers and illustrated how downturns can be especially challenging for this group. The recession spurred by COVID-9 cost millions their jobs, and, even with the economy recovering and unemployment low, older workers still seemed to have fewer chances to find work again. Besides, with the waning effectiveness of the vaccines over time and the prevalence of breakthrough cases, older workers—especially those engaged in face-to-face work—may not feel truly safe at work.

That different older people face different challenges makes it hard to devise retirement policies that work well for everyone. We need to encourage those who can work to keep working without punishing those who cannot. The bigger the payoff is to those who work longer, the greater the gap will be between those who work longer and those who cannot. While some inequality is inevitable and perhaps even desirable to reward those who continue to work, policymakers need to make sure that those who retire in their early 60s can avoid poverty as they age.

Americans who have worked their whole lives should not have to retire in poverty, and Social Security benefits should be robust enough to prevent it. As discussed earlier, policymakers can put a floor under the incomes of those who worked 30 or 40 years and cannot work longer by setting a minimum level of Social Security benefits. Other policies would both encourage work and reduce inequality, such as expanding the Earned Income Tax Credit (EITC), which goes to low- and moderate-income working families.

Private companies have a role to play, too. Employers, and their human resources departments, should make the best use they can of the experience and skills of older workers. Employers can run training programs for older workers to sharpen and update their skills, recognizing that older workers often remain at the same job longer than younger workers. Employers can also provide independent advice for workers nearing retirement about whether their plans are viable.

The government can increase the financial incentives for working longer and strengthen anti-discrimination laws to make sure that older workers can compete for jobs on a level playing field. Training and retraining programs should be an important part of the government's efforts to restore the economy after economic downturns. That would benefit workers of all ages, but government must make a special effort to help older workers, especially low-income and minority workers in this age group.

FINANCIAL INCENTIVES TO WORK LONGER

In the past, there were few incentives for people to keep working. Companies with pension plans often created incentives for workers to quit when they reached 65 or even younger, and many companies had mandatory retirement policies. Social Security also included financial incentives for people to stop working. That was not surprising: the program was created in the 1930s, at a time of chronically high unemployment, and it was designed to encourage older workers to retire in hopes that this would lower unemployment for those who remained in the workforce. America's health insurance system provides a considerable incentive for people to work until 65 because most people get their health insurance through their employer and, for most, buying insurance in the private market or through an exchange is expensive.[3] Once people turn 65, however, they are eligible for Medicare and lose this incentive.

Since the early 1980s, the financial incentives for people to keep working have expanded greatly. The Social Security reforms of 1983 changed the way benefits are structured, including—as we have described—a strong benefit to those who delay benefit receipt. Those who start collecting monthly benefits before the "full retirement age" receive benefits that are 5 percent smaller for each year back to age 62. Those who do not start collecting until after the full retirement age receive benefits that are 8 percent larger for each year up to age 70. By waiting beyond the retirement age, of course, beneficiaries miss out on a year or multiple years of benefits but, for many who do not need their benefits until later, waiting for the higher monthly benefits makes sense. Those who keep working until 70 receive an estimated 15 percent increase in their Social Security income.[4]

The shift from traditional (defined-benefit) pensions to 401(k)-type (defined-contribution) plans also changed incentives related to work decisions. Under 401(k) plans, employer matches and tax preferences are incentives for workers to keep working so they can build a larger retirement fund. Alternatively, incentives for working evaporate under private pension plans after workers have reached a certain age since, unlike 401(k)s, their retirement benefits do not appreciably increase with additional years of work.

Just how much the shift from pensions to 401(k)s changed incentives is hard to say. That's because the nationwide decline in pension offerings coincided with other economic changes and because private pensions vary in how they are structured. Still, compared to a typical pension plan of 40 years ago, the typical 401(k)-type plan of today boosts the financial incentive to keep working by the equivalent of 20–25 percent of one's income.[5] The old-style pension plans were often designed to provide a financial incentive to encourage retirement, whereas, with a 401(k) plan, the longer people work, the more they can accumulate for retirement.

Have these shifting incentives changed people's behavior? Older Americans are certainly working longer, which suggests that the greater work incentives have proved effective. Having said that, the increase in work by older Americans did not coincide with the changes in Social Security or pensions.[6] Still, one study of older workers argues that every 1 percent increase in take-home pay leads to a 2 percent increase in the amount that older people will work, which is a very large effect.[7] Older workers who can choose whether to retire or keep working will likely respond to work incentives.

We think that financial incentives are very important in shaping work decisions, even if the size of people's responses is hard to measure. Incentives change behavior only gradually. Given that, we support two measures that would boost the financial incentives already in place by changing the way that Medicare and the EITC distribute their benefits.

Medicare

Currently, employers that offer health insurance must offer the same coverage to all employees, regardless of age: a worker older than 65 is covered by the same plan and pays the same premiums as everyone else. That makes an older workforce an expensive proposition for employers because health insurance—which is already a high cost for many employers—is more expensive for older workers.

The pandemic may have exacerbated the problem. Naturally, the greater prevalence of serious consequences for older Americans correlates with higher rates of hospitalization,[8] which generates much higher medical costs. Businesses worried about the liability associated with their workers' health may try to mitigate their risks by hiring younger workers. While these concerns may subside as vaccine mandates are enacted in various workplaces, we suspect that concerns over health costs will linger.

One way to mitigate these higher health costs is to automatically enroll workers in Medicare when they reach 65, even if they are still working. That would shift the cost of health insurance away from the company employing older workers[9] and, in turn, encourage employers to retain older workers, pay them higher wages, and hire others. Small firms, in particular, understand the risks of providing health insurance for older workers; a heart surgery or cancer treatment could raise an employer's premiums substantially.[10]

The downside is that Medicare's trust fund, which is already projected to be exhausted in a few years, would carry the health costs of those working beyond age 65. The cost to the federal budget as a whole, however, might be small because those who work longer will continue to pay payroll and income taxes.[11]

The Earned Income Tax Credit

The EITC encourages low-income families to work by supplementing their incomes—by as much as 45 percent—when they do, and it has proved very important in helping struggling families with children. The EITC, however, offers much less to workers who do not have children at home and who work for low wages, providing a maximum subsidy of only around 8 percent of their wages, which means in effect that it merely offsets the payroll taxes that low-wage workers pay. Nor, critically—other than for a brief exception in 2021—are workers eligible for the EITC after they reach 65.

The EITC's eligibility rules and Social Security's tax and benefit formula mean that older workers, especially low-wage older workers, often pay a steep penalty for working. Low-wage workers pay substantial taxes because payroll taxes total 15.3 percent of earnings, or $4,590 on $30,000 in wages. To be sure, employers pay half of the 15.3 percent tax, but workers *effectively* pay the full tax because employers reduce wages to help cover their share of payroll taxes.[12]

Normally, workers eventually receive the benefit of these high payroll tax burdens in the form of higher Social Security benefits down the road. But Social Security benefits only account for the highest 35 years of earnings. So, if a worker is paying her payroll taxes one year, but her earnings that year are not among the 35 highest over the course of her working life, then the payroll taxes of that year don't boost her Social Security benefits.

As a result, older workers who earn low wages can face high implicit tax rates compared to a similarly situated younger worker, which would discourage them from working and encourage them to start taking Social Security benefits early.

A more generous EITC program could offset these penalties and help older workers postpone their retirements.[13] It would boost the incomes of low-wage workers, enabling them to save and increase their incentive to keep working for more years by making the jobs more worthwhile financially.

CHANGING ATTITUDES TOWARD RETIREMENT, OLDER WORKER PRODUCTIVITY

With few exceptions in the 1950s and 1960s, only white men worked in senior positions and well-paid jobs. Workplace discrimination against minorities and women has not ended—white males still earn more than others—but attitudes have evolved and more opportunities are now available to yesterday's targets of discrimination. Women and African Americans serve as CEOs and board members, and the economy is substantially better off with more equitable treatment of women and minority CEOs, scientists, and skilled workers.

For older workers, social norms affect employers' willingness to hire or retain them. Some employers view older workers as a liability because they block the hiring of younger, more productive, more adaptable workers. Older workers may receive higher pay than entry-level workers, and, as we have said, health benefits are more expensive for them.[14] Age discrimination is illegal, so employers do not admit that they prefer younger workers, making it hard to measure actual employer attitudes. Nevertheless, some employers almost certainly view older workers as less productive or less equipped to master new skills or technologies.

Are employers discriminating against older workers or simply responding to the reality that older workers are less productive? Clearly, cognitive ability declines with age.[15] Moreover, one survey found that just

25.5 percent of workers 65 and older had the resources and skills to enable them to telework, compared to 36.2 percent of workers aged 35 to 44.[16] Still, most if not all older workers are not necessarily less productive in all positions. In addition, the downside of cognitive decline is offset by the upside of more experience.[17] Also, other important factors affect the value of an employee.

First, workers excel at different tasks as they age. Within the same organization, younger workers can focus on tasks that require maximum cognitive ability while older workers can focus on such other tasks as team management or client meetings, for which experience is very important. Workers can change jobs as they age, moving from high-pressure positions that require intense work effort and long hours to less-pressurized jobs. Second, people within all groups vary greatly. Workers who use their cognitive abilities on a regular basis can remain sharp and creative as they age, and workers who remain fit can continue to use their physical abilities. Cognitive decline sets in gradually for many people, often well past the usual retirement age.[18] Third, with advances in medical science and nutrition, a large share of older workers are healthy and have more years during which they can work. In a 2010 survey, two in five Americans older than 65 self-reported that they are in good or excellent health.[19]

After working with consulting firm Aon Hewitt, which collected data from large employers,[20] AARP concluded that older workers are more "engaged" with employers, speak positively about their organization, want to be part of it, and are willing to work extra hard as needed. In addition, they are more motivated than younger workers and less likely to leave for another job. Moreover, they often have excellent skills in using technology.

AARP concluded as well that productivity can rise with age, citing one study that focused on production errors on an assembly line[21] and another that found that an aging workforce increases efficiency for the total labor force.[22] It also found that, among the large firms in their sample, the earnings of workers older than 50 did not keep up with those of younger workers, meaning that older workers are less expensive for companies to employ. Though an advocacy group for older Americans, AARP nevertheless makes a good case for the value of older workers and the need for employers to assess workers and applicants based on their skills and capabilities, not their ages.[23]

Americans are working longer partly because of economic necessity, but partly because perceptions about retirement are changing. Years ago, people retired early not only because employers pushed them out of their jobs but also because they, themselves, thought they could no longer be productive enough. Rising labor force participation for older Americans suggests that attitudes about retirement are changing, or at least that many older Americans are seeing the value of working longer. Not all, however. In 2018, nearly 29 percent of men and close to 41 percent of women were not in the workforce from ages 55 to 64. From ages 65 to 69, the percentage rose to 68 for men and 77 for women. Only a small fraction of Americans remains in the workforce through age 70 and an even smaller faction beyond it.[24] Early retirement is a valid choice for some, but we suspect that some Americans retired early without making a rational calculation of their financial position or factoring in how long they may live or the out-of-pocket health costs they may face as they age.

Older workers typically suffer when the economy falters, but the pandemic hit this group even harder than usual. The COVID-driven recession and its aftermath left millions of older Americans out of work—because they feared for their health, or they were laid off, or they simply decided that they didn't want to work any longer. Many of these people chose to retire early and not return to work, with more than a quarter of all workers saying that the pandemic prompted them to move up their retirement date.[25] The full impact of COVID-19 on retirement remains to be seen, but by 2022 there were clear signs that many retirees were returning to work, 1.5 million over the 12 months through May 2022.[26] The drivers of this trend are unclear, although it seems likely that some felt forced to return to work because of financial need.[27]

As more families recognize that they, themselves, must manage their retirement and weigh the benefits of continuing to work, attitudes and norms about the age to retire will evolve. Policymakers can speed that evolution in at least two ways.

Reframe the Social Security Administration (SSA) message.[28] When workers contact SSA to discuss their options for collecting benefits, the agency tells them about their "full retirement" age. As we have said, that age is now 66 and 2 months and will rise to 67 for those born in 1960 and later. Consequently, many people assume that they should start collecting benefits at that age. They learn about the penalty for starting to collect benefits earlier, but they rarely learn about the higher monthly benefits they will receive if they wait beyond the full retirement age. In essence, the full retirement age helps shape when people retire and start collecting benefits even though it should hold no special status for would-be retirees. To raise expected benefits for retirees, SSA can make it clear that retirees can receive higher benefit levels for the rest of their lives if they postpone collecting benefits beyond the full retirement age (up to age 70).

Foster a high-pressure economy. Before World War II, women did not often work on the production line in well-paid factory jobs. When men were drafted to fight the war, however, employers addressed the steep labor shortage by hiring female and minority workers to fill jobs that they had not done before. The war economy also affected retirement decisions, with older men and women encouraged to stay in their jobs and postpone retirement to help fuel war production.[29]

The high-pressure economy of the late 1960s drove upward mobility, as Arthur Okun famously wrote, with workers of limited skills securing upper-tier jobs. Under such conditions, companies may retain, or even hire, older workers to fill vacancies, which helps eliminate the barriers that older workers face and lets them prove that they remain capable. When, on the other hand, unemployment and underemployment are high, skilled and experienced workers accept lower-tier jobs that do not require their skills. That makes it harder for less-skilled workers to secure those jobs for themselves.

In 2018 and 2019, the labor market was historically strong, and workers could easily find jobs. The economy had recovered only slowly from the Great Recession of a decade earlier, but, by the last quarter of 2019, unemployment had fallen to the extraordinarily low 3.5 percent. Companies in many industries, trades, and professions struggled to find workers to fill their openings. The high-pressure labor market of that day was comparable to Arthur Okun's of the late 1960s.[30]

While a high-pressure economy breaks down barriers and helps shift social norms, an economic downturn may do the opposite. The booming economy of recent years was ravaged by COVID-19, and millions of workers were laid off. Then, just as quickly, millions were rehired, while muted immigration and sluggish labor force growth helped depress the size of the labor force (with older workers in particular helping to slow the growth in the labor force by leaving their jobs or choosing not to return to work). Taken together, these trends nourished a uniquely tight labor market, especially for those working for low wages. How long these trends will persist, especially in light of pandemic-related uncertainty, remains unclear with a new recession potentially looming in 2022. Sustaining a high-pressure labor market would help alleviate the barriers to work that older workers face while raising wages for those who continue to work.

Monetary and other macroeconomic policies cannot be geared only to the needs of older workers, of course. If the economy is too high-pressure, there is the danger of inflation.[31] Our point here is simply to note that when unemployment is low and the demand for workers is strong, this helps not only labor market groups such as disadvantaged youth, but it also helps older workers.

STRENGTHEN AGE DISCRIMINATION PROTECTIONS

The 1967 Age Discrimination in Employment Act (ADEA) prohibited discrimination against workers older than age 40 in hiring, promotions, wages, and layoffs. Employers also cannot deny benefits to older workers that they provide to younger workers. Amending the law in 1986, policymakers prohibited mandatory retirement, although with exceptions for highly compensated executives and for cases in which qualifications are age-related or public safety is at stake.

Nevertheless, age discrimination still exists in our economy. The strongest evidence comes from an experiment in which artificial résumés were sent in response to job advertisements for low- and moderate-wage positions, such as salespeople, security guards, janitors, or administrative assistants. The résumés described applicants who had the same backgrounds and qualifications but differed by age. Those aged 64–66 received fewer call-backs than those aged 29–31 or 49–51.[32]

The ADEA would seem a powerful weapon to ensure that older workers are treated fairly. In practice, it does not guarantee that older workers avoid discrimination any more than other laws eliminate discrimination against minorities and women. In addition, the courts have undercut the ADEA. Most important was the Supreme Court's "but for" ruling of 2009,[33] requiring that a worker suing an employer under the ADEA show that *but for* the worker's age, he or she would not have faced the layoff or other job action. If an employer can show that other factors also motivated the action, the worker cannot prove discrimination. That ruling has made discrimination cases much harder for older workers to win and much harder to convince lawyers to take, and employers are likely less concerned about litigation if they lay off or decide not to hire an older worker.[34]

As a result, lawmakers should modify the law so that it really provides equal protection. The Supreme Court and other federal courts have become more conservative, and, if the law is not clear, they will narrow the grounds under which plaintiffs can claim age discrimination. The president and Congress should clarify the law, granting the same protection to older workers that other groups, such as the disabled, now receive.

The free market can help undercut discrimination, as Gary Becker argued in *The Economics of Discrimination*. A company that does not discriminate has a larger labor force from which to choose diverse skillsets, giving them a comparative advantage over their competitors. Similarly, companies that recognize the value of older workers should be able to outcompete companies that discriminate against them. Becker's argument is important because it suggests that market forces can reinforce legal efforts to overcome discrimination against older workers.

RETRAIN OLDER WORKERS

Crises like COVID-19 cause huge economic dislocation, but the labor market changes enormously even in normal times. In each *month* of 2019, during a booming economy, there were well over 5 million job separations—1.7 million to 1.9 million workers were laid off or discharged, while another 3.5 million or so people quit their jobs. Employment still grew, however, with 5–6 million new hires per month.[35] Older workers generally enjoy more job stability than younger workers, but even older workers may lose their jobs or need to find others. And, as we have noted, older workers find it harder to secure other jobs. Re-employment for displaced workers aged 65 and older is only 31 percent, less than half of that for younger workers, the Bureau of Labor Statistics reported.[36]

People often learn the skills that make them productive and valuable to their employers on the job. Doctors, dentists, and other professionals do plenty of book learning, of course, but even they learn much of their craft in practical training. Older workers accumulate lots of "human capital" through years of work, and they can use some of it in a new job, but part of it is lost because a different job and employer require different skills. All employers have their own ways of working. Meanwhile, technology is shaping the nature of work, and most jobs now require knowledge of computers, testing equipment, or tablets. Changing jobs often means acquiring new skills.

America's retirement system assumes that people will keep working during their prime working years so policymakers and employers have an obligation to provide retraining opportunities for older workers to refresh their skills and ensure that they remain productive enough to earn a living wage. America's experience with training programs is mixed at best, but there is no alternative to providing good options for retraining older workers if our retirement system is to work properly.

Worker training is important for multiple reasons. First, it helps older workers build skills that enable them to work longer and ensure their retirement security. Second, it makes those looking for jobs more employable. Third, it may increase their productivity. Whether an older worker seeks training depends on the length of the training, the type of training, its cost, and the skill it teaches. Older workers in particular care about the length of training (since they have limited years before retirement) and its cost (since they want to avoid tapping their retirement savings). They will likely choose to learn skills tied to their existing knowledge rather than completely new ones.

The need to improve worker training. Older workers receive four kinds of training, according to an AARP report of 2015: (1) colleges and universities offer credentials for learning skills and programs; (2) trade and proprietary schools teach skills such as how to become an electrician or a medical technician; (3) nonprofit, community-based organizations offer low-cost and community-based trainings; and (4) employer and employee associations offer job-specific training to those on the payroll.[37] Older workers who want to switch jobs may lean toward any of the first three, while those who want to work longer may prefer the fourth. Employer-provided training can also boost the morale of older workers and raises retention rates since it signals an employer's interest in keeping its workers on the job.[38]

Training that is targeted to firms and sectors with well-paying jobs is more cost-effective, and employers should create more coherent workforce development systems that factor in the latest evidence to achieve better results, economist Harry Holzer argues.[39] Similarly, Matteo Picchio finds that training that accounts for the specific needs of older workers is more effective in ensuring improved skills.[40] There is, however, a dearth of programs in the market that are designed to serve the needs of older workers. *With the exception of one small program, AARP reported, no government-offered training or aid programs were geared toward older workers.*

Employers and governments would benefit from building and designing programs that serve older workers, but research into the effectiveness of training for older workers has been limited, due in part to the limited use of training by older workers, and in part to the extensive effort needed to track the progress of older workers during and after the training. The few available studies show that training increases the employability and retention of older workers to some extent.[41]

Not all older workers, of course, need training when they change jobs. In addition, training is costly for workers who forego paid work and may incur fees and potentially costly for employers who may incur training costs and sacrifice the work that workers in training would otherwise be doing. Nonetheless, the right kind of training can be a simple, effective, and desirable solution for some older workers, and employers and governments need to do more to provide it. Designing and offering training programs is ultimately an employer's investment in an employee, and these programs can be an effective tool in overcoming attitudinal and institutional barriers that older workers often face.

No matter how long they work, however, most Americans eventually will retire. At that point, they will need to decide how to spend their assets to meet their needs. To prepare for that day, many Americans would be well-advised to convert some of their assets into insurance products, as we explain in the next chapter.

Reforming Private Insurance Markets

America's retirement challenge is often viewed as a savings problem—that people save too little. What does not get enough attention is "decumulation"—how people spend down their retirement assets.

Retirees have two broad choices about how to spend their assets. They can take out money from their accounts as their spending needs arise, such as when IRA account holders take out a fixed dollar amount each month to supplement their Social Security payments. Or, they can convert some of their assets into insurance products that provide a stream of benefits throughout retirement.

With insurance, the benefits differ based on the products. Annuities traditionally provide cash. Long-term care insurance provides health-related benefits. A reverse mortgage, which is an insurance product of sorts, gives people access to tax-free funds and protection against losing their homes after drawing down their home equity.

The central benefit of insurance, as opposed to retirement accounts, is that it shifts the risk from the household to the insurance company. For long-term care, the approach is similar to home or auto insurance: policyholders pay their premiums into a pot of money, and the company compensates those who get sick or have an accident. But the "insurance" element of other products is less obvious to those planning retirement.

Take, for example, income annuities, in which an insurance company issues annuity policies to a collection of households and generally makes payments for as long as each household is alive. Some policyholders may only live a few years, while others live for decades. Just as the premiums of accident-free drivers subsidize the payments to those involved in accidents, annuity payments to those who die quickly subsidize the payments to those who live longer.

Insurance products are not perfect. Insurance companies are for-profit businesses that make a return by providing less in benefits than they receive in premiums. Although heavily regulated, insurers are not always as financially solid as consumers would like, and, on very rare occasions, their financial problems jeopardize consumers' benefits.[1] In addition, the products are often confusing and cumbersome, and the policy documents may be hard to understand, so policyholders may not get the insurance they expect and often have to spend time quizzing the insurer to learn the details of their benefits.

Yet, for households with any appreciable assets, there is no better option. The shift from company pensions to 401(k)-type accounts means that many retirees have large account balances but little assurance that they will not run out of cash. Meanwhile, with the absence of a healthy market for long-term care insurance, households must save for the possibility that they will need care. Retirees hoard their saving to protect against the unexpected (e.g., getting sick, watching the stock market crash, or living decades longer than they expected) so they cannot enjoy the retirement that their decades of work should provide.

The current retirement landscape includes lots of insurance-like products. For most retirees, Social Security is effectively a rock-solid income annuity; Medicare is a massive health insurance program; Medicaid offers long-term care for low-income, low-asset households; and Supplementary Security Income offers annuity-like payments to those with the lowest incomes. Even owning a home outright is an insurance program of sorts since a home is a bit like an annuity that pays the rent as long as you own your home while also protecting against rising housing costs.

For about half of households, however, this level of insurance is wholly inadequate for it leaves them to suffer large declines in their living standards if they face the unexpected. That is not a big concern for those who have not saved much for retirement or for those who have saved so much that their standard of living will not fall even if they face large health costs or live a long life. But for those in between, with sizable home equity or substantial financial wealth, better private insurance markets can mean a more secure retirement.

Together, reforms to reverse mortgages, annuities, and long-term care could dramatically improve the retirement outlook for roughly half of retirees, giving them more freedom to spend down their assets rather than save for unforeseen events.

WHY REFORM PRIVATE INSURANCE MARKETS?

Private insurance is not for everyone. Virtually all retirement-age Americans have access to social insurance programs—Social Security and Medicare—that provide an income annuity and health insurance benefits for life. That may be enough to give retirees with relatively little wealth and income an adequate retirement. That is, especially for retirees who own their homes, social insurance programs may give them about the same standard of living as they enjoyed during their working lives.

Consider the typical (i.e., median) retirement-age household on Social Security. The family receives benefits that equal 55 percent of their average earned income during their last 5 years of earnings.[2] (If they earned $60,000, their Social Security benefits would be $33,000.) Unlike with their wage income, they likely pay no payroll or income tax on their benefits. They have no commuting, lunch, or other work-related expenses. They pay premiums for their Medicare benefits but, at about $150 a month or $1,750 a year, the costs are reasonable.[3] They may own their home, so they do not make rent or mortgage payments, and they may live in a state that gives property tax breaks to older homeowners. All in all, they are not rich, but neither are they poor.

Many retirees, however, have financial and housing assets that they saved for retirement. In 2019, the median married household aged 65 and older held roughly $250,000 in financial assets and $210,000 in home equity and often received a small employer pension.[4] Beyond such assets, these retirees can expect sizable Social Security and Medicare benefits. For them, the question is how they should treat their financial and housing assets.

If they are like many households, they will choose to assume the risks associated with retirement by themselves. They will not buy an annuity; instead, if they live into their 90s or get sick, they will limit their spending. They will not tap their $210,000 in housing wealth unless they fall ill and need to move. Nor will they buy long-term care insurance unless they have a good reason to expect to use it.

Many families would enjoy a less risky retirement if they had better ways to turn part of their retirement wealth into insurance. The additional risk conferred on retirees in the post-pension environment demands better insurance markets.

Income annuities are perhaps the best way for families to secure their retirement, especially longevity annuities that they can buy at or before they reach retirement age and that begin paying benefits roughly two decades later. As we noted in Chapter 8, these annuities help mitigate the greatest source of risk in retirement: unknown lifespans. Long-term care insurance and reverse mortgages help as well, although they are probably more suitable for a smaller share of Americans unless policymakers reform these markets.

Consider how retirement might change for the median retirement couple described above. Rather than slowly draw down their $250,000 in retirement wealth and tap their home equity only in an emergency, they buy a longevity annuity for $45,000, which will pay $7,896 a year beginning at age 85.[5] They also buy a $60,000 long-term care policy that provides a monthly benefit in the event that care is needed (which would be more affordable under the reforms listed below), reducing the need to stockpile funds to prepare for illness.[6] If they want more funds, they take out a $100,000 reverse mortgage.

With these additional retirement vehicles, their planning is now considerably different. Rather than needing to spread $250,000 over a possible 40 years—a nearly impossible planning exercise—they now only need to spread $245,000 (their combined retirement wealth and reverse mortgage balance, less premiums for annuities and long-term care) over 20 years—just until their longevity annuity kicks in. This couple will have more money to spend each year, face less uncertainty, and may receive better long-term care.

This approach does have drawbacks, however. The couple now faces the miniscule risk that the life insurance company issuing their annuity goes bankrupt—although each state maintains a comprehensive backstop to protect annuity holders and defaults on annuity contracts are close to non-existent.[7] They may have less money to bequeath to their heirs. And, if the stock market rises in the years in which they hold this annuity, they will have foregone some investment income by sacrificing part of their savings to an annuity policy. Nevertheless, they have been able to reduce risk in their retirement.

With that in mind, we propose a series of reforms to transform America's retirement system into one in which private insurance products are more affordable and available. We focus on reverse mortgages, annuities, and long-term care insurance because they are most relevant to retirement. We also present the most promising reforms, rather than a laundry list of possible changes. The goal is a system in which retirees have reasonable ways to turn their savings into streams of income and benefits, enabling them to lock in a given standard of living while also generally raising their well-being—compared to a situation in which they assume most of the risk of retirement themselves.

REVERSE MORTGAGES

Reverse mortgages are mortgage loans that let homeowners access their home equity while keeping the home as their primary residence.[8] Unlike with traditional mortgages, borrowers do not have to make out-of-pocket payments during the life of the loan. Instead, borrowers take periodic distributions (or, in many cases, a single lump-sum distribution) that add to the loan balance and grow with interest. When the loans come due (usually when the borrower dies or sells the home), the borrowers or their heirs can pay the balance and keep the home, sell the home to settle the balance, or let the lender sell the home. Importantly, reverse mortgages are usually "non-recourse" loans—the borrower is not responsible for any loan balance that exceeds the proceeds from selling the property.

Reverse mortgages are not for every homeowner, but reforms to the market—which is run almost exclusively through the Housing and Urban Development (HUD) Department's Homeowner Equity Conversion Program (HECM)—would go a long way toward strengthening it and enable more retirees to access the equity in their homes. As we outlined in Chapter 10, the product currently has three main problems: it costs too much for potential borrowers who plan to stay in their homes, it does not let retirees convert traditional mortgages into reverse mortgages, and it has foreclosure rates that are too high.

We propose three strategies largely based on the research of reverse mortgage experts Donald Haurin and Stephanie Moulton, to improve the reverse mortgage market.[9]

Streamlined "small-dollar" HECM Loans: Many reverse mortgage borrowers do not need "open-ended" products through which they can take large amounts of home equity, exposing lenders to *crossover risk*—the chance that the loan balance will exceed the home's value. Instead, the HECM program could offer small-dollar reverse mortgages that create essentially no risk that lenders will suffer a loss.

For example, the streamlined HECM could enable homeowners to withdraw up to $20,000 in a "closed-end" draw, meaning that the withdrawal could not exceed this figure. These borrowers would pay a fixed interest rate. Of the roughly 25.7 million older homeowners who could be candidates for this product, roughly half could take out the full $20,000 and still owe less than about a quarter of their home's value in debt.[10] That means, in effect, that about half of older homeowners could take out a small-dollar HECM that could come with virtually no chance that the loan would be worth more than the home.

The streamlined HECM would mostly benefit older households with limited financial wealth. If someone needs $20,000 for an unexpected expense, the best option at the time is typically to dip into retirement saving accounts, which impose the lowest fees. Paying the $20,000 with credit card debt may also be a possibility, but credit card interest rates are very high and the borrower must repay the loan with monthly payments. Moulton and Haurin estimate that more than 6 million homeowners have less than $10,000 in financial wealth but more than $20,000 in home equity, so a wide swath of older Americans could use this product to weather financial shocks.

Those familiar with reverse mortgages will remember that, from 2010 to 2013, the HECM Saver program offered a similar product, with an up-front premium of just 0.01 percent compared to 2 percent for a standard mortgage. Consumers and regulators, however, found the product unappealing due to the combination of unusual housing volatility and problematic design characteristics, such as lower maximum draws and variable interest rates. In a less unusual time for housing prices, a better-designed product should receive a more positive reception.

Forward conversion mortgages: While both reverse and traditional (forward) mortgages are both debts that are secured by a home, they differ in the timing of the payments. Traditional mortgages are paid off in monthly installments, while reverse mortgages are paid off when the home is sold. A growing share of older Americans today are starting retirement with sizable outstanding balances on their traditional mortgages, so they will owe monthly payments, perhaps for several years. Many families have refinanced their mortgages, partly to take advantage of lower interest rates, but also to take out cash to cover college costs for children or other expenses. That is fine for those with enough income to live comfortably and those who want to accumulate assets to leave to their heirs. But for retirees who want more discretionary income each month, converting a traditional mortgage to a reverse mortgage can enable them to avoid monthly mortgage payments indefinitely.

While a substantial share of reverse mortgage holders have effectively used them to pay off their traditional mortgages, the conversion is costly and cumbersome. In one promising reform, HUD could explicitly offer a conversion reverse mortgage that would let homeowners seamlessly convert one into the other. Under this reform, older adults with traditional mortgages and substantial home equity could convert their traditional mortgage to a reverse mortgage with a fixed interest rate. They could borrow only up to the balance on their traditional mortgage, and borrowers who could not pay property taxes and maintenance would have to set aside additional money that acted like an escrow account.[11]

Assume, for instance, that a 65-year-old homeowner is 20 years into a 4 percent $220,000 mortgage on a $350,000 home. The monthly payment is $1,050. After two decades, she would still owe about $95,000 on the mortgage. With a conversion, she could take out a reverse mortgage for the full $95,000, not pay a monthly mortgage going forward, and incur lower fees than for a typical reverse mortgage. The cost would come when she sells the home, and she would have less equity to pass on to heirs. But retirees who need money for food and healthcare each month and who would sacrifice some of the value of their home when they sell it or die would benefit from a conversion product.

The fees associated with a product for conversions, Moulton and Haurin explain, would be lower because homeowners could only take out loans that total no more than their remaining balances and because the product would have lower marketing fees since lenders could market directly to homeowners.

Preventive servicing: One of the reverse mortgage market's biggest shortfalls is its high foreclosure rate. Media stories about reverse mortgages often stress the dangers of foreclosure, with older families forced out of their homes. Indeed, borrowers must reside in their home or repay the loan if they move, and local authorities may initiate foreclosure proceedings if borrowers persistently do not pay their taxes, regardless of whether there is a mortgage on the property. The danger is real, but these stories do not provide the full picture. In recent years, about 18 percent of reverse mortgages ended in foreclosure, but three-quarters of these foreclosures occurred because homeowners were no longer living in their homes and the other quarter occurred because property taxes were not paid.[12]

Still, foreclosures hurt both lenders and borrowers, and both want to avoid them.[13] A promising strategy is to provide preventive servicing to help reduce foreclosures. That can include quarterly reminders from lenders to borrowers through email to make property tax and home insurance payments—which can cut non-payment of these expenses by half. Another option is to expand the federally supported "cash for keys" program, for loans originated after 2017, which allows servicers to provide a $3,000 payment to help high-risk borrowers transition into a property they can better afford. Last, lenders can simply remind borrowers of the consequences of not making payments since, according to a report by the Consumer Financial Protection Bureau, some borrowers did not know that their non-payment of these obligations could result in a foreclosure.[14]

ANNUITIES

As we have said, just a small fraction of families that retire with significant financial assets buy an annuity. And those that do often buy products that are not pure annuities and do not guarantee lifetime income, making the products more comparable to mutual funds. Income annuities remain a niche product in America.

As we have also said, economists are perplexed that consumers have so little interest in annuities, terming the phenomenon "the annuity puzzle." Most employer-provided retirement accounts do not offer annuities, and retirees often do not recognize their insurance value and will not buy them because they will "lose out" if they die after only a few years. Making annuities available in retirement accounts and framing them as insurance products are necessary to boost interest in them.

Adding annuities to employer accounts: Few employees can buy an annuity as part of their employer retirement plan.

To be sure, employees who are facing retirement could buy annuities on their own, but fees in the individual market are high, and these employees may think they do not know enough to choose a good product. Employers can offer annuities as part of their 401(k) options and negotiate a group rate that would lower fees, but few employers do, in part because they believe that offering annuities would expose them to serious fiduciary risk; they worry that they will have to make the annuity payments themselves if the annuity provider they choose for their workers goes broke.

Employers' risks are typically not significant if they choose an annuity provider sensibly and monitor its financial health, but many employers will not take the risk. In a 2016 Willis Towers Watson survey, 81 percent of plan sponsors indicated that fiduciary risk was an important barrier to including lifetime income solutions in their retirement options. Similarly, a 2016 Government Accountability Office survey found that of the 39 plan sponsors that did not offer an annuity, 26 said that was partly due to concerns over the "resources required to obtain liability relief."[15]

The SECURE Act, which President Trump signed into law in December of 2019, sought to address the problem by making it easier for employers to protect themselves from future liability. It included "safe harbor" provisions that the insurance industry largely developed to protect employers from potential fiduciary liability for selecting annuity providers.[16] Employers still must conduct an objective, thorough, and analytical search for annuity providers, but the safe harbor provisions are designed to make the process much more explicit, objective, and attainable.[17] Most importantly, employers are not deemed responsible if the annuity provider goes bankrupt as long as they followed a reasonable path in choosing the provider.

If liability concerns are really a major obstacle for employers, this law should help drive more annuity offerings. If, however, employers remain reluctant, then policymakers should revisit the safe harbor's design so that it gives employers a more reasonable assurance that offering an annuity from a licensed life insurance company would not make them liable if the company goes under.

Changing the framing of annuities: Employers, advisers, and the financial media often frame annuities as a portfolio decision for employees, equating them with other investments, such as mutual funds, and comparing such elements as rates, returns, and fees. That framing is appropriate for variable annuities that account holders can rarely convert into income payments, but is misleading for income annuities.

How can we change the framing? One way is through financial education. Throughout this book, we have framed the decision to buy an annuity as essentially an insurance decision, protecting households against running out of money if they live longer than expected. We have stressed that consumers should think of annuities as a product that adds stability to a retirement portfolio by essentially providing a monthly "paycheck." No one asks about the rate of return on home or auto insurance, and no one should ask such questions about income annuities.

Financial education would help people visualize what their lives will be like at age 85 or 90, depending on how much money they have available. What will their housing situation look like if they are living just on Social Security? Will they have funds to pay for cleaning or meal preparation? Will they have enough to pay for a Medicare Advantage program and make co-payments on drugs and doctor visits? No one likes to imagine being old and infirm, but a secure income would make that situation much better. We are not overly optimistic about the impact of financial education, but it could help savers who want to learn about financial concepts and markets and to act on what they learn.

Perhaps the most promising approach is for employers to provide guidance to employees, including access to retirement plan administrators who can clarify the merits of and drawbacks to annuities. Employers can help older workers avoid thinking of life expectancy as a guaranteed date of death and instead as a series of possible outcomes with varying chances of occurring. And by simply framing annuities as insurance products rather than financial investments, employers can increase consumer interest in them.[18] The financial media can also help shed light on the tradeoff between annuities and bonds.

Automatically enrolling in longevity annuities: In a compelling paper,[19] economists Vanya Horneff, Raimond Maurer, and Olivia S. Mitchell suggested that certain employees with 401(k)-style plans should be automatically enrolled in deferred-income annuities (DIAs) unless they specifically choose to opt out. Under their proposal, any individual who reached age 66 with more than a minimum amount in a retirement account would have 10 percent of their account balance defaulted into a DIA that began paying benefits at age 85. On average, the authors found, DIAs enable older workers to spend more at advanced ages.[20]

Policymakers will not likely mandate that private-sector employers adopt such a strategy. One possible way to make default investments in DIAs more widespread is for public-sector defined-contribution plans to adopt the practice or for the automatic enrollment plans described in the previous chapter to include a similar provision. Government agencies also could encourage employers to pursue such a strategy. These steps, coupled with a more accommodating safe harbor for income annuities, could begin to move the needle on worker demand for these products.

Including income annuities in a retirement portfolio: We can think about regular income annuities as part of a retirement decumulation decision. Investment advisors often suggest that investors hold 60 percent of their assets in stocks and the other 40 percent in bonds. This 60–40 (or perhaps 70–30) rule can help retirees watch their assets grow and their bonds provide a regular income payout with less overall volatility. Bonds are included in portfolios to reduce risk, at the cost of low expected returns (given low interest rates).

We are not recommending any specific retirement drawdown strategy. However, in looking at ways in which annuities could be used, we note that many retirees use a 60–40 strategy, meaning 60 percent of their retirement portfolio in stocks and 40 percent in bonds. Or for those with greater tolerance for risk, a 70–30 strategy with a larger percentage in stocks. An alternative approach is to use part, or all, of the bond portion of the retirement portfolio to buy an annuity: for example, 60 percent in stocks, 30 percent to purchase an annuity, and 10 percent in bonds. That would reduce a retiree's exposure to market volatility and provide regular guaranteed income for life. Retirees would keep 60 (or 70) percent of their retirement funds in the stock market but have an annuity to supplement Social Security and mitigate risk. Annuities may be a worthy alternative to bonds in a retirement portfolio because of the insurance value they provide. To reiterate, we are *not* making specific portfolio recommendations, which must depend on each family's circumstances and risk tolerance.

LONG-TERM CARE

Long-term care is among the hardest and most pressing problems for households. As we explained in Chapter 9, the long-term care market has complex, extensive problems. Medicaid serves as a public backstop on private insurance, discouraging individuals from buying private policies. The private market suffers from failures that drive up costs. Americans are often poor planners, so they widely eschew long-term care policies that would seem to serve their interests. Few employers offer policies that cover long-term care needs in old age. And a poorly designed tax incentive for private insurance has done little to drive more consumer demand.

Consequently, too few Americans get the care they need and too many unpaid caregivers—often the adult daughters and daughters-in-law of patients—bear the burden of providing care. Moreover, COVID-19's sky-high fatality rate among seniors in nursing homes reflected the long-term care system's stark inability to respond to a pandemic that made facility-based care so expensive.

The system's shortcomings suggest the need for a comprehensive solution. The Community Living Assistance Services and Supports (CLASS) Act, which was enacted as part of the 2010 Affordable Care Act, was supposed to provide it. Ultimately, it proved unworkable and did not generate expected participation rates of more than 4 percent.[21] Since the Obama administration shut down the program, policymakers have done little to revisit a comprehensive solution.

If policymakers were ready to enact a comprehensive solution, they might create a new entitlement program through which individuals paid into a program that funded their long-term care needs across their lifetimes. Or, they might adopt a proposal, like one from economists Karen Dynan and Jason Brown, through which Social Security beneficiaries could divert some of their benefits to long-term care.[22] But political prospects for a new government insurance program, or even the expansion of an existing one, seem highly problematic; policymakers will not likely enact such bold measures for the foreseeable future.

As a result, we propose politically feasible solutions. They would not completely fix the problems with the long-term care market, but they would help alleviate the problems and reduce the burden on unpaid caregivers.

Securing state waivers for in-home and community-based care: The care for someone who does not live in a facility is typically called *home or community-based services* (HCBS). It can include an aide providing in-home nursing care, a dietician providing dietary management, caregiver training, or hospice care. Caregivers can deliver this care in homes or other facilities, such as senior centers or adult daycares.

Medicaid gives states latitude in what services they provide and how they set eligibility for them. The program requires that each state provide personal nursing services, but states can provide a host of optional services to increase the amount of care that caregivers provide in the home, such as mental health care, assistance with self-care (like bathing or food preparation), and assistance for family caregivers.

HCBS offers three main benefits over facility-based care. First, it is generally cheaper. A home health aide for 20 hours a week cost an average of $23,920 a year in 2019, compared to $48,612 for a room in an assisted living facility.[23] Second, most people prefer to receive care outside of institutions. Third, in the wake of COVID-19's tragically high fatality rate in nursing homes, in-home care may be safer for older Americans.

In recent decades, Medicaid-funded care has moved away from institutional settings and toward HCBS. From 1995 to 2016, the share of Medicaid spending that went for long-term services and supports for HCBS rose from 18 to 57 percent.[24] Meanwhile, states are expanding access to HCBS for Medicaid beneficiaries. In recent years, 34 states provided personal care to residents, 8 adopted the Community First Choice program that provides in-home support to people who would otherwise need institutional care, and 11 adopted Section 1915(i) waivers that let states provide targeted services to people who might not need an institution. Many more states can adopt these options.

By relying more on HCBS, states can reduce their costs while better meeting the wishes of Medicaid beneficiaries. A wide range of studies have demonstrated the cost containment benefits of this approach. As an AARP review of 38 studies on the cost impact of these programs found, "The studies consistently provide evidence of cost containment and a slower rate of spending growth as states have expanded HCBS."[25] Over time, the switch could extend beyond Medicaid: proposed legislation, which has some bipartisan support, seeks to test strategies for letting Medicare beneficiaries (a much larger share of the 65-plus population) receive long-term care services at home.

Reforming the tax treatment of long-term care: The federal tax subsidy for buying long-term care insurance is poorly designed and available to few people, as we discussed in Chapter 9. Taxpayers can get a tax break for buying long-term care insurance only by including it as an excess medical expense in their itemized deductions. The problem is that few older Americans itemize their deductions, the per-dollar benefit is higher for upper-income people in higher tax brackets, and the amount that people can deduct at younger ages is extremely low (i.e., a person aged 40 and younger can deduct only $430 in annual premiums, while someone between 60 and 70 can deduct $4,350). The 2017 tax law included tax changes that sharply lowered the rates of itemization, especially for middle-income families, so this benefit is now virtually nonexistent for most older Americans.

Policymakers should convert the tax benefit to a refundable credit— equal to, say, 15 percent of the cost of a policy up to a limit—that phases out as a taxpayer's income rises.[26] That would help low- and middle-income taxpayers. In effect, a middle-class taxpayer buying a long-term care insurance policy would get 15 percent off the cost as long as the policy was below the typical value of long-term care. Such a tax credit would reduce Medicaid costs, lessen the burden on unpaid caregivers, and generate better care for older Americans. The credit would likely be available only to consumers who buy long-term care insurance outside of retirement accounts (which carry their own tax break), as we discuss in further detail below.

A separate tax-based approach could ease the burden on unpaid caregivers. A bill in Congress would let unpaid caregivers claim a tax credit of up to $3,000 a year against the costs of providing unpaid care, including expenses like transportation and equipment. Under the Credit for Caring Act, caregivers with less than $7,500 in earnings could claim 30 percent of the costs above $2,000, up to the maximum credit of $3,000. A healthcare professional would need to certify that the person receiving long-term care needs at least 180 days of it per year. Though this legislation would not fully address the financial burdens on unpaid caregivers, it would be an important first step for this overworked group. An AARP study suggests that this provision would boost GDP by allowing some family caregivers to go to work if they chose to.[27]

Revising distribution channels for private long-term care insurance: The current system for buying long-term care insurance does not work well enough. One way to fix it is for policymakers to enact policies that encourage a transition away from the individual market and toward employer-provided plans; another is to let insurance companies sell long-term care policies on the health exchanges that the Affordable Care Act created.

Strengthening the market for employer-provided policies can help ease underwriting burdens (the cost of evaluating risk) and drive other product improvements. A thoughtful proposal from the Bipartisan Policy Center (BPC) would let employers offer standardized products to workers starting at age 45, and these workers could use their savings to pay for them. The products would carry premiums that rise only with inflation. To control costs and keep products affordable, standardized options would include long elimination periods (the number of days one pays for care before insurance kicks in) and coinsurance arrangements (under which the insurance company and policyholder share costs).[28]

The tax benefit to help low- and middle-income taxpayers buy long-term care insurance also could help address concerns about adverse selection—in which only the most likely to need care buy insurance—that affect the market for private long-term care insurance. As we discussed in Chapter 10, the market suffers from adverse selection and asymmetric information concerns: buyers know much more about whether they will likely need long-term care than insurance companies do, prompting companies to raise the cost of insurance and pricing out lower-cost consumers. Encouraging people to buy long-term care insurance earlier in adulthood can help mitigate this concern.

Policymakers could let state healthcare marketplaces offer long-term care policies for retirement. As the BPC proposed, these exchanges could let workers 45 and older buy these policies by withdrawing funds from their workplace saving plans or IRAs. These policies would likely feature standardized benefits, which may help alleviate the confusion associated with the product, and they would feature lower costs because companies would spend less on advertising and distribution.[29]

Improving communication among family members: To improve the outlook for long-term care, families should talk about the future and plan for caring for the older generation. Social norms dictate a peculiar dynamic between generations: younger generations, including daughters- or sons-in-law, are often tacitly expected to provide care for older family members, but families often do not discuss such taboo topics as finances and planning. Better communication would help.

Because older adults provide so much care to their parents—with nearly 6 out of 10 reporting that they provided care over the course of a 12-year span[30]—long-term care is an especially salient topic for discussion, and those who will potentially receive the care can reasonably ask about it. AARP[31] suggests speaking with relatives over the holiday season; approaching the conversation with "compassion and sensitivity"; and discussing long-term care planning and preferences, including one's inclination to live in an institution versus a home or community facility.

Where, then, are we when it comes to retirement? In our next and final chapter, we will summarize what we have learned over the preceding pages and what we must do to address our challenges.

A Vision for a New Retirement Paradigm

The traditional three-legged stool of retirement—household saving, Social Security, and pensions—has lost one leg as pensions are disappearing. Another leg, Social Security, is under financial stress because its current funding will not fully its cover costs over time. The new leg of the retirement paradigm, gradually replacing pensions, is, of course, contributory pensions (401(k) type plans), but these bring new challenges. Moreover, even for families that retire with otherwise adequate resources, private insurance markets are not properly positioned to reduce the risks associated with longevity and long-term care. We need a new paradigm, one that builds on the current system and adds feasible measures to improve it. That means government policies that are politically viable, changes in family behavior, and human resources policies through which companies can make meaningful contributions to workers' retirement security.

Historically, elderly poverty fell in tandem with the growth of Social Security and Medicare. Today, nevertheless, 9 percent of persons 65 and older remain in poverty.[1] Too many families on the cusp of retirement have few if any financial assets. Private long-term care is prohibitively expensive for most Americans, while average out-of-pocket spending on healthcare eats up about a third of Social Security benefits. Americans are living longer but starting their retirement with less.

Many of our retirement challenges stem from the shift away from pensions and toward personal saving accounts. Every year, more than half of workers lack reasonable opportunities to save, and savers lack affordable pathways to turn their wealth into security. The labor market has yet to fully satisfy the desire of older workers to keep working, especially those who are not well-prepared for retirement. Most tax breaks for saving go to the wealthiest fifth of workers, too few people begin retirement with substantial assets besides their home, and families bear an unprecedented level of risk. In short, America's predominant retirement paradigm is to save as much as possible and hope you don't live too long.

The system, however, is not completely broken. Social Security will be solvent for the next 15 or so years and, even after that, will still be able to make most of its promised payments. Medicaid will continue paying long-term care benefits. And millions of Americans have accumulated assets in retirement accounts that will give them a healthy, secure retirement.

The near disappearance of traditional pensions has placed a much greater burden on families to manage their own retirements, and some have the resources and skills to do that well. Others, however, have lacked access to employer-run retirement plans and have struggled to save enough during their working years. They remain too dependent on Social Security and other government programs in retirement.

All of that suggests both the need and the opportunity to improve the system. But, for the past four decades, policymakers have largely avoided the problem. Despite a rapidly aging population and other major demographic changes, policymakers last reformed Social Security in a significant way in 1983. They have modified tax breaks for retirement saving only marginally since 401(k)s were created in the late 1970s. And in the decade since they tried and failed at reforming long-term care and they have not seriously advanced an alternative. The lone exception to Washington's large-scale inaction came in 2003, when President George W. Bush and Congress added prescription drug coverage to Medicare.

To be sure, presidents and Congresses have enacted modest reforms. The 2006 Pension Protection Act helped to advance automatic enrollment in saving plans. The 2019 SECURE Act opened the door for employers to include more annuities in their benefit plans for workers and made it easier for small employers to establish 401(k) plans. These reforms, while generally positive, were incremental at best. We need sweeping change to address our retirement challenge.

The Most Important Steps to Improve Retirement

We laid out a summary agenda for improving retirement in the first chapter of this book and, of course, we have talked about different aspects of this agenda throughout the book. However, even though this box repeats that material, it may be helpful for some readers to have a summary of the specific steps needed to reach the new retirement paradigm. We start with the policy agenda.

1. *Shore-Up Social Security and Medicare.* The policy reform agenda laid out in this book is the centerpiece of the new retirement paradigm and the most important policy change is to put Social Security and Medicare on stable financial footing.[2] This is the hardest change to make but it is the most important. Americans, from the poor to the upper-middle class, rely on these programs as they age, and the program trust funds are running out. Some adjustments to the programs can be used to lower costs, such as adjustments in Social Security benefits for upper-income families and allowing Medicare to negotiate with healthcare providers. But the hardest policy shift is also the most important: increasing payroll tax revenues.

2. *Change the structure of retirement tax preferences.* The tax code today provides the biggest saving incentives to the richest Americans. The hundreds of billions in tax preferences should be provided in a fairer way so as to provide a stronger saving incentive to low- and moderate-income families, even if they pay little or no federal income tax in the years when contributions are made.

3. *Provide access to retirement saving vehicles for all American workers.* Most large companies have set up 401(k)-type plans for

their employees and many of them make employer contributions of a percentage of the employee's salary, up to a limit. Some smaller companies also offer such plans, as do nonprofits, but many do not. Ultimately, only about half of the workforce has access to a retirement plan at work. Policymakers should either provide incentives to all employers to offer such plans or set up government-run programs. There should be automatic enrollment in retirement saving plans, with an opt-out provision for employees. A government-run program (perhaps run by the states) can cover the self-employed as well as employees whose employers have no plan.

4. *Provide better tax incentives for long-term care insurance and unpaid caregivers.* The current system of tax-based subsidies is both insufficient and poorly designed. A better system would convert the current, limited subsidy into a refundable tax credit, while also providing more generous tax benefits for unpaid caregivers.

5. *Reform the market for reverse mortgages to make the products cheaper and more appealing.* Reverse mortgages have a theoretical appeal for those households with limited financial assets, but relatively high wealth in their homes. Low levels of take-up in the reverse mortgage market are likely due, in part, to poor policy design that drives up the cost and makes the products unappealing to consumers. Reforms can help.

A paradigm shift requires more than just public policy reforms; it also demands redoubled efforts by employers to meaningfully contribute to their workers' retirement security. Key changes from employers include the following:

1. *Leverage new policy incentives for retirement saving accounts to achieve universal coverage.* Employers have phased out their traditional pension programs, but they have a responsibility

to provide an alternative retirement vehicle, like a 401(k) plan where they contribute a percentage of the employee's salary.

2. *Employers should ensure that their workers have a source of trusted, comprehensive, and unbiased information.* Workers need information and help with their retirement decisions, and employers should meet this need by arranging for unbiased outside advisors to counsel employees on how much to save and how to choose retirement products.

3. *Offer more insurance-like products in their retirement plans.* In addition to equity and bond funds, employers should make sure their workers can choose annuities and long-term care insurance and that they understand these products. Employers should negotiate group rates for their employees.

4. *Employers should aim to ease the burden on employees of administering their retirement plans.* In particular, employers should assist employees who quit or are laid off to consolidate their retirement funds through easily executed rollover between accounts.

Government policy reforms and an evolution in the role of human resources departments are critical to achieving a new paradigm, but families have an important role, too. Households can help bolster their own retirement security through the following steps:

1. *Well before reaching retirement age, working age adults should establish a plan.* Families need a retirement plan and they should talk with their spouses and other family members about it. It should include estimated retirement dates, the adequacy of saving, and how the family will deal with long-term care needs, should they arise. Most families would benefit from obtaining professional advice for this plan, and employers should help with this, especially in making sure an advisor does not have a conflict of interest. Last, as family members approach retirement age,

they should look at the tradeoff between retiring sooner or later against their standard of living in retirement. People are living longer, often into their 80s and 90s or even beyond. Some have plenty of money to retire early, but others should look at working longer (if they can) and postponing the date at which they collect Social Security in order to receive a larger monthly benefit for the rest of their lives.

2. *Families should look at ways to de-risk their retirement.* Risk is inevitable and all families must manage it. Taking too much investment risk jeopardizes retirement security but taking too little risk can do so also. Longevity annuities can reduce the risk of outliving one's money, while long-term care insurance can reduce the risk of full-time care (although at present this type of insurance is very expensive). Reverse mortgages, while certainly not for everyone, should be on the table for families with plenty of housing equity but few other assets.

3. *Many workers need to save more.* While Americans have amassed trillions in retirement, the large share of workers who enter retirement with a low level of savings, or even no liquid assets, are doing themselves a disservice. While it is unreasonable to expect the lowest-income working families to build a sizable nest egg, middle-income workers should take advantage of more equitable retirement saving incentives and more widespread access to workplace accounts to save for retirement.

WHY ALTERNATIVE PROPOSALS WILL NOT WORK

Two alternative reforms could solve the problems with America's retirement system. Businesses could return to the old system of providing generous pensions, or policymakers could raise Social Security benefits enough to ensure that all retirees live comfortably even if they have not saved for retirement. We see the attraction of either or both options, but neither is feasible for policy or political reasons. Our approach is the only realistic path to retirement security for all Americans.

Why Traditional Private Pensions Will Not Return

About 12 percent of non-union workers in the private sector had traditional defined-benefit pension plans in 2015, but many of them were legacy plans—that is, carried over from the days before companies no longer offered pensions to new employees. Younger workers rarely have traditional pensions. Some 70 percent of union workers still have traditional pensions, but only 10 percent of the workforce are unionized.[3] Can we return to the "good old days" when most workers were covered by such programs?

Traditional pensions disappeared mainly because they became subject to regulation under the 1974 Employee Retirement Income and Security Act (ERISA). The law's requirements were extremely detailed and forced companies with pension plans to make substantial policy changes. ERISA still plays an important role in protecting workers, but its rules prompted employers to re-evaluate their retirement programs and most switched to 401(k)-type plans. Increasing lifespans were also making defined-contribution plans more expensive over time, and, starting in the late 1980s, interest rates began to fall, making it harder for companies to fund pensions. Even if policymakers now loosened ERISA's rules, employers probably would not shift back to traditional pensions. Moreover, the rules were enacted for good reasons: to avoid fraud and other problems that arose with unregulated pensions. Policymakers could require all or most employers to offer defined-benefit plans, but legislation to do so would face too much strong opposition in Congress to pass.

Defined-benefit pension plans also have problems, which means that a return to the good old days actually would not be so good. These days, most people do not stay with one employer through their working lives, so employer-provided pensions would be scattered among different companies. Workers with traditional company pensions are often locked into their jobs at age 50, even if they dislike them and would rather change jobs. When companies go broke, their pension obligations are addressed in bankruptcy court or pushed into a federal program that can reduce the benefits workers receive. Companies restructure to meet rising competition or changing technologies, forcing some employees to leave and look for other jobs. In short, because workers move around and companies rise and fall, a return to traditional company pensions would be hard to administer, requiring extensive government involvement. That is the case in European economies, but it would be hard to duplicate in the United States. In Europe, moreover, some governments were forced to adjust their retirement rules because their pension programs became unaffordable with the decline in labor force growth.

Why Social Security Benefits Will Not Grow More Generous

Social Security is a pay-as-you-go system in which today's workers pay payroll (or FICA, "Federal Insurance Contributions Act") taxes that finance most of the benefits of today's retirees.[4] In the past, FICA tax revenues were larger in total than the benefits that Social Security was paying out, and the government put the excess revenue into a trust fund, used that revenue to buy US Treasury securities, and accumulated a large reserve fund. Then, with the fall in the nation's birth rate and, subsequently, a fall in the labor force growth rate, FICA revenue fell below the total amount of benefits that Social Security was paying out.

As we have noted elsewhere, the share of older people in America's population has increased. That has put tremendous financial pressure on Social Security (and Medicare). The Social Security trust fund is expected to be exhausted by 2034, while the Medicare trust fund will run out in 2026.[5] To keep Social Security solvent, policymakers will have to raise FICA payroll taxes or cut benefits (at least for some retirees), or they will have to use other tax revenue to pay benefits.

The federal government, however, is facing huge fiscal constraints. Deficits and debt have exploded due to large tax cuts, the financial crisis and Great Recession of 2008 and beyond, the pandemic-induced recession, and the policies enacted in response to the financial crisis and both recessions. At some point, policymakers will face limits on how much they can spend without triggering increases in interest rates or perhaps inflation. We believe that policymakers should raise Social Security's minimum level of benefits to ensure that workers who paid FICA taxes for many years can avoid poverty when they retire. It is, however, neither politically feasible nor good policy to raise benefits for most recipients enough to replace the traditional employer-funded retirement programs of the past. That would require a large tax increase that the electorate would oppose and that could dampen employment.

WHY OUR VISION FOR RETIREMENT SHOULD PREVAIL

We can do better. Employers, families, and policymakers can all do more to strengthen the nation's retirement system. All employers must offer retirement savings programs to their employees and hold discussion sessions so that everyone understands the range of investment choices and financial products available to ensure a secure retirement. Families must save consistently for retirement and not withdraw money prematurely from retirement funds, except for extreme emergencies.

In addition, policymakers have real opportunities to improve retirement. They can reform the labor market for older workers to address age discrimination. They can make work-based retirement saving programs more equitable and universal while applying the insights of behavioral economics. They can expand and reform private insurance markets so that older Americans can turn their wealth into better safeguards against outliving assets and needing long-term care insurance.

These would not be radical changes, but they would prove important. Together, they would transform retirement. Many more workers would build up liquid retirement assets, and most savers would save more. Entering retirement would be more gradual for some, and working a few extra years to shore up saving would be more viable. Fewer people would start claiming Social Security benefits in their early 60s, and that would boost average monthly benefits across the board. Longevity annuities would become widespread, so retirees could depend on a reliable stream of income if they lived past their life expectancy. Long-term care insurance would be more affordable and more widespread, easing the caregiving burden on middle-aged offspring, mainly women. And homeowners could affordably tap their housing equity in case of emergency or as a general retirement strategy.

This new system would not be perfect. More saving means less spending, with working-age families foregoing more of their paycheck to build up a nest egg. Broader taxpayer use of tax incentives for saving would force the federal government to make up for lost revenue. Insurance companies and reverse mortgage lenders would increase their share of the retirement market, drawing a slightly greater share of household retirement funds toward corporate profits—but with commensurate benefits. Some inheritances would shrink as retirees no longer need to stockpile as many assets.

Structural problems would remain. Low-income workers would continue to be low-income retirees who are very dependent on Social Security benefits. Health costs would continue to rise, requiring more revenue for Medicare. Policymakers would continue to face the long-term threat of an exhausted Social Security Trust Fund. And high rates of inequality would persist into retirement.

But retirement in America would be substantially better. New retirees could spend more freely, and they would not need to stockpile their assets for fear of outliving their savings. Older Americans would rely on their children less, which would let those middle-aged individuals spend more time preparing for their own retirement. And, most importantly, retirees would feel more secure in their retirement, knowing that bad luck would be much less likely to derail their retirement plans.

No president and Congress will completely abandon the current system, so we see no value in advocating for sweeping but implausible changes. Instead, policymakers can substantially improve the system through a series of common-sense, moderate reforms. And while there is no silver bullet, these reforms together can bring dramatic improvement. In some form, lawmakers have introduced bills that would enact many of these reforms, and we are optimistic that lawmakers will seriously consider the others.

Our nation's politics is very polarized, but improving our retirement system has broad, bipartisan support in Congress and across the country. We can fix the current system without abandoning its structure. Let's fix it by plugging the holes in the hull rather than trying and failing to buy a whole new ship.

CHAPTER 1

1. Median annual income adjusted for inflation, compiled by the US Bureaus of the Census. Reported by the St. Louis Federal Reserve Bank, https://fred.stlouisfed.org/series/MEHOINUSA672N.
2. US Bureau of Labor Statistics (2012), "The Recession of 2007–2009."
3. Social Security Administration (2020), "Life Expectancy for Social Security."
4. Statista (2020), "Number of Retired Workers Receiving Social Security in the United States from 2010 to 2020."
5. Congressional Budget Office (2021), "The 2021 Long-Term Outlook."
6. The Urban Institute, "State and Local Government Pensions," accessed October 27, 2021.
7. Scholz, Seshadri, and Khitatrakun (2006), "Are Americans Saving 'Optimally' for Retirement?," 607–643.
8. The diversity of retirement saving reflects the wide gap between rich and poor in earnings and wealth at younger ages, a gap that has risen over time. A useful primer on inequality comes from the Stanford Center on Poverty and Inequality. See https://inequality.stanford.edu/publications/americas-poverty-course.
9. Vernon, Harrati, and Streeter (2018), "Are Americans Saving Enough for an Adequate Retirement?," 20–29.
10. $12.6 trillion in individual retirement accounts and $9.9 trillion in defined contribution accounts in the first quarter of 2021, according to the Investment Company Institute, "The US Retirement Market, First Quarter 2021."
11. We examine the market for reverse mortgages later in the book.
12. Alexandra Thornton (2019), "Taking Stock of Spending Through the Tax Code," Center for American Progress.

CHAPTER 2

1. The date at which the trust fund is exhausted is reviewed and revised each year. For the latest information, see https://www.ssa.gov/oact/TRSUM/.

2. For decades, these have been described as the "three-legged stool" of retirement.

3. This means that half of households had incomes above $44,400 and half had incomes below this amount.

4. See Bee and Mitchell (2017), "Do Older Americans Have More Income." This study, from researchers at the US Census Bureau, reported higher income and a lower poverty rate than in prior research based on their conclusion that households responding to surveys often understate their incomes, particularly pension income.

5. This provision also penalizes anyone trying to "game the retirement system." For example, someone who had a very variable income over time could put money into their retirement account in years when they had a high income and take money out when they had a low income, thereby avoiding taxes.

6. US Department of Labor, Employee Benefits Security Administration (2021).

7. It is hard to provide an exact and complete definition of economic rationality but, in this context, it means people use the best available estimates of future economic outcomes and weigh, for example, what benefit they will get from current consumption versus future consumption. People will avoid impulsive purchases that they later regret. Furthermore, people will make the best available estimates of their own expected lifetimes and the probability that they will suffer a prolonged illness or dementia in future years.

8. See Aguiar and Hurst (2008), "Deconstructing Life Cycle Expenditure."

9. Undersaving is defined relative to the model in the study, based on the idea that retirees will want to maintain their standard of living while retired.

10. Again, the optimal wealth target is based on the model the authors use; it is the amount of retirement saving that allows maintenance of living standards.

11. The findings require quite a few caveats. Part of the reason for the low wealth targets was that the average age of the household was just 55.7—meaning that any of the households still have years to accumulate wealth before reaching retirement age. Among lower-income savers, the presence of a progressive Social Security formula meant that much of the earnings would be replaced through Social Security benefits. Also, this cohort still had received pension benefits at relatively high rates, meaning that they needed to save less than a worker today without a workplace pension.

12. The median undersaving gap of $5,260 in 1992 dollars is equal to about $7,000 in 2004—substantially smaller than the finding from the later paper.

13. This figure includes the Supplementary Security Income, or SSI, which provides about 30 percent of income to the lowest income group.

14. See Bee and Mitchell (2017), "Do Older Americans," table 1 and table 9.

15. See Poterba (2014), "Retirement Security," table 9.

16. See Smith, Soto, and Penner (2009), "How Seniors"; Poterba, Venti, and Wise (2013), "Health Education"; Love, Palumbo, and Smith (2009), "The Trajectory of Wealth"; and Ameriks et al. (2019), "Long-Term Care."

17. Kahneman's popular book *Thinking Fast and Slow* gives an introduction to his ideas. Amos Tversky died before he could share the Nobel Prize.

18. See Thaler and Sunstein (2008), "Improving Decisions."

19. Laibson's web page at the Harvard economics department has lucid presentations that give his ideas.

20. The figures here are based on the 2019 Survey of Consumer Finances.

21. Federal Reserve Board (2021), "Report in the Economic."

22. Life expectancies are quoted, for example, in terms of how long, on average, a baby born today would be expected to live. This is the life expectancy of the cohort of people who are just starting their lives. Life expectancy can also be estimated for people at different ages. Someone at age 60, for example, has a shorter life expectancy than someone just born. However, if the life expectancy of a newborn is, say, 75 years, the life expectancy of someone aged 60 is longer than just 15 years because the person at age 60 has avoided all the hazards and illnesses that can afflict children or young people. The life expectancy of those who are age 60 today is the amount, on average, that this "cohort" of people can be expected to live. Of course, actual life expectancy for each individual will be different, as Figure 2.1 illustrates.

23. James Poterba, in an enlightening Richard T. Ely lecture, notes two important life expectancy trends with respect to retirement. One is the persistent increase in life expectancy conditional on reaching age 65. Men born in 1950 who reach age 65 can expect to live 4.1 years longer, on average, than a man born 50 years earlier; women born in 1950 can similarly expect to live an additional 2.3 years. A second important trend is the divergence between low and high earners, with the gap widening from under 1 year for those born in 1912 to 5.4 years for men and women born in 1941.

24. The life expectancy figures cited are derived from the Social Security Administration's 2010 period life tables. Median life expectancies based on the 1950 cohort life table, which allow for continuing mortality declines, are about a year longer than those based on the 2010 period life table, as are the anticipated lifespans for the longest-lived 30 percent and longest-lived 10 percent of the 1950 cohort.

25. Bosworth and Burke (2014), "Differential Mortality and Retirement Benefits in the Health and Retirement Study."

26. A. Chiu, L. Bever, and A. Eunjung Cha, A. (2021), "Driven by Covid Deaths, U.S. Life Expectancy Dropped by 1.5 Years in 2020," *The Washington Post*, July 21.

27. The Health and Retirement Study (Weir 2008), University of Michigan.

28. See, for example, Hurd and McGarry (2002), "The Predictive Validity"; Sloan, Smith, and Taylor (2001), "Longevity Expectations"; and Elder (2013), "The Predictive Validity."

29. Hurd and Rohwedder (2011), "Economic Preparation for Retirement."

30. There are two main types of retirement saving accounts in the United States: traditional accounts and Roth-type accounts. Traditional accounts typically exempt contributions from tax initially, allow earnings to grow tax free, and then tax distributions at normal rates when taken in retirement. Roth-type accounts do not allow for the initial exemption for contributions but allow earnings to grow tax free and do not levy a tax on withdrawal. The determination of which account is more appropriate depends on a variety of factors, including, in particular, the relative tax rates during working years and retirement.

31. In 2017, married savers in the 25 percent tax bracket with $100,000 would expect the account to yield roughly $75,000 in distributions after tax; in 2018, with the relevant tax rate lowered to 22 percent, this account could be expected to yield $78,000 (before any changes due to investment returns).

CHAPTER 3

1. Increased saving adds to availability of funds for long-run growth. In a recession, there can be too much saving and too little aggregate demand. Here we are talking about the long run.

2. Today, we recognize that this population growth came at the expense of Native Americans and included African Americans brought forcibly to this country, but these ugly facts do not change the important arithmetic of growth. US population chart data from https://courses.lumenlearning.com/suny-ushistory2os2xmaster/chapter/united-states-population-chart/ for early years and then the US Bureau of the Census.

3. Center on Budget and Policy Priorities (2022), "Policy Basics: Understanding the Social Security Trust Funds."

4. In the 1980s, concerns about the long-term solvency of Social Security triggered a change in the benefit system. To receive a full benefit, workers had to postpone the age at which they first collected benefits. This was effectively a cut in benefits.

5. Data from database at the World Bank, "Fertility Rate, Total (Births per Woman)—United States for 2020."

6. The United Nations population division has estimated that a fertility rate of 2.1 is needed to keep a population stable.

7. Hamilton et al., "Births: Provisional Data for 2020."

8. As we discuss in more detail later in the book, the labor force includes everyone who is employed plus those looking for work, the unemployed. Contributions to Social Security come from the employed.

9. Board of Trustees of the Federal Old-Age and Survivors Insurance and Federal Disability Insurance Trust Funds (2006), table IV B-2.

10. Congressional Budget Office, "The Budget and Economic Outlook, 2022 to 2032," Potential Labor Force, from Table 2-3, p. 42.

11. Ibid.

12. Sawhill and Pulliam (2019), "Six Facts About Wealth."

13. Two influential contributions to this literature were the books *The Limits to Growth*, by Donnella Meadows et al. (1972); and *Small Is Beautiful: A Study of Economics As If People Mattered*, by E. F. Schumacher, published in 1973.

14. If the population and labor force rise each year, this means more people are working relative to the number who are retired. In a pay-as-you-go system like Social Security (benefits are mostly paid for by the tax contributions of those currently working), an increasing labor force enables higher benefit payments to retirees without having the system run out of money.

15. There has also been a shift among economists in the attitude toward public debt because the interest rates on Treasury bills and bonds has been so low for so long. The

argument is that as long as interest rates remain low in relation to the growth rate of the economy, there is no need ever to repay the debt; it can always be rolled over. And even the interest on the debt can be financed through additional borrowing. This argument is impeccable, given its assumptions, but there is a danger if borrowing and the debt become too large. It may no longer be possible to sell Treasury securities at such low interest rates, at which point the debt becomes a real burden and borrowing may become difficult.

16. In 2017, Jason Furman laid out the identity linking potential GDP growth to labor productivity, weekly hours, labor force participation, and population. (Potential GDP growth abstracts from the business cycle and hence from changes in the unemployment rate.)

    Real potential GDP growth = Percent change in potential labor productivity + Percent change in average weekly hours + Percent change in potential labor force participation rate + Percent change in population

17. Since both dates are close to cyclical peaks, we can take it that this decline in labor force participation has subtracted about 0.4 percent a year from real potential GDP growth.

18. FRED (2021), "Labor Force Participation Rate," https://fred.stlouisfed.org/series/CIVPART.

19. Eppsteiner, Furman, and Powell (2019), "Adjusted for Aging."

20. The importance of the aging of the population obscures some offsetting trends within the population. Young people have lower participation rates than in the past, males older than 50 without a college education have experienced a very pronounced decline in participation, while female participation increased, followed by a modest decline in recent years. Of course, in earlier periods, population growth was faster and labor force participation was growing, not declining, so the contrast to earlier time periods is much larger than 0.4 percent a year.

21. This assumes that the contributions start at age 25 and the return accrues annually. The amount at age 70 would be $137,579. A worker who had periods of unemployment, who left the labor force for a period (to have children, for example), or who retired earlier than age 70 would accrue less.

22. The contribution of capital is the growth in the amount of capital per hour worked, multiplied by the share of capital in total income. Sometimes the term *multifactor productivity growth* or MFP is used instead of TFP.

23. We discuss the deficit issue further in Chapter 4.

24. This book is not the place for an extended analysis of the issues around foreign borrowing. It is hard to explain intuitively, but large-scale borrowing from overseas has to be balanced by large trade deficits. The US government is fighting a trade war with China and other countries that we blame for our trade deficits, but we will never make much inroad into the trade deficit while we continue to borrow so much from overseas.

25. Alex Gailey (2021), "How Has the Pandemic Impacted US Savings Rates?," *Time*.

26. The concept of personal saving from the National Income and Product Accounts is subject to revision over time and does not equal the change in the net worth of

households because capital gains and losses are excluded. Companies save and invest, and this increases their valuations. Households own the companies and therefore participate in this value creation. Personal saving is a useful number, though, reflecting the extent to which households do not spend all their disposable income, which makes resources available for investment. COVID-19 triggered a sharp rise in the saving rate because people could not spend on vacations, restaurants, and so on. The saving rate has started to come down as the economy has gradually opened.

CHAPTER 4

1. Social Security Administration (2021).
2. Bee and Mitchell (2017), "Do Older Americans." It seems that many of those responding to the Current Population Survey had not reported the income they received from traditional (defined-benefit) pensions or withdrawals from IRAs. We do not know exactly why, but perhaps families judged that moneys from these sources represented benefits or income they had earned in earlier years while they were working and did not consider them to be current income.
3. The largest amount of underreporting was from traditional pensions, which are gradually disappearing, so the importance of Social Security benefits may increase in the future unless households can replace traditional pensions with retirement savings (such as 401(k)s).
4. This is done by multiplying earnings in various years by a factor to account for inflation and then computing the average over the worker's career. If a worker's career lasted less than 35 years, "$0" is imputed for those years. For the purposes of Social Security, only wages below an inflation-adjusted maximum are relevant. As we explain below, taxes (and benefits) are determined up to a certain limit.
5. Specifically, this formula separates the average monthly wage into three buckets and provides a share of the wages in each bucket. For example, in 2020, the benefit for someone who retires at the "full retirement age" equals the sum of 90 percent of the first $960 in wages, 32 percent of wages between $960 and $5,785, and 15 percent of earnings over $5,785—up to a maximum annual benefit of $36,132. An example might be helpful. Assume that over 35 years of labor, a given worker's average annual earnings were $72,000 in 2020 dollars—or $6,000 per month. This worker would receive about $2,890 per month, calculated as 0.90*($960) + 0.32*($2,785 − 960) * 0.15 * ($6,000 − $2,785).
6. In 2020, the earnings threshold was $18,240 for workers who were not reaching their full retirement age in 2020.
7. Most recipients do not realize they will get their money back (eventually) and view the deduction as a tax.
8. SSI eligibility is based on a complex set of income and asset tests designed to ensure that only households with very limited resources receive the benefit. For example, the asset test requires that single households own less than $1,000 in assets and married couples own less than $3,000.
9. Social Security Administration (2021), "Social Security Basic Facts."
10. Authors' own calculations from Social Security Administration July 2021 data.

11. See Cubanski et al. (2019), "How Much Do Medicare Beneficiaries Spend Out of Pocket on Health Care," figure 1.

12. Medicaid beneficiaries are eligible for long-term care based on a series of asset and income tests to ensure that the individual is in need and on a set of state-specific criteria around health status.

13. For much of Social Security's history, roughly 90 percent of total wages earned in the US economy were subject to Social Security taxes. Today, that share is about 83 percent.

14. The Affordable Care Act (ACA) added an Additional Medicare Tax of 0.9 percent, which took effect in 2013, increasing the effective Medicare Tax rate to 3.8 percent.

15. Technically, these programs are funded out of the Supplementary Medical Insurance Trust Fund, but this "fund" is a bit of a misnomer because it receives roughly 70 percent of its funding from general government funding and subsequently will always be solvent. With Medicare Part B, the remaining funding mostly comes from beneficiary premiums, which are designed to cover one-quarter of the program's cost. For Part D, the remaining funding comes from a mix of beneficiary premiums, also designed to cover about one-quarter of program costs, and payments from the states related to people who are eligible for both Medicare and Medicaid.

16. Data for the figure taken from https://www.ssa.gov/oact/TRSUM/images/LD_ChartE.html.

17. US Library of Congress, Congressional Research Service (2020), "Social Security," p. i.

18. Other factors play a role, as well. A series of tax cuts under President George W. Bush on a temporary basis, and largely extended under President Obama on a permanent basis, have further eroded revenues.

19. The figures here are for debt held by the public. Data from the Office of Management and Budget reported by FRED, the Federal Reserve Bank of St. Louis.

20. The CBO projects the FY2020 deficit to be 4.6 percent of GDP, hitting 5.4 percent by 2030.

21. Source data as follows: historical budget data, https://www.cbo.gov/system/files/2021-02/51134-2021-02-11-historicalbudgetdata.xlsx; 10-year budget projection data, https://www.cbo.gov/data/budget-economic-data#3.

22. Auerbach, Gale, and Harris (2014), "Federal Health Spending and the Budget Outlook: Some Alternative Scenarios." Note that these projections were published in 2014, which did not foresee the sharp run-up in public debt owing to the pandemic.

23. A unified deficit includes the deficit and surplus in Social Security and Medicare and net interest payments.

24. In fact, the current situation has given rise to a new set of assertions, under the rubric of *modern monetary theory* (MMT), which suggests that Washington can and should spend aggressively to address its social and economic problems. Though a complex and nuanced theory, MMT essentially argues that America's ability to both tax and to issue its own currency means that it can borrow and print additional money without substantial consequence. If inflation becomes a problem—and

many MMT advocates believe that it probably won't—the federal government can raise taxes to reduce its deficits.

25. Furman and Summers (2020), "A Reconsideration of Fiscal Policy."
26. J. D. Tuccille (2021), "Shaky Social Security Trust Fund May Run Out in 11 Years."
27. OECD (2019), "Revenue Statistics," table 1.

CHAPTER 5

1. The overall labor force participation rate has risen in the past few years with the economic recovery, but this is after a prolonged period of decline.
2. Rau (2017), "Why Glaring Quality Gaps Among Nursing Homes Are Likely to Grow If Medicaid Is Cut."
3. Modigliani (1966) gives a good review of the life cycle model and the evidence for it. The model itself was developed in earlier research by Franco Modigliani and Richard Brumberg.
4. Munnell and Chen (2015), "Trends in Social Security Claiming."
5. 2021 Annual Statistical Supplement figures are adjusted to take out conversions from disability.
6. Coile and Levine (2010), "Reconsidering Retirement," found that the net impact of the Great Recession was to increase retirement.
7. Richard Fry (2021), "Amid the Pandemic, a Rising Share of Older US Adults Are Now Retired."
8. Bhattarai (2022), "Millions Retired Early."
9. The rate of return that savers receive on their retirement assets can also influence the retirement decision, again with offsetting effects. Higher returns mean people accumulate money more quickly and are able to retire early (the income effect, where higher interest rates encourage early retirement). Conversely, a higher return on saving makes it more attractive to keep working and keep saving (the substitution effect delays retirement).
10. This point is often lost in discussions of tax policy. The Urban-Brookings Tax Policy Center estimates that 85 percent of tax units pay more in payroll taxes than in income taxes, including more than 95 percent of those with less than $50,000 in income.
11. Poterba (2014), "Retirement Security."
12. Economists rely on various metrics to determine the extent to which Americans are working. One key term is the labor *force participation rate* (LFPR), which measures the share of Americans who are working or looking for work. The LFPR is defined as the proportion of adults age 16 and older, and who are not in an institution such as a nursing home or in the armed forces, who report either being employed or being actively engaged in a job search. Another key indicator is the share of adults who are working, which is known as the *ratio of employment to population* (EPOP). The difference between the LFPR and EPOP is that the LFPR includes adults who are unemployed but looking for work, while the EPOP measures the share of adults who have a job. In this section, we focus on the LFPR because it is

less sensitive to changes in the business cycle—that is, recessions and recoveries—that can influence the share of adults who are working.

13. Between 2000 and 2014, the LFPR for prime-age women declined from 77 to 74 percent, rising by about 1 percentage point since then.

14. We illustrate this trend in Figure 3.1 in Chapter 3.

15. All labor force statistics are from the US Bureau of Labor Statistics (2020), "Labor Force Statistics from the Current Population Survey."

16. Based on output from the US Bureau of Labor Statistics' "One Screen" Labor Force Statistics Database.

17. US Bureau of Labor Statistics (2020), "Civilian Labor Force Participation Rate by Age, Sex, Race, and Ethnicity."

18. This terminology is widely used but a bit misleading. The population is aging 1 year at a time, as it always has. The reason for the "aging of the population" is the decline in the birth rate, hence fewer young people.

19. Similarly, a study by researchers at the International Monetary Fund found that about half the declining LFPR between 2007 and 2013 was due to population shifts, although the precise share varied substantially by time periods and gender. For example, the researchers find that, of the decline of 0.7 percentage point in women's LFPR between 2010 and 2013, a full 0.5 percentage point was due to population shifts—compared with just a 0.6 percentage point out of the drop of 2.0 percentage points for men over the same period. See Balakrishnan et al. (2015), "Recent US Labor Force."

20. For discussion, see Council of Economic Advisers (2016), "The Long-Term Decline," and Krause and Sawhill (2017), "What We Know."

21. Aaronson et al. (2014), "Labor Force Participation."

22. Prior research supports the finding of a weak relationship between the business cycle and the overall LFPR. For example, Aaronson et al. (2014) found that a sustained increase of 1 percentage point in the unemployment rate will only depress the total LFPR by 0.2 percentage points.

23. Social Security benefits are based on the highest 35 years of a worker's earnings. An extra year of labor for an older worker would boost their Social Security benefits if it qualified as one of the worker's 35 highest years of earnings and it did not replace a year of earnings that was above the taxable maximum.

24. Research confirms the steep drop in work penalties for older workers. A working paper by Courtney Coile (2018), "The Evolution of Retirement," finds that the implicit tax on workers age 65–69 has plummeted by more than half since 1980. For example, the implicit tax for a 67-year-old worker fell from 32 percent in 1980 to 10 percent today. Coile found similar declines for other workers in their late 60s, driven mainly by gradual changes in Social Security rules.

25. Bosworth, Burtless, and Zhang (2016), "Later Retirement," found that there has been a substantial decline in the availability of employer-provided retiree health insurance and that health insurance coverage as an employee or retiree has a strong influence on labor force participation.

26. Coile, Milligan, and Wise (2016), "Health Capacity to Work."

27. While it is clear that workers are living longer lives, trends in disability and mortality introduce the question about whether workers are healthy enough to work at older ages. For example, Crimmins and Beltrán-Sánchez (2011), "Mortality and Morbidity," document widespread increases in morbidity experience by older Americans between 1998 and 2006.

28. Aísa, Pueyo, and Sanso (2012), "Life Expectancy and Labor Supply."

CHAPTER 6

1. This argument holds from the perspective of a household's saving behavior. From a national saving perspective, the issue is more nuanced and complicated. As explained in Gale and Sabelhous (1999), "Perspectives on the Household Saving Rate," the capital gain should only be classified as saving if it is due to an underlying increase in productivity rather than a change in tastes. This theoretical issue is of great interest to economists but probably worthless to the average household saver.

2. Angeletos et al. (2001), "Hyperbolic Consumption Model."

3. Choi et al. (2002), "Defined Contribution Pensions."

4. Madrian and Shea (2001), "The Power of Suggestion." A wide range of studies have confirmed this result, leading many to adopt this approach as a way to boost saving. A nuanced point is that while the literature has established the link between automatic enrollment and increased contributions to retirement accounts, it is less clear whether automatic enrollment boosts total saving. That is, economists are still debating whether the increased contributions are new saving or whether workers simply substitute workplace saving for other types of saving.

5. The most common questions, often used in Lusardi's research, are "Suppose you had $100 in a savings account and the interest rate was 2% per year. After 5 years, how much do you think you would have in the account if you left the money to grow?"; "Imagine that the interest rate on your savings account was 1% per year and inflation was 2% per year. After 1 year, how much would you be able to buy with the money in this account?"; and "Please tell me whether this statement is true or false. 'Buying a single company's stock usually provides a safer return than a stock mutual fund.'"

6. Lusardi (2008), "Financial Literacy." The three questions concern understanding interest rates and compounding, the impact of inflation, and risk diversification.

7. For example, in a review of the financial education literature, Gale, Harris, and Levine (2012), "Raising Household Saving," find that workplace financial education programs often have an impact, although the magnitude varies; high school education programs have generally not been shown to work; and there is limited conclusive evidence around credit- or mortgage-based counseling.

8. Some studies find that these asset tests tend to reduce all types of saving, including "liquid" assets like 401(k) balances, while others find that the tests have impacts on ownership of certain types of assets (such as cars), but not on retirement saving. See Chen and Lerman (2005), "Do Asset Limits." Still, the literature is sufficiently conclusive to warrant the Bipartisan Policy Center (Isom 2015), "Barriers to Saving," to state that, "Asset tests are clearly a strong savings disincentive for

Americans who benefit from means-tested programs. Those individuals are effectively penalized for saving—even what little they may be able to—for retirement or other purposes."

9. Looney and Yannelis (2015), "A Crisis in Student Loans?," and Johnson (2021), "The U.S. Has a Record-Breaking $1.73 Trillion in Student Debt."

10. While we are unaware of a comprehensive decomposition quantifying all of these factors, Akers and Chingos (2014), "Is a Student Loan Crisis," find that more than half of the change in mean debt between 1989 and 2010 was due to increased tuition and that roughly one-quarter was due to increased educational attainment. Similarly, Looney and Yannelis (2015), "A Crisis in Student Loans," attribute much of the increase in debt between 2000 and 2011 to a soaring rise in "non-traditional" borrowers—namely students at for-profit institutions and in 2-year degree programs.

11. Rutledge et al. (2016), "Risk Taking." An interesting finding in this study, however, was that, among borrowers, the size of student debt seemed not to impact retirement saving.

12. Munnell, Hou, and Webb (2016), "Will the Explosion."

13. Diamond and Rajan (1999), "Liquidity Risk."

14. US Government Accountability Office (2019), "Retirement Savings."

15. Gale and Scholz (1994), "Intergenerational Transfers and the Accumulation of Wealth."

16. Wolff and Gittleman (2014), "Inheritances and the Distribution of Wealth."

17. In this example, with a 20 percent tax rate on capital gains and a 7 percent annual rate of return, the value of the account is $1,000 * (1 + 0.07)^n$ after "n" years (not accounting for the initial benefit of not paying taxes on the contribution. If the account was not provided preferential treatment, it would be worth $1,000 *(1 + 0.07(1-0.20))^n$. So, after 10 years, the difference due to non-taxation is worth $243, but grows to $2,485 after 30 years.

18. Burman et al. (2004), "Distributional Effects of Defined-Benefit Contribution Plans."

19. See Harris et al. (2014), "Tax Subsidies," for a review of the distribution of tax benefits for saving more broadly.

20. Duflo, Glennerster, and Kremer (2007), "Using Randomization."

21. Gale and Sholtz (1994), "Intergenerational Transfers"; Chetty et al. (2020), "Opportunity Insights."

22. Economists often note that the "true" housing subsidy is the exclusion of imputed rent on owner-occupied homes. The rationale for this assertion is that investment in housing should be taxed like any other investment in which profits—revenue less expenses—are taxed. With owner-occupied housing, imputed rent is the revenue, and mortgage interest and property taxes paid are the housing expenses. (For those not used to this concept, an easy way to understand imputed rent is to consider a person and a neighbor each owning a house and renting to each other, paying taxes on rent less interest and property tax and other expenses paid.) Thus, if housing were treated analogously to other investments, imputed rent less deductible expenses would be taxed. In practice, imputed rent is difficult to tax and thus

economists often mainly cite mortgage interest and property tax deductions as tax preferences for homeownership.

23. See Bourassa et al. (2012), "Mortgage Interest Deduction," for a survey the international literature.

24. Poterba and Sinai (2011), "Revenue Costs and Incentive Effects."

25. Tax Policy Center (2020), "Key Elements of the US Tax System."

CHAPTER 7

1. In looking at this figure, keep in mind that labor force participation declines strongly with age, as we saw in Chapter 6. The figure plots the shares among those who are working. The tabulations in Figure 7.1 were carried out by Brad Hershbein of the Upjohn Institute and Katharine Abraham of the University of Maryland and are used with permission and with thanks.

2. Calculations made by the authors from Bureau of Labor Statistics (BLS) data (2018). The distinction between voluntary and involuntary reasons is based on whether the respondent was unable to find a full-time job. If someone had a medical problem such that they did not feel able to work full time, this was counted as voluntary. During bad economic times the amount of involuntary part-time work increases as a share of total older worker employment; it was 17 percent in 2010 as a result of the Great Recession and there was high unemployment in that year also. BLS reviews the different reasons and what they mean in Dunn.

3. See Case and Deaton (2017). These facts about the older workforce are positive, but do not say all older workers are satisfied with their labor market options. We know that wages for workers without any college education are poor, that many people drop out of the workforce in their 50s, and that the death rate for this group has risen, especially for men.

4. This section draws on the work of Maestas (2010), "Back to Work."

5. Ibid.

6. Abraham, Hershbein, and Houseman (2019), "Contract Work." These authors worked with Gallup in creating the questions used in the survey.

7. When people are asked if they have worked for an employer, they may say "yes" even if they are an independent contractor and not on the payroll of the company that is paying them. Specific follow-up questions in the Gallup survey improved the accuracy of the answers and revealed the miscoding. To illustrate their findings: among those aged 65–69 who reported working, the fraction who are self-employed in the sample was 45.5 percent, but this fraction would have been reported as only 36.5 percent had the misclassification not been corrected.

8. Abraham, Hershbein, and Houseman (2020), "Contract Work."

9. See the data from the National Center for Health Statistics (2022). The fertility rate reflects the expected number of children born to a woman over the course of her life.

10. Adrian Raftery (June 21, 2021), "The Dip in US Birthrate."

11. Gretchen Livingston (2019), "Is U.S. Fertility at an All-Time Low?," Pew Research Center.

12. US Bureau of Labor Statistics (2020a, 2020b), "Employment, Hours, and Earnings." Data on the share of production workers from Haver Analytics, which is drawn from BLS.

13. Perry (2018), "The Main Reason for the Loss of US Steel Jobs."

14. Many women also worked in manufacturing, and the number of their jobs has declined a lot also. The apparel industry has a largely female workforce, and apparel jobs have been decimated. Jobs in the apparel industry were not well-paid compared to jobs in autos or machine tools.

15. Hecker et al. (2021), "Digital Skills."

16. Gould (2019), "State of Working America Wages, 2018."

17. Brynjolfsson and McAfee (2014), *The Second Machine Age*. See also Lund et al. (2019), "The Future of Work in America." (Martin Baily was an advisor to this project.)

18. Johnson (2019), "The Case Against Early Retirement."

19. See Sullivan and von Wachter (2009), "Job Displacement."

20. National Academies (2020), "Social Isolation."

21. Centers for Disease Control (2020), "Loneliness and Social Isolation."

22. See Xue et al. (2017), "The Effect of Retirement"; Rohwedder and Willis (2010), "Mental Retirement"; and C. Grotz et al. (2016), "Why Is Later Age."

CHAPTER 8

1. With variable annuities, income protections and principal guarantees can take several forms, all grouped under a "living benefit" umbrella. Individuals, for example, can buy a *guaranteed minimum accumulation benefit* to ensure a certain contract value after a set period of time, a *guaranteed minimum benefit amount* that establishes a set lifetime income after a waiting period for collecting benefits (such as a decade), and a *guaranteed minimum withdrawal benefit* (or *guaranteed lifetime withdrawal benefit*) that—like the guaranteed minimum benefit amount—provides a set minimum distribution for life. These protections typically cost from half to three-quarters of a percent of the annuity value a year and are backed by the financial strength of the insurance company in question.

2. Several analyses report a positive correlation between the length of the surrender period and commissions, with shorter surrender periods driving some of the decline in average commissions.

3. The Vanguard life expectancy tool can be found here: https://personal.vanguard. com/us/insights/retirement/plan-for-a-long-retirement-tool.

4. The economic case for annuities was first laid out by Menahem Yaari (1965), "Uncertain Lifetime," where he demonstrated assumptions under which rational individuals would use all their retirement savings to purchase an annuity rather than holding bonds. The assumptions were strong ones—for example, he assumed retirees did not wish to leave a bequest to their children, and he ignored the fees charged on annuities. Subsequent literature has generalized Yaari's analysis, relaxing his assumptions while preserving the case for placing at least a part of retirement wealth into an annuity product. Benartzi, Previtero, and Thaler (2011),

"Annuity Puzzles," provide an excellent and intuitive summary of this literature. To take one example of generalizing Yaari's result: households can set aside money for bequests and then annuitize the remainder of their retirement assets. Or a second example from Gong and Webb (2010), "Evaluating the Advanced Life Deferred Annuity": allowing for the fees that are incurred when buying an annuity does not eliminate the case for annuities as long as the fees are moderate.

5. Retirement Income Journal (2020), "One Bright Spot in First Quarter."

6. The assets held as annuities outside of retirement accounts have grown from $1.4 trillion in 2009 to $2.1 trillion today, including both variable and fixed annuities, according to the Investment Company Institute (ICI). The data imply that this amount is roughly split between fixed and variable annuities, with $1.2 trillion held in variable annuities outside of retirement accounts.

7. Brien and Panis (2011), "Annuities."

8. Kahneman and Tversky (1979), "Prospect Theory."

9. In prospect theory, people are assumed to overweight small-probability events and this helps explain why people buy lottery tickets where they overestimate their chances of winning. Prospect theory also assumes individuals weigh losses more than gains from an initial starting point. Overweighting small-probability events would suggest that 30-year-olds will overweight the probability they will live until age 90, whereas in practice there is a tendency to underweight this probability. Another example of underweighting small-probability events occurred in the financial crisis, where banks and regulators underestimated the small probability of a collapse of the housing market.

10. The economic analysis of annuities typically compares the flow of benefits from an annuity to the flow of returns from the purchase of a safe bond (a Treasury security, for example). The global economy today is one where interest rates are very low but where corporate profitability and the return on equities have been high. No one knows how these patterns may change in the future, but a retiree managing his or her own funds can choose to invest in equities.

11. For those interested in economic history, the deferred annuity has its origins in a 17th-century financial product called a *tontine*. This was an investment product used to raise capital in which the payoffs went increasingly to those investors who survived longest. They are still common in France and are getting new consideration in the United States. See McKeever (2009), "A Short History," and Iwry et al. (2020), "Retirement Tontines."

12. Quotes calculated using ImmediateAnnuities.com. Amounts reflect the estimated premium of a lifetime income policy with no guaranteed income in the event of the death of the policy holder.

13. There is a schedule of required minimum distributions (RMDs) specifying a rising percentage of the tax-preferred assets that must be withdrawn each year from 72 on.

14. The rules contributions to retirement accounts are explained by the IRS at the following site: https://www.irs.gov/retirement-plans/plan-participant-employee/retirement-topics-catch-up-contributions.

15. *Arizona Governing Comm. v. Norris*, 463 U.S. 1073 (1983).

16. Economic analysis has clearly shown that it is total worker compensation that is determined by the marketplace, so that health insurance premiums, payroll taxes, and pension contributions are all effectively paid for by wage rates that are lower than they would be in the absence of these costs. Many firms introduced pensions during wartime controls. They were not able to raise wages, and so they used pensions and health insurance as a way of attracting workers during a time of labor shortage. At that time, the fringe benefits were probably a net plus to workers, but that changes once controls are lifted.

CHAPTER 9

1. Morrissey (2019), "The State of American Retirement Savings."
2. US Census Bureau (2020), "65 and Older Population Grows Rapidly as Baby Boomers Age."
3. Hado and Komisar (2019), "Long-Term Services and Supports."
4. Richard W. Johnson (2019), "What Is the Lifetime Risk of Needing and Receiving Long-Term Services and Supports."
5. Hado and Komisar (2019).
6. Congressional Budget Office (2013), "Rising Demand."
7. Alzheimer's Association, 2022 Alzheimer's Disease Facts and Figures, p. 20. The ADAMS study is the Aging, Demographics, and Memory Study, based on the Health and Retirement Study.
8. Ibid., p. 18.
9. Ibid., p. 62.
10. AARP Family Caregiving (2020), "Caregiving in the US."
11. Ibid.
12. This section draws on Mudrazija and Johnson (2020), "Economic Impacts of Programs to Support Caregivers." The report is dated January 2020 but records that it was completed and submitted in September 2017 from the Urban Institute.
13. Hado and Komisar (2019).
14. Freedman and Spillman (2014), "Disability and Care Needs"; Spillman (2014), "Why Do Elders Receiving Informal Home Care Transition."
15. American Association of Retired Persons (2018), "2018 Home and Community Preferences Survey."
16. Rowland (2013), "Testimony to the Commission on Long-Term Care."
17. Konetzka et al. (2020), "Is Being Home Good for Your Health?"
18. US Bureau of Labor Statistics (2022), "Home Health and Personal Care Aides."
19. Hado and Komisar (2019).
20. AARP Public Policy Institute (2019), "Valuing the Invaluable: 2019 Update."
21. Money Geek (2020), "The Sobering Cost of Long-Term Care"; Congressional Budget Office (2013)." CBO estimates of costs are consistent with this survey except they report that a part-time home health aide working part-time cost only $20,000 a year in 2012.
22. Brown and Finkelstein (2011), "Insuring Long-Term Care"; CBO (2013). The figures are drawn from the Health and Retirement Surveys of 2008 and 2010. The CBO

also reports the percent of the population that is covered by long-term care insurance (compared the percent of those receiving care), and this figure is much lower at 3 percent.

23. Stark (2018), "5 Things You Should Know About Long-Term Care Insurance."

24. Figures from "Health and Retirement Survey" (2018).

25. This and the next three paragraphs draw on Brown and Finkelstein (2011).

26. Cornell et al. (2016), "Medical Underwriting."

27. The amount of long-term care premiums that can be deducted rises with age. For example, a person aged 40 and younger can deduct just $430, while a person aged 70 or older can deduct $5,430. However, after the 2017 tax bill, only a small share of taxpayers itemize deductions—with especially low rates for households with low or moderate income. Combined with the limited benefit for medical expense deductions, this means that very few families will claim a tax break for purchasing long-term care insurance.

28. There is another way to express the cost of long-term care policies. Any insurance policy has a "load factor" reflecting the fact that not all premiums are paid out to beneficiaries. Any insurance company must cover administrative costs and make a profit. The load factors on long-term care policies are very high, such that a person buying a policy will receive an expected return of 67.9 cents for every dollar of premiums they pay (i.e., the policy will have a load factor of 32.1 percent). Since men are much less likely to go into long-term care, their load factor is 55.4, meaning that over half of their premium is lost on what they can expect to receive. In practice, the load factor is even worse than these numbers indicate because a high percentage of buyers of the policies stop paying premiums before they take advantage of the coverage. Allowing for policy terminations, the load factor for men is 66.4 percent. It may still make sense for a man to buy a policy, but he is getting a terrible deal relative to most insurance products. The very high load factors may suggest profiteering by the insurance companies offering the policies, but that does not seem to be the case. Insurance companies are exiting this market, concerned about the rising costs of care and uncertainty about the liability they will incur. The market for long-term care policies is a thin one where most people do not buy policies, costs increase, and suppliers decide to exit. It is not clear if the private market for individual long-term care policies will survive.

29. CBO (2013). This figure reflects their projection of 2019 expenditure.

30. Benz (2020), "100 Must-Know Statistics."

31. AARP and the National Alliance for Caregiving (2020), "Caregiving in the U.S."

32. Butrica and Karamcheva (2014), "The Impact of Informal Caregiving." There is an extensive literature exploring employment impacts of caregiving; see Mudrazija and Johnson (2020), "Economic Impacts of Programs to Support Caregivers." They report that relatively few men provide long-term care. In other countries the employment effects of providing care are larger than in the United States.

33. Mudrazija and Johnson (2020), Ibid.

34. Hado and Komisar (2019).

35. Joint Center for Housing Studies (2019), "Housing America's Older Adults."

36. Center for Medicare and Medicaid Services (2021), "COVID-19 Nursing Home Data."

37. Brown and Finkelstein (2011) argue that purchases of long-term care insurance would increase in the absence of Medicare but would still not cover a large fraction of the population.

38. Kaiser Family Foundation (2019), "Distribution of Medicaid Spending by Service."

39. US Census Bureau (2019), "Real Median Household Income in the United States." Median family income is higher, at $86,011. Families consist of two or more related individuals living together. Households may include unrelated individuals and include single parents.

40. Life expectancy is uncertain so a fully optimal plan would also require a longevity annuity, something we discuss elsewhere in this book.

41. Ruseski and Wadsworth (2019), "Adverse Selection and Long-Term Care."

42. Oster, Shoulson, Quaid, and Dorsey (2009), "Genetic Adverse Selection."

43. Cornell et al. (2016).

44. This paragraph draws on Feder, Komisar, and Friedland (2007), "Long-Term Care Financing: Policy Options for the Future."

CHAPTER 10

1. Nakajima and Telyukova (2017), "Reverse Mortgage Loans."

2. Harris (2013), "Tax Reform."

3. Haurin, Loibl, and Moulton (2019), "Debt Stress," surveyed those who had decided against a reverse mortgage and those who had taken one out.

4. The implication of this difference is that the balances on traditional mortgages tend to decline with time, while the balances on reverse mortgages typically grow over time.

5. To our knowledge, reverse mortgages are the only product that offers both longevity protection and provides a hedge against falling homes prices.

6. Shan (2011), "Reversing the Trend."

7. For example, in 2020 a 70-year-old borrowing at 4 percent has a principal limit factor of 0.522, while a 65-year-old borrowing at the same rate has a factor of 0.490. Thus, a 65-year-old borrower with a $300,000 house (an amount below the FHA cap) can borrow $147,000 at 4 percent, while the 70-year-old can borrow $156,600 at 4 percent. The principal limiting factor is determined by FHA, and it changes with time periods. The numbers used here are applicable for loans originating on or after October 2, 2017. The principal limiting factors for all time periods, interest rates, and ages can be found here: https://www.hud.gov/program_offices/housing/sfh/hecm.

8. Pinnacle Actuarial Resources (2018), "Fiscal Year 2018 Independent Review."

9. Moulton, Haurin, and Shi (2015), "An Analysis of Default Risk."

10. Twomey and Jurgens (2019), "Subprime Revisited"; Paz Garcia, Cole, and Reeves (2010), "Examining Faulty Foundations."

11. Moulton, Loibl, and Haurin (2017), "Reverse Mortgages, Motivations."

12. Consumer Financial Protection Bureau (2012), "Report to Congress on Reverse Mortgages."

13. Ibid.

14. A Congressional Research Service report speculates that the trend away from single women was driven by two factors. One, until recently, couple borrowing increased due to a practice of removing the younger spouse (typically a woman) from the deed to increase the amount that could be borrowed. Two, the new HUD rule that the age of the younger non-borrowing spouse be accounted for may help explain the increase in couple borrowing (Perl [2017], "HUD's Reverse Mortgage Insurance Program").

15. Perl (2017).

16. Munnell and Sass (2014), "The Government's Redesigned Reverse Mortgage Program."

17. Golding and Goodman, "To Better Assess the Risk of FHA Programs." Reverse mortgages only comprise 6.5 percent of the fund but are a highly volatile component. See Congressional Budget Office (June 2019), "The 2019 Long-Term Budget Outlook," for a discussion of the budgetary considerations with HECMs.

18. According to a 2012 report by Consumer Financial Protection Bureau, fixed-rate loans previously constituted roughly 70 percent of the market. The popularity of fixed-rate loans, which allows mortgagors to draw down all funds at the time of loan closing, caused higher payouts of insurance claims and increased risks to the FHA Mutual Mortgage Insurance Fund. To improve the fiscal safety and soundness of the program, FHA decided to build on the existing fixed-interest rate mortgage policy guidance and put a loan-to-value ratio on these loans. After the change made by FHA in 2013, fixed-rate loans accounted for less than 4 percent of new HECM loans as of May 2019.

19. Redfoot, Scholen, and Brown (2007), "Reverse Mortgages."

20. This demand is almost exclusively for traditional HECM loans. Over the first 5 months of 2019, for example, there were 13,816 new HECM loans, of which 12,259 were traditional HECM loans, 898 purchase loans, and 659 HECM for refinance loans. See National Reverse Mortgage Lenders Association (2019), "HECM Endorsement Analytics."

21. Shan (2011).

22. Haurin et al. (2016), "Spatial Variation in Reverse Mortgages."

23. Nakajima and Telyukova (2017), "Reverse Mortgage Loans."

24. US Government Accountability Office (September 2019), "Reverse Mortgages"; Michelangeli (2010), "Does It Pay to Get a Reverse Mortgage"; Nakajima and Telyukova (2017), "Reverse Mortgage Loans."

25. Nakajima and Telyukova (2017).

26. Venti and Wise (1990), "But They Don't Want to Reduce Housing Equity"; Venti and Wise (1990), "Aging Moving and Housing Wealth"; Venti and Wise (2004), "Aging and Housing Equity"; Davidoff (2010), "Home Equity Commitment."

27. Davidoff (2015), "Can High Costs Justify Weak Demand."

28. Lucas (2015), "Hacking Reverse Mortgages," quantifies the benefits to various entities engaged in reverse mortgages. She finds that HECMs are largely beneficial to lenders with a net present value (NPV) of $31,000 per loan, compared to negative $27,000 for borrowers (and a government subsidy NPV of $4,000). However, she also finds that undertaking the "ruthless" strategy described by Davidoff and Wetzel ("Do Reverse Mortgage Borrowers Use Credit Ruthlessly?") will result in an average NPV gain of more than $53,000 for the borrower, largely at the expense of the government backstop. In addition, Nakajima and Telyukova (2017) explore a model in which the insurance features of reverse mortgages (called the *non-recourse feature*) would not be included in a hypothetical reverse mortgage. By excluding the non-recourse feature there would be a corresponding reduction in upfront mortgage costs. They argue that this would boost take-up by 43 percent so that 2.9 percent of eligible households would undertake a reverse mortgage. As we have said, it would be very difficult or impossible to have reverse mortgages like this in practice, but this hypothetical analysis helps us understand an important reason why the demand for reverse mortgages is so low. They point out that most borrowers expect their loans to be fully repaid and in fact most are fully repaid, so the insurance only "pays off" to a minority of borrowers (of course, that is always true of insurance). One reason the insurance element of reverse mortgages is undervalued is because, despite the housing crisis of 2009, most people underestimate the chances that their own house could fall in value.

29. Miceli and Sirmans (1994), "Reverse Mortgages and Borrower Maintenance Risk."

30. Moulton and Haurin (2019), "Unlocking Housing Wealth."

31. As noted by Davidoff and Welke (2007), "Selection and Moral Hazard," long expected durations are only a concern in the reverse mortgage market if interest rates exceed home price appreciation.

32. Moulton and Haurin (2019).

33. Davidoff and Welke (2007), *Selection and Moral Hazard*.

34. The Davidoff and Welke finding that many homeowners sell soon after taking out a reverse mortgage likely also reflects timing; there had been rapid house price increases prior to 2007.

35. Kutty (1998), "The Scope for Poverty Alleviation"; Mayer and Simons (1994), "Reverse Mortgages and Liquidity"; Merrill, Finkel, and Kutty (1994), "Potential Beneficiaries"; Nakajima and Telyukova (2017); Rasmussen, Megbolugbe, and Morgan (1995), "Using the 1990 Public Use Microdata"; Shan (2011); and Venti and Wise (1991).

36. Merrill, Finkel, and Kutty (1994) give the 9 percent estimate. Rasmussen, Megbolugbe, and Morgan 1995 ("Using the 1990 Public Use Microdata") argue the 80 percent figure for elderly women. Other studies are cited in note 34.

37. Venti and Wise (1990), "Aging, Moving"; Venti and Wise (1990), "But They Don't Want to Reduce Housing Equity"; Venti and Wise (2004).

38. Bayer and Harper (2000), "Fixing to Stay."

39. Haurin, Loibl, and Moulton (2019), "Debt Stress and Mortgage Borrowing."

40. Valentina Michelangeli (2007), "Does It Pay?"
41. US Government Accountability Office (September 2019), "Reverse Mortgages."
42. Ibid.

CHAPTER 11

1. Investment Company Institute (2021), "The US Retirement Market, First Quarter 2021."
2. For example, see Chetty et al. (2014), "Active vs. Passive Decisions."
3. Pew Research Center (2016), "Who's In, Who's Out."
4. The plan, described in US Treasury (2017), "General Explanations of the Administration's Fiscal Year 2017 Revenue Proposals," allows for a maximum of $250 in per employee credits for up to 6 years.
5. Harris and Johnson (2012), "Economic Effects of Automatic Enrollment."
6. Harris and Fischer (2012), "Population of Workers Covered by the Auto IRA."
7. See Georgetown Center for Retirement Initiatives (2020), "State-Facilitated Retirement Savings Programs," for a description of state characteristics.
8. For a discussion of dashboards, see John et al. in Gale, Iwry, and John (2021), "Wealth After Work."
9. Gale (2011), "Tax Reform Options: Promoting Retirement Security."
10. Economic research confirms that lack of information plays a role. For example, a 2005 experiment offered tax filers in various H&R Block offices similar match rates to the Saver's Credit when they contributed to an IRA—but filers also received guidance and explanations from their tax preparers. The share of people contributing to IRAs rose substantially. Duflo et al. (2006), "Saving Incentives."
11. Tax Policy Center (2018), "Tax Units with Zero or Negative Income Tax," table 18-0128.
12. These options are described in more detail, including potential economic impact, in Gale, Iwry, and Orszag (2004), "The Saver's Credit."
13. Correia (2021), "Contribution Catch-Up for Caregivers Gaining Favor."
14. Society for Human Resource Management (2017), "2017 Employee Benefits."
15. Lusardi and Tufano (2019), "Teach Workers About the Perils of Debt."
16. When interest rates change, the price of bonds rises or falls, generating a temporary increase or decrease in returns. This calculation is based on a situation where rates remain stable. Bonds are not totally secure and can fluctuate in value and suffer from defaults.
17. These numbers are not adjusted for inflation, which would reduce the real returns in both cases.
18. Executive Office of the President (2015), "The Effects of Conflicted Investment Advice."
19. Johnson (2021), "How Low Can Fund Fees Go?"

CHAPTER 12

1. See Ellis et al. (2014), "Falling Short."

2. Burtless (2013), "Is an Aging Workforce Less Productive?"

3. The Affordable Care Act made health insurance more accessible.

4. Coile (2018), "Evolution of Retirement Incentives."

5. Ibid.

6. Ibid.

7. Clark and Shoven (2019), "Enhancing Work Incentives."

8. Fiedler and Song (2020), "Estimating Potential Spending on COVID-19 Care."

9. Burtless (2017), "Age-Related Health Costs."

10. This policy would be especially beneficial to those with moderate wage levels. For someone earning $100,000 a year or more, health insurance costs are not a large part of their total compensation. For someone earning $30,000–50,000, health insurance costs are a big deal.

11. Clark and Shoven (2019).

12. Workers at the legal minimum wage will not face lower wages because of the employer contribution to FICA taxes.

13. Munnell and Walters (2019), "Proposals to Keep Older People in the Labor Force."

14. Even if all workers were to move to Medicare at age 65, the cost of health insurance rises for people in their 50s and 60s.

15. Agarwal et al. (2010), "What Is the Age of Reason?"

16. This finding likely reflects a combination of factors, including ability to master telework technology and nature of work by age. Agovino (2020), "COVID-19 Deals a Dual Threat."

17. Agarwal et al. (2010).

18. Glisky (2007), "Changes in Cognitive Function"; Miklos and Sterns (1995), "The Aging Worker." Citations in this note and in Note 4 are highlighted in the work of the Sloan Center on Aging and Work at Boston College.

19. Centers for Disease Control (2011), "Health, United States."

20. Hewitt (2015), "A Business Case for Workers."

21. Borsch-Supan and Weiss (2013), "Productivity and Age."

22. Weir (2008), "The Health and Retirement Study."

23. Peter Cappelli and Bill Novelli, in their 2010 book, argue that there are many myths about the productivity of older workers, and they look at strategies companies can use to get the most out of older workers. Cappelli is a professor at Wharton while Novelli is the former CEO of AARP.

24. US Bureau of Labor Statistics (2020), "Civilian Labor Force Participation Rate," table 3.3.

25. Marcus (2021), "In One Year, Pandemic Forced Millions of Workers to Retire Early."

26. Bhattarai (2022), "Millions Retired."

27. Casselman (2022), "I Had to Go Back."

28. See Munnell and Walters (2019), "Keeping Older Workers"; Behaghel and Blau (2012), "Framing Social Security Reform."

29. Bernstein (2018), "Americans in Depression and War."

30. After World War II, there was concern among policymakers that the economy might return to the depressed labor market conditions of the 1930s. The American government's priority was to find civilian jobs for returning Gis, and, as a result,

women and older workers were encouraged or forced to leave their jobs. One could argue, therefore, that the high-pressure economy of the war caused only a temporary shift in the labor market and the position of women, African Americans, and older workers also faced a return to prewar norms. However, we think the experience during World War II and the high-pressure economy of the 1960s were important in showing the capabilities of disadvantaged workers, and it laid the groundwork for the civil rights movement and the women's movement of the 1960s and 1970s. There was also progress in providing a more open labor market for older workers and an anti-age discrimination law was passed in 1967, which we will discuss shortly. A high-pressure economy is helpful in breaking down barriers.

31. Inflation has emerged as a problem in 2022. In part, this is because there is strong demand pressure as the economy recovers from the pandemic. Likely the larger part of the blame for inflation, though, comes from the supply chain problems that the pandemic has caused and from the war in Ukraine.

32. Neumark (2020), "Strengthening Age Discrimination Protections."

33. *Gross v. FBL Financial Services, Inc.*, 557 U.S. 167 (8th Cir. 2009).

34. Harris (2020), "Increasing Employment."

35. US Bureau of Labor Statistics (2020), "Job Openings and Labor Turnover Survey."

36. Data reported in US Bureau of Labor Statistics (August 27, 2020), "Displaced Workers Summary."

37. Van Horn et al. (2015), "Improving Education and Training."

38. It is vital to use the right type of training for older workers, as shown by Zwick (2011), "Why Training Older Employees," or else the results will be poor.

39. Holzer (2011), "Raising Job Quality." Holzer's recommendations do not focus on older workers and are intended for the entire workforce.

40. Picchio (2015), "Is Training Effective?"

41. Peter Berg et al. (2017), "The Relationship Between Employer-Provided Training," match German establishment survey data with employee Social Security records to examine the relationship between worker training and employee retention. They find that training programs increase the working years of older, especially low-wage, women, but a similar association does not exist for older men. Like Holzer and Picchio, Berg et al. also find evidence to support the effectiveness of targeted training. Jacobson et al. (1993), "Earnings Losses," match longitudinal earnings data to community college records in Washington state to estimate the impact of community college schooling on the earnings of older displaced workers who seek retraining around the time of their job losses. They find that older workers are less likely to enroll in community colleges than their younger counterparts. However, those who do experience an 8–10 percent increase in long-term earnings per year of academic education.

CHAPTER 13

1. Harris (2018), "Why Annuities May Be Safer."

2. Chen et al. (2018), "How Much Income Do Retirees Have?"

3. Medicare covers hospital insurance (Part A coverage) for covered beneficiaries. Part B, covering outpatient treatment had a monthly premium of $148.50 per person for moderate income households, rising as high as $504.90 a month for very high-income individuals. Part D is the prescription drug plan, and the premiums depend on both the plan that people choose and their incomes. Figures are for 2021, and information is available at medicare.gov.

4. US Census Bureau (Revised 2020), "Wealth, Asset Ownership, & Debt...Tables 2017."

5. Charles Schwab (2020), "Income Annuity Estimator."

6. Mutual of Omaha (2020), "Long-Term Care Insurance Calculator."

7. For example, in a *Wall Street Journal* op-ed, one of us noted, "The Government Accountability Office estimates that of the 1,100 life insurers operating during the crisis, just 12 were placed into liquidation. And the life-insurance industry is quick to point out that those insurance companies that failed were all small, with less than $1 billion in total liabilities." See Harris (2018).

8. Not all older households own their own homes, but the majority do—about fourth-fifths of households older than 55 are homeowners; see Harvard Joint Center for Urban Studies (2011).

9. These proposals are largely based on the work of reverse mortgage experts Donald Haurin and Stephanie Moulton, who presented a series of potential reforms in a 2019 report that we commissioned as part of an ongoing project on retirement.

10. Moulton and Haurin (2019), "Unlocking Housing Wealth."

11. Moulton and Haurin suggest this set-aside be required for borrowers with poor credit or limited financial assets to ensure that they can stay current on their mortgage.

12. US Government Accountability Office (September 2019), "Reverse Mortgages."

13. For example, the Congressional Budget Office estimates that disposition costs owing to the federal government amount to 25 percent of the home's value. And for consumers, the rates of foreclosure are often substantially higher in African American or poorer communities among those who may have undertaken these loans after being targeted by predatory lenders. See Penzenstadler and Lowenstein (2019), "Seniors."

14. Consumer Financial Protection Bureau (2012), "Report on to Congress on Reverse Mortgages."

15. US Government Accountability Office (2016), "401(K) Plans."

16. It is worth noting, too, that state insurance commissions provide an elaborate back-stop to life insurance companies, whereby commissions restrict the riskiness of insurers' investments, monitor their financial health, and intervene if it appears that contracts cannot be honored.

17. In essence, employers can satisfy the safe harbor if they obtain written verification that the insurance company is properly licensed and has been for at least 7 years.

18. Brown et al. (2008), "Why Don't People Insure Late-Life Consumption?"

19. Horneff, Maurer, and Mitchell (2019), "Automatic Enrollment in 401(k) Annuities." We commissioned this paper as part of an ongoing project devoted to retirement security.

20. Part of this is due to the pooling of benefits, whereby the premiums of deceased policyholders subsidized the benefits of still-living retirees, and part of it was due to the ability of policyholders to take on more risk (and thus reap higher rewards) in the portion of their portfolio not invested in a DIA.

21. Congressional Budget Office (2009), "Letter." Implementation of the CLASS Act was halted in 2011, and the Act was formally repealed in 2013.

22. Brown and Dynan (2017), "Increasing the Economic Security." In this paper, Brown and Dynan propose two modifications to the Social Security system to address poverty among women over the age of 65, whom they argue fall into poverty largely due to two factors: loss of spouse and experiencing disability. To address the first factor, they argue that married couples should be able to elect to receive less in Social Security benefits while both spouses are alive in order to partially offset the decrease in benefits after one spouse passes away. To address the second, they propose that newer recipients of Social Security benefits should be able to elect to receive lower benefits when younger in exchange for supplemental benefits in the event of disability later in life (effectively diverting a portion of their benefits to a public form of long-term care insurance).

23. Genworth (2019), "Cost of Care Survey."

24. O'Malley Watts, Musumeci, and Chidambaram (2013), "Medicaid Home and Community-Based Services Enrollment and Spending."

25. Fox-Grage and Walls (2013), "State Studies Find Home and Community-Based Services Are Cost-Effective."

26. Some long-term care policies are geared to those seeking luxury care. That is fine, but the tax advantage should be restricted to good but not super-expensive policies.

27. Kerr (2021), "Credit for Caring Act Would Provide Tax Credit to Family Caregivers."

28. Bipartisan Policy Center (2016), "Initial Recommendations." The BPC report outlined a number of specifications for the employer-provided long-term care insurance (LTCI) products it proposes. These include incorporating deductibles and co-insurance into LTCI products in order to reduce premiums; protecting against inflation by adjusting LTCI benefits according to rises in the employment cost index; imposing non-level premiums that increase incrementally with inflation instead of level premiums that are subject to large intermittent rate increases, including a nonforfeiture benefit such that lapsed policyholders could still claim benefits up to the level of premiums already paid; ensuring that LTCI policies would be deemed "Partnership-qualified" for Medicaid-covered LTSS; and allowing employees to use retirement assets to purchase retirement LTCI. See Appendix I-B of the report for further information.

29. Bipartisan Policy Center (2016).

30. Butrica and Karamcheva (2014), "Impact of Informal Caregiving."

31. Khalfani-Cox (2013), "5 Tips."

CHAPTER 14

1. Congressional Research Service (2022). "Poverty in the United States." The poverty rate for older Americans is lower than the average for all Americans, largely thanks to Social Security. However, it is very troubling when people in their 80s and 90s fall into poverty as they typically cannot work and add to their incomes.
2. We include the Supplemental Security Income program and Medicaid as vital support programs also.
3. US Bureau of Labor Statistics (2022), "Union Membership."
4. FICA revenues also cover disability insurance and payments to children whose parents have died.
5. Estimates from the Congressional Budget Office (2021).

Aaronson, Stephanie, Tomaz Cajner, Bruce Fallick, Felix Galbis-Reig, Christopher Smith, and William Wascher. "Labor Force Participation: Recent Developments and Future Prospects." *Brookings Papers on Economic Activity* (Fall 2014): 197–275. doi:10.1353/eca.2014.0015.

AARP Bulletin. "Working at 50 Plus." (November 2018). https://www.aarp.org/work/working-at-50-plus/info-2018/boeing-rehires-retired-employees.html.

AARP Public Policy Institute. "Fact Sheet: Long-Term Support and Services." (March 2017). https://paperzz.com/doc/6776012/long-term-support-and-services.

AARP Public Policy Institute. "Valuing the Invaluable 2019 Update: Charting a Path Forward." (November 14, 2019). https://www.aarp.org/ppi/info-2015/valuing-the-invaluable-2015-update.html.

AARP Social Security Resource Center. "The Maximum Social Security Benefit Explained." (December 24, 2020). https://www.aarp.org/retirement/social-security/questions-answers/maximum-ss-benefit.html.

AARP and the National Alliance for Caregiving. "Caregiving in the U.S." (May 2020). https://doi.org/10.26419/ppi.00103.001.

Abraham, Katherine G., and Benjamin H. Harris. "The Market for Longevity Annuities." *Journal of Retirement* 3, no. 4 (2016): 12–27.

Abraham, Katherine G., Brad Hershbein, and Susan Houseman. "Contract Work at Older Ages." NBER Working Paper No. 26612. (January 2020). https://www.nber.org/papers/w26612.

Acemoglu, Daron, David H. Autor, and David Lyle. "Women, War, and Wages: The Effect of Female Labor Supply on the Wage Structure at Midcentury." *Journal of Political Economy* 112, no. 3 (2014): 497–551. doi:10.1086/383100.

Agarwal, Sumit, John C. Driscoll, Xavier Gabaix, and David Laibson. "What Is the Age of Reason?" Center for Retirement Research at Boston College, Issue in Brief 10-12. (2010). https://scholar.harvard.edu/files/laibson/files/ageofreason_supplement.pdf.

Agovina, Theresa. "COVID-19 Deals a Dual Threat to Older Workers." *SHRM.* (July 18, 2020). https://www.shrm.org/hr-today/news/all-things-work/pages/covid-19-deals-a-dual-threat-to-older-workers.aspx.

Agnew, Julie. "Australia's Retirement System: Strengths, Weaknesses, and Reforms." Center for Retirement Research, Issues in Brief 13-5. (2013). https://ideas.repec.org/p/crr/issbrf/ib2013-5.html.

Aguiar, Mark, and Erik Hurst. "Deconstructing Life Cycle Expenditure." NBER Working Paper No. 13893. (March 2008). https://www.nber.org/papers/w13893.

Aísa, Rosa, Fernando Pueyo, and Marcus Sanso. "Life Expectancy and Labor Supply of the Elderly." *Journal of Population Economics* 25, no. 2 (2012): 545–568.

Akers, Beth, and Matthew M. Chingos. "Is a Student Loan Crisis on the Horizon?" The Brookings Institution. (June 2014). https://www.brookings.edu/research/is-a-student-loan-crisis-on-the-horizon/.

Alzheimer's Association. "2022 Alzheimer's Disease Facts and Figures." (2022). https://www.alz.org/media/documents/alzheimers-facts-and-figures.pdf.

American Association for Long Term Care Insurance (AALTCI). *Long-Term Care Insurance Facts – Data – Statistics – 2019 Report.* (2019). https://www.aaltci.org/long-term-care-insurance/learning-center/ltcfacts-2019.php#2019costs.

American Association of Retired Persons (AARP). "A National Survey of Adults 45 and Older; Loneliness and Social Connections." AARP Research. (2018). doi.org/10.26419/res.00246.001.

American College of Surgeons. *COVID-19: Recommendations for Management of Elective Surgical Procedures.* (2020). https://www.facs.org/-/media/files/covid19/recommendations_for_management_of_elective_surgical_procedur0es.ashx.

Ameriks, John, Joseph Briggs, Andrew Caplin, Matthew D. Shapiro, and Christopher Tonetti. "Long-Term-Care Utility and Late-in-Life Saving." Vanguard Research Initiative Working Paper. (March 2019). https://ebp-projects.isr.umich.edu/VRI/papers/VRI-LTC-U.pdf.

Ang, James S., James Wuh Lin, and Floyd Tyler. "Evidence on the Lack of Separation Between Business and Personal Risks among Small Businesses." *Journal of Small Business Finance* 4, no. 2 (Fall 1995): 197–2102. https://digitalcommons.pepperdine.edu/jef/vol4/iss2/7.

Angeletos, George-Marios, David Laibson, Andrea Repetto, Jeremy Tobacman, and Stephen Weinberg. "The Hyperbolic Consumption Model: Calibration, Simulation, and Empirical Evaluation." *Journal of Economic Perspectives* 15, no. 3 (2001): 47–68. doi:10.1257/jep.15.3.47.

Arizona Governing Comm. v. Norris, 463 U.S. 1073 (1983).

Auerbach, Alan J., William G. Gale, and Benjamin H. Harris. "Federal Health Spending and the Budget Outlook: Some Alternative Scenarios." Engelberg Center for Health Care Reform, The Brookings Institution. (April 11, 2014). https://www.brookings.edu/wp-content/uploads/2016/06/federal_health_spending_budget_outlook_auerbach_gale_harris.pdf.

Barrero, José María, Nick Bloom, and Steven Davis. "COVID-19 Is Also a Reallocation Shock." *Brookings Papers on Economic Activity* (Summer 2020). https://www.brookings.edu/bpea-articles/covid-19-is-also-a-reallocation-shock/.

Bayer, Ada-Helen, and Leon Harper. "Fixing to Stay: A National Survey of Housing and Home Modification Issues." AARP Research. (May 2000). https://www.aarp.org/content/dam/aarp/research/surveys_statistics/general/fixing-to-stay.pdf.

Balakrishnan, Ravi, Mai Dao, Juan Sole, and Jeremy Zook. "Recent U.S. Labor Force Dynamics: Reversible or Not?" IMF Working Paper 15–76. (2015). doi:10.5089/9781484315620.001.

Becker, Gary S. *The Economics of Discrimination*. Chicago: University of Chicago Press, 1957.

Bee, Adam, and Joshua Mitchell. "Do Older Americans Have More Income Than We Think?" SESHD Working Paper 2017-39. (July 2017). https://www.census.gov/content/dam/Census/library/working-papers/2017/demo/SEHSD-WP2017-39.pdf.

Behaghel, Luc, and David Blau, "Framing Social Security Reform: Behavioral Responses to Changes in the Full Retirement Age." *American Economic Journal: Economic Policy* 4, no. 4 (2012): 41–67. doi:10.1257/pol.4.4.41.

Benartzi, Shlomo, Alessandro Previtero, and Richard H. Thaler. "Annuity Puzzles." *Journal of Economic Perspectives* 25, no. 4 (2011): 143–164. https://doi.org/10.1257/jep.25.4.143.

Benz, Christine. "100 Must-Know Statistics About Long-Term Care: Pandemic Edition." *Morningstar*. (December 8, 2020). https://www.morningstar.com/articles/1013929/100-must-know-statistics-about-long-term-care-pandemic-edition.

Berg, Peter B., Mary K. Hamman, Matthew M. Piszczek, and Christopher J. Ruhm. "The Relationship Between Employer-Provided Training and the Retention of Older Workers: Evidence from Germany." *International Labour Review* 156, no. 3–4 (2017): 495–523. doi:10.1111/ilr.12031.

Bernstein, Irving. "Americans in Depression and War." US Department of Labor. (2018). https://www.dol.gov/oasam/programs/history/chapter5.htm.

Bhattarai, Abha. "Millions Retired Early During the Pandemic. Many Are Now Returning to Work, New Data Shows." *Washington Post*. (May 5, 2022). https://www.washingtonpost.com/business/2022/05/05/retirement-jobs-work-inflation-medicare/.

Bipartisan Policy Center. "Initial Recommendations to Improve the Financing of Long-Term Care." (February 2016). https://bipartisanpolicy.org/wp-content/uploads/2019/03/BPC-Health-Long-Term-Care-Financing-Recommendations.pdf.

Blasi, Joseph, and Douglas Kruse. "2018 Annual Business Survey Analysis." Unpublished note based on survey data. (July 2020). https://www.census.gov/data/tables/2018/econ/abs/2018-abs-company-summary.html.

Blay, Joyce. "Annuity Sales Increase 14% In 2018, LIMRA Says." *Financial Advisor*. (February 20, 2019). https://www.fa-mag.com/news/limra-reports-best-total-annuity-sales-quarter-since-q1-2009-43407.html.

Board of Trustees of the Federal Old-Age and Survivors Insurance and Federal Disability Insurance Trust Funds. US Government Printing Office. (2006). https://www.ssa.gov/OACT/TR/TR06/tr06.pdf.

Borsch-Supan, Axel, and Matthias Weiss. "Productivity and Age: Evidence from Work Teams at the Assembly Line." Munich Center for the Economics of Aging. (2013). https://cris.maastrichtuniversity.nl/ws/portalfiles/portal/1625281/guid-ffe3dad9-d860-439b-b4fc-bbd33c359973-ASSET1.0.pdf.

Bosworth, Barry, and Kathleen Burke. "Differential Mortality and Retirement Benefits in the Health and Retirement Study." The Brookings Institution. (April 2014). https://

www.brookings.edu/wp-content/uploads/2016/06/differential_mortality_retirement_benefits_bosworth_version_2.pdf.

Bosworth, Barry, Gary Burtless, and Kan Zhang. "Later Retirement, Inequality in Old Age, and the Growing Gap in Longevity Between Rich and Poor." The Brookings Institution. (2016). https://www.brookings.edu/wp-content/uploads/2016/02/BosworthBurtlessZhang_retirementinequalitylongevity_012815.pdf.

Bourassa, Steven, Donald Haurin, Patric H. Hendershott, and Martin Hoesli. "Mortgage Interest Deductions and Homeownership: An International Survey." Swiss Finance Institute. (2012). https://econpapers.repec.org/paper/chfrpseri/rp1206.htm.

Brady, Peter J., Steven Bass, Jessica Holland, and Kevin Pierce. "Using Panel Tax Data to Examine the Transition to Retirement." SSRN Electronic Journal. (March 2017). doi:10.2139/ssrn.2928375.

Brien, Michael J., and Constantin W. A. Panis. "Annuities in the Context of Defined Contribution Plans." US Department of Labor. (November 2011). https://www.dol.gov/sites/default/files/ebsa/researchers/analysis/retirement/annuities-in-the-context-of-defined-contribution-plans.pdf.

Brown, Jason, and Karen Dynan. "Increasing the Economic Security of Older Women." The Brookings Institution. (October 2017). https://www.hamiltonproject.org/assets/files/increasing_economic_security_older_women_BrownDynan.pdf.

Brown, Jeffrey R., and Amy Finkelstein. "Insuring Long-Term Care in the United States." Journal of Economic Perspectives 25, no. 4 (2011): 119–142. https://doi.org/10.1257/jep.25.4.119.

Brown, Jeffrey R., Jeffrey R. Kling, Sendhil Mullainathan, and Marian V. Wrobel. "Framing and Annuities." TIAA Institute. (2009). https://www.tiaainstitute.org/sites/default/files/presentations/2017-02/report_ti_framingannuities_0109.pdf.

Brown, Jeffrey R., Jeffrey R. Kling, Sendhil Mullainathan, and Marian V. Wrobel. "Why Don't People Insure Late-Life Consumption? A Framing Explanation of the Under-Annuitization Puzzle." American Economic Review 98, no. 2 (May 2008): 304–309.

Browning, Martin, and Thomas F. Crossley. "The Life-Cycle Model of Consumption and Saving." Journal of Economic Perspectives 15, no. 3 (2001): 3–22. doi:10.1257/jep.15.3.3.

Brynjolfsson, Erik, and Andrew McAfee. The Second Machine Age: Work, Progress, and Prosperity in a Time of Brilliant Technologies. New York: W. W. Norton & Company, 2014.

Bui, Truc Thi Mai, Patrick Button, and Elyce G. Picciotti. "Early Evidence on the Impact of COVID-19 and the Recession on Older Workers." NBER Working Paper 27448. (June 2020). https://www.nber.org/papers/w27448.

Burman, Leonard, William Gale, Matthew Hall, and Peter Orszag. "Distributional Effects of Defined Benefit Contribution Plans and Individual Retirement Accounts." Urban Institute and Brookings Institution Tax Policy Center, Discussion Paper No. 16. (August 2004). https://www.urban.org/sites/default/files/publication/57696/311029-Distributional-Effects-of-Defined-Contribution-Plans-and-Individual-Retirement-Accounts.PDF.

Bursztyn, Leonardo, Florian Ederer, Bruno Ferman, and Noam Yuchtman. "Understanding Mechanisms Underlying Peer Effects: Evidence from a Field Experiment on Financial Decisions." Econometrica 82, no. 4 (2014): 1273–1301. https://doi.org/10.3982/ECTA11991.

Burtless, Gary. "Age-Related Health Costs and Job Prospects of Older Workers." Stanford Institute for Economic Policy Research. (October 2017). https://siepr.stanford.edu/system/files/BURTLESS_Age-Related-Health-Costs_1st-Draft_Oct-2017.pdf.

Burtless, Gary. "Is an Aging Workforce Less Productive?" The Brookings Institution. (June 2013). https://www.brookings.edu/blog/up-front/2013/06/10/is-an-aging-workforce-less-productive/.

Burtless, Gary. "The Growing Life-Expectancy Gap Between Rich and Poor." The Brookings Institution. (February 2016). https://www.brookings.edu/opinions/the-growing-life-expectancy-gap-between-rich-and-poor/.

Burtless, Gary. "Social Norms, Rules of Thumb, and Retirement: Evidence for Rationality in Retirement Planning." The Brookings Institution. (November 2004). https://www.brookings.edu/wp-content/uploads/2016/06/CSED37.pdf.

Burtless, Gary, Barry Bosworth, and Kan Zhang. "Later Retirement, Inequality in Old Age, and the Growing Gap in Longevity between Rich and Poor." The Brookings Institution. (February 2016). https://www.brookings.edu/wp-content/uploads/2016/02/BosworthBurtlessZhang_retirementinequalitylongevity_012815.pdf.

Butrica, Barbara, and Nadia Karamcheva. "The Impact of Informal Caregiving on Older Adults' Labor Supply and Economic Resources." Congressional Budget Office. (October 2014). https://www.researchgate.net/publication/286448788_The_Impact_of_Informal_Caregiving_on_Older_Adults'_Labor_Supply_and_Economic_Resources.

Cajner, Tomaz, Leland D. Crane, Ryan A. Decker, John Grigsby, Adrian Hamins-Puertolas, Erik Hurst, Christopher Kurz, and Ahu Yildirmaz. "The U.S. Labor Market During the Beginning of the Pandemic Recession." Becker Friedman Institute Working Paper 2020-58, University of Chicago. (July 2020). https://bfi.uchicago.edu/wp-content/uploads/BFI_WP_202058-1.pdf.

Cappelli, Peter, and William D. Novelli. *Managing the Older Worker: How to Prepare for the New Organizational Order*. Boston: Harvard Business Review Press, 2010.

Case, Anne, and Angus Deaton. "Mortality and Morbidity in the 21st Century." The Brookings Institution. (March 2017). https://www.brookings.edu/wp-content/uploads/2017/08/casetextsp17bpea.pdf.

Casselman, Ben. "I Had to Go Back: Over 65 and Not Retired After All." *New York Times*. (May 19, 2022). https://www.nytimes.com/2022/05/19/business/economy/older-workers-labor-force.html.

Center for Medicare and Medicaid Services. "COVID-19 Nursing Home Data." (Data through September 5, 2021). https://data.cms.gov/covid-19/covid-19-nursing-home-data.

Centers for Disease Control. "Health, United States 2010: With Special Feature on Death and Dying." No. 2011-1232. National Center for Health Statistics. (February 2011). https://www.cdc.gov/nchs/data/hus/hus10.pdf.

Centers for Disease Control. "Loneliness and Social Isolation Linked to Serious Health Conditions." (2020). https://www.cdc.gov/aging/publications/features/lonely-older-adults.html.

Centers for Disease Control. "Long-term Care Providers and Services Users in the United States, 2015–2016." No. 2019–1427. *National Center for Health Statistics* 3, no. 43 (2019).

Centers for Disease Control. "Nursing Home Care Data." National Center for Health Statistics. (Last modified May 20, 2020). https://www.cdc.gov/nchs/fastats/nursing-home-.htm.

Centers for Disease Control. "Provisional Death Counts for Coronavirus Disease 2019 (COVID-19)." National Center for Health Statistics. (Updated September 30, 2020). https://www.cdc.gov/nchs/nvss/vsrr/covid_weekly/index.htm#Race_Hispanic.

Center on Budget and Policy Priorities. "Policy Basics: Understanding the Social Security Trust Funds." (2022). https://www.cbpp.org/sites/default/files/atoms/files/policy_basics_soc_sec_trust_funds.pdf.

Charles Schwab Corporation. "Income Annuity Estimator." (2020). https://www.schwab.com/annuities/fixed-income-annuity-calculator.

Chen, Henry, and Robert I. Lerman. "Do Asset Limits in Social Security Programs Affect the Accumulation of Wealth?." Urban Institute. (August 2005). https://www.urban.org/sites/default/files/publication/51686/311223-Do-Asset-Limits-in-Social-Programs-Affect-the-Accumulation-of-Wealth-.PDF.

Chen, Anqi, Alicia H. Munnell, and Geoffrey T. Sanzenbacher. "How Much Income Do Retirees Actually Have? Evaluating the Evidence from Five National Datasets." Center for Retirement Research at Boston College. (November 2018). https://crr.bc.edu/wp-content/uploads/2018/11/wp_2018-14__.pdf.

Chetty, Raj, John N. Friedman, Nathaniel Hendren, Michael Stepner, and the OI Team. "Opportunity Insights Economic Tracker." (2020). https://www.tracktherecovery.org/.

Chetty, Raj, John N. Friedman, Søren Leth-Petersen, Torben Heien Nielsen, and Tore Olsen. "Active vs. Passive Decisions and Crowd-Out in Retirement Savings Accounts: Evidence from Denmark." *Quarterly Journal of Economics* 129, no. 3 (2014): 1141–1219. https://doi.org/10.1093/qje/qju013.

Chiu, A., L. Bever, and A. Eunjung Cha. "Driven by Covid Deaths, U.S. Life Expectancy Dropped by 1.5 Years in 2020." *The Washington Post*. (July 21, 2021). https://www.washingtonpost.com/health/2021/07/21/life-expectancy-covid/.

Choi, James J., David Laibson, Brigitte C. Madrian, and Andrew Metrick. "Defined Contribution Pensions: Plan Rules, Participant Choices, and the Path of Least Resistance." *Tax Policy and the Economy* 16 (January 2002): 67–113. doi:10.1086/654750.

Coile, Courtney. "The Evolution of Retirement Incentives in the U.S." NBER Working Paper 25281. (2018). doi:10.3386/w25281.

Coile, Courtney, and Phillip B. Levine. *Reconsidering Retirement: How Losses and Layoffs Affect Older Workers*. Washington, DC: Brookings Institution Press, 2010.

Coile, Courtney, Kevin S. Milligan, and David A. Wise. "Health Capacity to Work at Older Ages: Evidence from the U.S." NBER Working Paper 21940. (2016). doi:10.3386/w21940.

Committee for a Responsible Federal Budget. "Analysis of CBO's 2020 Long-Term Budget Outlook." (September 21, 2020). https://www.crfb.org/papers/analysis-cbos-2020-long-term-budget-outlook.

Congressional Budget Office. "The 2019 Long-Term Budget Outlook." (June 2019). http://www.cbo.gov/publication/55331.

Congressional Budget Office. "The 2021 Long-Term Outlook." (2021). https://www.cbo.gov/publication/57038.

Congressional Budget Office. "Budget and Economic Data." (July 2021). https://www.cbo.gov/data/budget-economic-data#3.

Congressional Budget Office. "The Budget and Economic Outlook: 2019 to 2029." (2019), 45, table 2-5. https://www.cbo.gov/system/files/2019-03/54918-Outlook-3.pdf.

Congressional Budget Office. "The Budget and Economic Outlook 2022 to 2032." https://www.cbo.gov/system/files?file=2022-05/57950-Outlook.pdf.

Congressional Budget Office. "Historical Budget Data." (February 2021). https://www.cbo.gov/system/files/2021-02/51134-2021-02-11-historicalbudgetdata.xlsx.

Congressional Budget Office. "Letter to the Honorable Kay R. Hagan." (July 6, 2009). https://www.cbo.gov/sites/default/files/cbofiles/ftpdocs/104xx/doc10436/07-06-class act.pdf.

Congressional Budget Office. "Rising Demand for Long-Term Services and Supports for Elderly People." Pub. No. 4240. (June 2013). https://www.cbo.gov/sites/default/files/cbofiles/attachments/44363-LTC.pdf.

Congressional Research Service. "Poverty in the United States in 2020." CRS Report, R47030. (February 2022).https://crsreports.congress.gov/product/pdf/R/R47030.

Consumer Financial Protection Bureau. "Report to Congress on Reverse Mortgages." (June 2012). https://www.consumerfinance.gov/data-research/research-reports/reverse-mortgages-report/.

Cornell, Portia Y., David C. Grabowski, Marc Cohen, Xiaomei Shi, and David G. Stevenson. "Medical Underwriting in Long-Term Care Insurance: Market Conditions Limit Options for Higher-Risk Consumers." Health Affairs 35, no. 8 (August 2016). https://doi.org/10.1377/hlthaff.2015.1133.

Council of Economic Advisers (CEA). "The Long-Term Decline in Prime-Age Male Labor Force Participation." Executive Office of the President of the United States. (June 2016). https://obamawhitehouse.archives.gov/sites/default/files/page/files/201 60620_cea_primeage_male_lfp.pdf.

Clark, Robert L., and John B. Shoven. "Enhancing Work Incentives for Older Workers: Social Security and Medicare Proposals to Reduce Work Disincentives." The Brookings Institution. (January 31, 2019). https://www.brookings.edu/wp-cont ent/uploads/2018/12/2-Clark-Shoven.pdf.

Correia, Margarida. "Contribution Catch-up for Caregivers Gaining Favor." Pensions & Investments. (March 8, 2021). https://www.pionline.com/washington/contribution-catch-caregivers-gaining-favor.

Crimmins, Eileen M., and Hiram Beltrán-Sánchez. "Mortality and Morbidity Trends: Is There Compression of Morbidity?" The Journals of Gerontology. Series B, Psychological Sciences and Social Sciences 66, no. 1 (2011): 75–86. doi:10.1093/geronb/gbq088.

Cubanski, Julitette, Wyatt Koma, Anthony Damico, and Tricia Neuman. "How Much Do Medicare Beneficiaries Spend Out of Pocket on Health Care?" KKF. (November 2019). https://www.kff.org/medicare/issue-brief/how-much-do-medicare-beneficiar ies-spend-out-of-pocket-on-health-care/.

Davidoff, Thomas. "Can 'High Costs' Justify Weak Demand for the Home Equity Conversion Market?" *Review of Financial Studies* 28, no. 8 (August 2015): 2364–2398. https://www.jstor.org/stable/24466881.

Davidoff, Thomas. "Home Equity Commitment and Long-Term Care Insurance Demand." *Journal of Public Economics* 94, no. 1 (2010): 44–49. doi:10.1016/j.jpubeco.2009.09.006.

Davidoff, Thomas, and Gerd Welke. *Selection and Moral Hazard in the Reverse Mortgage Market.* Berkeley: University of California, Berkeley, Haas School of Business, 2007.

Davidoff, Thomas, and Jake Wetzel. "Do Reverse Mortgages Borrowers Use Credit Ruthlessly?" Working Paper. (July 22, 2014). https://ssrn.com/abstract=2279930.

Deloitte. "Defined Contribution Benchmarking Survey: From Oversight to Participant Experience: Plan Sponsors Are Taking Their Fiduciary Role Up a Notch." (2017). https://www2.deloitte.com/us/en/pages/human-capital/articles/annual-defined-contribution-benchmarking-survey.html.

Diamond, Douglas W., and Raghuram G. Rajan. "Liquidity Risk, Liquidity Creation and Financial Fragility: A Theory of Banking." NBER Working Paper 7430. (December 1999). http://www.nber.org/papers/w7430.

Duflo, Esther, William Gale, Jeffrey Liebman, Peter Orszag, Emmanuel Saez. "Saving Incentives for Low- and Middle-Income Families: Evidence from a Field Experiment with H&R Block." *Quarterly Journal of Economics* no. 1 (2006). doi:10.3386/w11680.

Duflo, Esther, Rachel Glennerster, and Michael Kremer. "Using Randomization on Development Economics Research: A Toolkit." Development Economics, Discussion Paper No. 6059. (January 2007). https://economics.mit.edu/files/806.

Duflo, Esther, and Emmanuel Saez. "The Role of Information and Social Interactions in Retirement Plan Decisions: Evidence from a Randomized Experiment." *Quarterly Journal of Economics* 118, no. 3 (2003): 815–842. https://doi.org/10.1162/0033553036 0698432.

Dunn, Megan. "Who Chooses Part Time Work and Why?" *BLS Monthly Labor Review* 141, no. 3 (March 2018): 1–25. https://www.bls.gov/opub/mlr/2018/article/pdf/who-chooses-part-time-work-and-why.pdf.

Dweck, Carol S. *Mindset: The New Psychology of Success.* New York: Random House, 2006.

Eisen, Ben, and Lisa Beilfuss. "Steak Dinner and Annuities: Retirement Product Surges After Fiduciary Rule's Demise." *Wall Street Journal.* (October 27, 2018). https://www.wsj.com/articles/steak-dinner-and-annuities-retirement-product-surges-after-fiduciary-rules-demise-1540656000.

Elder, Todd E. "The Predictive Validity of Subjective Mortality Expectations: Evidence from the Health and Retirement Study." *Demography,* 50, no. 2 (April 2013): 569–589. https://link.springer.com/article/10.1007/s13524-012-0164-2.

Ellis, Charles D., Alicia H. Munnell, and Andrew D. Esctruth. "Falling Short: The Coming Retirement Crisis and What to Do About It." Oxford Scholarship Online. (2014). https://oxford.universitypressscholarship.com/view/10.1093/acprof:oso/9780190218898.001.0001/acprof-9780190218898.

Eppsteiner, Harris, Jason Furman, and Wilson Powell. "Adjusted for Aging, the US Employment Rate Continued to Rise Above Its Pre-Recession Level in 2018." *Peterson Institute for International Economics.* (January 2019). https://www.piie.com/

blogs/realtime-economic-issues-watch/adjusted-aging-us-employment-rate-contin
ued-rise-above-its-pre.

Eppsteiner, Harris, Jason Furman, and Wilson Powell III. "An Aging Population Explains
Most—but Not All—of the Decline in the U.S. Labor Force Participation Rate Since
2007." Peterson Institute for International Economics. (July 7, 2017). https://piie.
com/blogs/realtime-economic-issues-watch/aging-population-explains-most-not-
all-decline-us-labor-force.

Executive Office of the President of the United States. "The Effects of Conflicted
Investment Advice on Retirement Savings." (February 2015). https://obamawhiteho
use.archives.gov/sites/default/files/docs/cea_coi_report_final.pdf.

Family Caregiver Alliance. "Caregiver Statistics: Demographics." National Center on
Caregiving. (April 17, 2019). https://www.caregiver.org/resource/caregiver-statistics-
demographics/.

Favreault, Melissa, and Judith Dey. "Long-Term Services and Supports for Older
Americans: Risks and Financing Research Brief." US Department of Health and
Human Services, Office of the Assistant Secretary for Planning and Evaluation. (July
1, 2015). https://aspe.hhs.gov/reports/long-term-services-supports-older-americans-
risks-financing-research-brief-0.

Fiedler, Matthew, and Zirui Song. "Estimating Potential Spending on COVID-19 Care."
The Brookings Institution. (May 7, 2020). https://www.brookings.edu/research/est
imating-potential-spending-on-covid-19-care/.

Feder, Judith, Harriet L. Komisar and Robert B. Friedland. "Long-Term Care
Financing: Policy Options for the Future." Georgetown University Long-Term Care
Financing Project. (June 2007). https://www.thescanfoundation.org/sites/default/
files/georgetown_importance_federal_financing_ltc_2.pdf.

Federal Reserve Board. "Report on the Economic Well-Being of U.S. Households in
2020–May 2021." (2021). https://www.federalreserve.gov/publications/2021-econo
mic-well-being-of-us-households-in-2020-retirement.htm.

Federal Reserve Economic Data. "Federal Outlays: Interest as Percent of Gross Domestic
Product." (July 29, 2021). https://fred.stlouisfed.org/series/FYOIGDA188S.

Federal Reserve Economic Data. "Labor Force Participation Rate." (September 3, 2021).
https://fred.stlouisfed.org/series/CIVPART.

Federal Reserve Economic Data. "Real Median Household Income in the United States."
(September 15, 2021). https://fred.stlouisfed.org/series/MEHOINUSA672N.

Fox-Grage, Wendy, and Jenna Walls. "State Studies Find Home and Community-Based
Services to Be Cost-Effective." AARP Public Policy Institute. (March 2013). https://
www.aarp.org/content/dam/aarp/research/public_policy_institute/ltc/2013/state-
studies-find-hcbs-cost-effective-spotlight-AARP-ppi-ltc.pdf.

Freedman, Vicki A., and Brenda C. Spillman. "Disability and Care Needs of Older
Americans." Milbank Quarterly 92, no. 3 (2014): 509–541.

Fry, Richard. "Amid the Pandemic, a Rising Share of Older U.S. Adults Are Now Retired."
Pew Research Center. (November 4, 2021). https://www.pewresearch.org/fact-tank/
2021/11/04/amid-the-pandemic-a-rising-share-of-older-u-s-adults-are-now-retired/.

Furman, Jason. "What Is the Potential Growth Rate of the U.S. Economy and How Might
Policy Affect It? Business Economics 52, no. 3 (July 2017): 158. https://go.gale.com/ps/

anonymous?id=GALE%7CA506828473&sid=googleScholar&v=2.1&it=r&linkacc
ess=abs&issn=0007666X&p=AONE&sw=w.

Furman, Jason, and Lawrence Summers. "A Reconsideration of Fiscal Policy in the Era of Low Interest Rates." The Brookings Institution. (November 2020). https://www. brookings.edu/wp-content/uploads/2020/11/furman-summers-fiscal-reconsiderat ion-discussion-draft.pdf.

Gailey, Alex. "How Has the Pandemic Impacted U.S. Savings Rates?" *Time*. August 30, 2021. https://time.com/nextadvisor/banking/savings/us-saving-rate-soaring/.

Gale, William. "Tax Reform Options: Promoting Retirement Security." Testimony Submitted to United States Senate Committee on Finance. (September 15, 2011). https://www.brookings.edu/wp-content/uploads/2016/06/0915_retirement_savings_ gale-1.pdf.

Gale, William G., Benjamin H. Harris, and, Ruth Levine. "Raising Household Saving: Does Financial Education Work?" *Social Security Bulletin* 72, no. 2 (May 2012): 39–48. https://ssrn.com/abstract=1953629.

Gale, William G., J. Mark Iwry, and Peter R. Orszag. "The Saver's Credit: Issues and Options." The Brookings Institution. (April 2004). https://www.brookings.edu/wp-content/uploads/2016/06/20040419.pdf.

Gale, William G., and John Sabelhaus. "Perspectives on the Household Saving Rate." *Brookings Papers on Economic Activity*. (May 1999). https://ssrn.com/abstract=1754682.

Gale, William G., and John Karl Scholz. "Intergenerational Transfers and the Accumulation of Wealth." *Journal of Economic Perspectives* 8, no. 4 (1994): 145–160. doi:10.1257/jep.8.4.145.

Gale, William G., J. Mark Iwry, and David C. John. "Wealth After Work: Innovative Reforms to Expand Retirement Security." The Brookings Institution. (2021), 82–115. https://www.brookings.edu/book/wealth-after-work/.

Garfield, Rachel, Gary Claxton, Anthony Damico, and Larry Levitt. "Eligibility for ACA Health Coverage Following Job Loss." Kaiser Family Foundation. (2020). https:// www.kff.org/coronavirus-covid-19/issue-brief/eligibility-for-aca-health-coverage-following-job-loss/.

Genworth Financial, Inc. "Cost of Care Survey." (2022). https://www.genworth.com/ aging-and-you/finances/cost-of-care.html.

Georgetown Center for Retirement Initiatives. "State-Facilitated Retirement Savings Programs: A Snapshot of Program Design Features." Georgetown University McCourt School of Public Policy, Center for Retirement Initiatives. State Brief 20-02. (August 31, 2020). https://cri.georgetown.edu/wp-content/uploads/2018/12/ CRI-State-Brief-20-02.pdf.

Glisky, E. L. "Changes in Cognitive Function in Human Aging." In *Brain Aging: Models, Methods, and Mechanisms*, edited by David R. Riddle. Boca Raton, FL: CRC Press/ Taylor & Francis, 2007. https://www.ncbi.nlm.nih.gov/pubmed/21204355.

Golding, Edward, and Laurie Goodman. "To Better Assess the Risk of FHA Programs, Separate Reverse and Forward Mortgages." *Urban Wire: The Blog of the Urban Institute*. (Last modified November 29, 2017). https://www.urban.org/urban-wire/bet ter-assess-risk-fha-programs-separate-reverse-and-forward-mortgages.

Gong, Guan, and Anthony Webb. "Evaluating the Advanced Life Deferred Annuity: An Annuity People Might Actually Buy." *Insurance: Mathematics and Economics* 46, no. 1 (2010): 210–221. http://dx.doi.org/10.1016/j.insmatheco.2009.08.010.

Gould, Elise. "State of Working America Wages 2018." Economic Policy Institute. (February 2019). https://www.epi.org/publication/state-of-american-wages-2018/.

Gross v. FBL Financial Services, Inc., 557 U.S. 167 (8th Cir. 2009).

Grotz, C., C. Meillon, H. Amieva, Y. Stern, J-F Dartigues, S. Adam, and L. Letenneur. "Why Is Later Age at Retirement Beneficial for Cognition? Results from a French Population-based Study." *Journal of Nutrition, Health and Aging* 20, no. 5 (2016): 514–519. https://doi.org/10.1007/s12603-015-0599-4.

Gurley-Calvez, Tami, Kandice A. Kapinos, and Donald Bruce. "Retirement, Recessions and Older Small Business Owners." Office of Small Business Administration Advocacy. (2020). http://dx.doi.org/10.2139/ssrn.2199615.

Hado, Eden, and Harriet Komisar. "Long-Term Services and Supports." AARP Public Policy Institute. (August 26, 2019). http://www.advancingstates.org/node/71725.

Hamilton, Brady E., Joyce Martin, and Michelle J. K. Osterman. "Births: Provisional Data for 2020." Report No. 012 NVSS. (May 2021). https://stacks.cdc.gov/view/cdc/104993.

Hannon, Kerry. "How Older Workers Can Learn New Job Skills." AARP. (February 14, 2018). https://www.aarp.org/work/job-search/info-2018/work-skills-resume-fd.html.

Harris, Benjamin. "Tax Reform, Transaction Costs, and Metropolitan Housing in the United States." Urban-Brookings Tax Policy Center. (June 2013). https://www.taxpolicycenter.org/publications/tax-reform-transaction-costs-and-metropolitan-housing-united-states.

Harris, Benjamin. "Why Annuities May Be Safer Than You Think." *Wall Street Journal.* (July 8, 2018). https://www.wsj.com/articles/why-annuities-may-be-safer-than-you-think-1531102216.

Harris, Benjamin, and Ilana Fischer. "The Population of Workers Covered by the Auto IRA: Trends and Characteristics." AARP Public Policy Institute. No. 2012-03. (February 2012). https://studylib.net/doc/14297682/the-population-of-workers-covered-by-the-auto-ira--trends...

Harris, Benjamin, and Rachel Johnson. "Economic Effects of Automatic Enrollment in Individual Retirement Accounts." AARP Public Policy Institute. No. 2012-04. (February 2012). https://documents.pub/document/the-population-of-workers-covered-by-the-auto-iratrends-auto-iras-with-an-expanded.html.

Harris, Benjamin H., C. Eugene Steuerle, Signe-Mary McKernan, Caleb Quakenbush, and Caroline Ratcliffe. "Tax Subsidies for Asset Development: An Overview and Distributional Analysis." (August, 2014). https://www.urban.org/sites/default/files/publication/22381/413048-Tax-Subsidies-for-Asset-Development-An-Overview-and-Distributional-Analysis.PDF.

Harris, Seth. "Increasing Employment for Older Workers with Effective Protections Against Employment Discrimination." The Brookings Institution. (November 2020). https://www.brookings.edu/wp-content/uploads/2020/11/ES-11.19.20-Harris.pdf.

Haurin, Donald, Cäzilia Loibl, and Stephanie Moulton. "Debt Stress and Mortgage Borrowing in Older Age: Implications for Economic Security in Retirement."

University of Wisconsin-Madison, Center for Financial Security, Retirement & Disability Research Center. (November 2019). https://cfsrdrc.wisc.edu/project/wi19-06.

Haurin, Donald, Chao Ma, Stephanie Moulton, Maximilian Schmeiser, Jason Seligman, and Wei Shi. "Spatial Variation in Reverse Mortgages Usage: House Price Dynamics and Consumer Selection." *Journal of Real Estate and Financial Economics* 53, no. 3 (2016): 392–417. doi:10.1007/s11146-014-9463-2.

Harvard Joint Center for Housing Studies. "America's Rental Housing: Meeting Challenges, Building on Opportunities." 2011. https://www.jchs.harvard.edu/sites/default/files/ahr2011-3-demographics.pdf.

"Health and Retirement Survey." (2018). Database maintained by the University of Michigan, in collaboration with the National Institute of Aging and the Social Security Administration. https://hrs.isr.umich.edu/about.

Hecker, Ian, Shayne Spaulding, and Daniel Kuehn. "Digital Skills and Older Workers." Urban Institute. (September 2021). https://www.urban.org/sites/default/files/publication/104771/digital-skills-and-older-workers_1.pdf.

Hewitt, Aon. "A Business Case for Workers Age 50+: A Look at the Value of Experience 2015." AARP Research. (2015). https://doi.org/10.26419/res.00100.001.

Holzer, Harry. "Raising Job Quality and Skills for American Workers: Creating More-Effective Education and Workforce Development Systems in the States." The Brookings Institution. (November 2011). http://www.brookings.edu/research/papers/2011/11/workforce-holzer.

Horneff, Vanya, Raimond Maurer, and Olivia Mitchell. "Automatic Enrollment in 401(k) Annuities: Boosting Retiree Lifetime Income." The Brookings Institution. (June 2019). https://www.brookings.edu/wp-content/uploads/2019/06/ES_20190620_HorneffMaurerMitchell.pdf.

Hurd, Michael, and Kathleen McGarry. "The Predictive Validity of Subjective Probabilities of Survival." *The Economic Journal* 112, no. 482 (October 2002): 966–985. https://doi.org/10.1111/1468-0297.00065.

Hurd, Michael, and Susan Rohwedder. "Economic Preparation for Retirement." RAND Working Paper Series WR-872. (June 2011). https://papers.ssrn.com/sol3/papers.cfm?abstract_id=1931775.

Hurst, Eric. "The Retirement of a Consumption Puzzle." NBER Working Paper 13789. (2008). doi:10.3386/w13789.

Hurwitz, Abigail. "Using Behavioral Insights to Increase Annuitization Rates: The Role of Framing and Anchoring." Brookings Institution. (June 2019). https://www.brookings.edu/wp-content/uploads/2019/06/ES_201906_HurwitzAnnuities.pdf.

Investment Company Institute. *2009 Investment Company Fact Book*. 49th ed. (2009). https://www.ici.org/pdf/2009_factbook.pdf.

Investment Company Institute. *2018 Investment Company Fact Book*. 58th ed. (2018). https://www.ici.org/pdf/2018_factbook.pdf.

Investment Company Institute. "The US Retirement Market, First Quarter 2021." (2021). https://www.ici.org/system/files/2021-06/ret_21_q1_data.xls.

Isom, Kelly. "Barriers to Savings: Assets Tests." Bipartisan Policy Center. (March 13, 2015). https://bipartisanpolicy.org/blog/barriers-to-savings-asset-tests/.

Iwry, J. Mark, Claire Haldeman, William G. Gale, and David C. John. "Retirement Tontines: Using a Classical Finance Mechanism an Alternative Source of Retirement Income." The Brookings Institution. (October 2020). https://www.brookings.edu/wp-content/uploads/2020/10/Retirement-Security-Project-Tontines-Oct-2020.pdf.

Jacobson, Louis S., Robert J. LaLonde, and Daniel G. Sullivan. "Earnings Losses of Displaced Workers." *American Economic Review.* (September 1993): 685–709.https://www.princeton.edu/~davidlee/wp/0.pdf.

John, David C., Grace Enda, William G. Gale, and J. Mark Iwry. "A Retirement Dashboard for the United States." In *Wealth After Work,* edited by William G. Gale, J. Mark Iwry, and David C. John. Washington, DC: The Brookings Institution, 2021, pp. 90-92.

Johns Hopkins University. "COVID-19 Dashboard by the Center for Systems Science and Engineering." Coronavirus Resource Center. (July 22, 2020). https://coronavirus.jhu.edu/map.html.

Johnson, Ben. "How Low Can Fund Fees Go?" *Morningstar.* (August 24, 2021). https://www.morningstar.com/articles/1055229/how-low-can-fund-fees-go.

Johnson, Richard W. "The Case Against Early Retirement." *The Wall Street Journal.* (April 21, 2019). https://www.wsj.com/articles/the-case-against-early-retirement-11555899000.

Johnson, Richard W. "What Is the Lifetime Risk of Needing and Receiving Long-Term Services and Support?" US Department of Health and Human Services, Office of Disability, Aging and Long-Term Care Policy. (April 4, 2019). https://www.urban.org/research/publication/what-lifetime-risk-needing-and-receiving-long-term-services-and-supports.

Johnson, Richard W. "Who Is Covered by Private Long-Term Care Insurance?" Program on Retirement Policy, Urban Institute. (2016). https://www.urban.org/sites/default/files/publication/83146/2000881-Who-Is-Covered-by-Private-Long-Term-Care-Insurance.pdf.

Johnson, Richard W., and Peter Gosselin. "How Secure Is Employment at Older Ages?" The Urban Institute. (2018). https://www.urban.org/research/publication/how-secure-employment-older-ages.

Johnson, Richard W., and Corina Mommaerts. "Age Differences in Job Loss, Job Search, and Reemployment." Retirement Policy Discussion Paper Series, Urban Institute. (January 2011). https://www.urban.org/research/publication/age-differences-job-loss-job-search-and-reemployment.

Johnson Hess, Abigail. "The U.S. Has a Record-Breaking $1.73 Trillion in Student Debt: Borrowers from These States Owe the Most on Average." *CNBC.* (September 9, 2021). https://www.cnbc.com/2021/09/09/america-has-1point73-trillion-in-student-debtborrowers-from-these-states-owe-the-most.html.

Joint Center for Housing Studies of Harvard University. "Housing America's Older Adults 2019." Harvard University. (2019). https://www.jchs.harvard.edu/sites/default/files/Harvard_JCHS_Housing_Americas_Older_Adults_2019.pdf.

Kahneman, Daniel. *Thinking Fast and Slow.* New York: Farrar, Straus and Giroux, 2011.

Kahneman, Daniel, and Amos Tversky. "Prospect Theory: An Analysis of Decision Under Risk." *Econometrica* 47, no. 2 (1979): 263–91. https://doi.org/10.2307/1914185.

Kaiser Family Foundation. "Distribution of Medicaid Spending by Service." (2019). https://www.kff.org/medicaid/state-indicator/distribution-of-medicaid-spend ing-by-service/?currentTimeframe=0&sortModel=%7B%22colId%22:%22Locat ion%22,%22sort%22:%22asc%22%7D.

Kerr, Nancy. "Credit for Caring Act Would Provide Tax Credit to Family Caregivers." AARP. (July 15, 2021). https://www.aarp.org/caregiving/financial-legal/info-2021/ new-credit-for-caring-act.html.

Khalfani-Cox, Lynnette. "5 Tips for Discussing Money Matters with Family." AARP. (November 18, 2013). https://www.aarp.org/caregiving/financial-legal/info-2017/fam ily-finances-money.html.

Konetzka, R. Tamara, D. Jung, R. Gorges, and P. Sanghavi. "Is Being Home Good for Your Health? Outcomes of Medicaid Home- and Community-Based Long-Term Care Relative to Nursing Home Care." *Health Services Research* 55, no. 51 (August 2020). https://doi.org/10.1111/1475-6773.13354.

Krause, Eleanor, and Isabel V. Sawhill. "What We Know and Don't Know About Declining Labor Force Participation: A Review." The Brookings Institution. (May 2017). https://www.brookings.edu/research/what-we-know-and-dont-know-about- declining-labor-force-participation-a-review/.

Kutty, Nandinee. "The Scope for Poverty Alleviation Among Elderly Home-Owners in the United States through Reverse Mortgages." *Urban Studies* 35, no. 1 (January 1998): 113–129. https://www.jstor.org/stable/43083795.

Laibson, David. "Behavioral Economics and Aging." RAND Corporation. (July 8, 2009). https://scholar.harvard.edu/laibson/publications/behavioral-economics-and-aging.

Livingston, Gretchen. "Is U.S. Fertility at an All-Time Low? Two of Three Measures Point to Yes." Pew Research Center. (May 22, 2019). https://www.pewresearch.org/ fact-tank/2019/05/22/u-s-fertility-rate-explained/.

Looney, Adam, and Constantine Yannelis. "A Crisis in Student Loans? How Changes in the Characteristics of Borrowers and in the Institutions They Attended Contributed to Rising Loan Defaults." *Brookings Papers on Economic Activity* (Fall 2015). https:// www.brookings.edu/wp-content/uploads/2015/09/LooneyTextFall15BPEA.pdf.

Love, David, Michael Palumbo, and Paul A. Smith. "The Trajectory of Wealth in Retirement." *Journal of Public Economics* 93, nos. 1–2 (2009): 191–208. https://econpap ers.repec.org/article/eeepubeco/v_3a93_3ay_3a2009_3ai_3a1-2_3ap_3a191-208.htm.

Lucas, Deborah J. "Hacking Reverse Mortgages." MIT Sloan Working Paper 5401-15. (October 2015). https://mitsloan.mit.edu/shared/ods/documents/?PublicationDoc umentID=4596.

Lund, Susan, James Manyika, Liz Hilton Segel, André Dua, Bryan Hancock, Scott Rutherford, and Brent Macon. "The Future of Work in America: People and Places, Today and Tomorrow." McKinsey Global Institute. (July 2019). https://www.mckin sey.com/featured-insights/future-of-work/the-future-of-work-in-america-people- and-places-today-and-tomorrow.

Lusardi, Annamaria. "Financial Literacy: An Essential Tool for Informed Consumer Choice?" NBER Working Paper 14084. (2008). https://www.nber.org/papers/w14 084.pdf.

Lusardi, Annamaria, and Peter Tufano. "Teach Workers About the Perils of Debt." *Harvard Business Review*. (November 2019). https://hbr.org/2009/11/teach-workers-about-the-perils-of-debt.

Madrian, Brigitte C., and Dennis F. Shea. "The Power of Suggestion: Inertia in 401(k) Participation and Savings Behavior." *Quarterly Journal of Economics* 116 (November 2001): 1149–1187. doi:10.3386/w7682.

Maestas, Nicole. "Back to Work: Expectations and Realizations of Work After Retirement." *Journal of Human Resources* 45, no. 3 (Summer 2010): 718–748. doi:10.1:353/jhr.2010.0011.

Maestas, Nicole, and Julie Zissimopoulos. "How Longer Work Lives Ease the Crunch of Population Aging." *Journal of Economic Perspectives* 24, no. 1 (2010): 139–160. doi:10.1257/jep.24.1.139.

Marcus, John. "In One Year, Pandemic Forced Millions of Workers to Retire Early." AARP. (March 10, 2021). https://www.aarp.org/work/working-at-50-plus/info-2021/pandemic-workers-early-retirement.html.

Mastrobuoni, Giovanni. "Labor Supply Effects of the Recent Social Security Benefit Cuts: Empirical Estimates Using Cohort Discontinuities." *Journal of Public Economics* 93, no. 11–12 (2009): 1224–1233. doi:10.1016/j.jpubeco.2009.07.009.

Mayer, Christopher J., and Katerina V. Simons. "Reverse Mortgages and the Liquidity of Housing Wealth." *Journal of the American Real Estate and Urban Economics Association* 22, no. 2 (1994): 235–255. doi:10.1111/1540-6229.00634.

McKeever, Kent. "A Short History of Tontines." *Fordham Journal of Corporate & Financial Law* 15, no. 2 (2009): 491–521.

Meadows, Donella H., Dennis L. Meadows, Jorgen Randers, and William W. Behrens III. *The Limits to Growth*. (March 2, 1972). Potomac Associates-Universe Books, ISBN 0-87663-165-0.

Merrill, Sally R., Meryl Finkel, and Nandinee K. Kutty. "Potential Beneficiaries from Reverse Mortgage Products for Elderly Homeowners: An Analysis of American Housing Survey Data." *Journal of the American Real Estate and Urban Economics Association* 22, no. 2 (1994): 257–299. doi:10.1111/1540-6229.00635.

Miceli, Thomas J., and C. F. Sirmans. "Reverse Mortgages and Borrower Maintenance Risk." *Journal of the American Real Estate and Urban Economics Association* 22, no. 2 (1994): 433–450. doi:10.1111/1540-6229.00641.

Michelangeli, Valentina. "Does It Pay to Get a Reverse Mortgage?" Researchgate. (September 15, 2007). https://www.researchgate.net/profile/Valentina-Michelangeli/publication/241120546_Does_it_Pay_to_Get_a_Reverse_Mortgage/links/5fa953b62 99bf10f73302800/Does-it-Pay-to-Get-a-Reverse-Mortgage.pdf.

Miklos, Suzanne M., and Harvey L. Sterns. "The Aging Worker in a Changing Environment: Organizational and Individual Issues." *Journal of Vocational Behavior* 47, no. 3 (1995): 248–268.

Mirrlees, J. A. "An Exploration in the Theory of Optimum Income Taxation." *Review of Economic Studies* 38, no. 2 (1971): 175–208. doi:10.2307/2296779.

Modigliani, Franco. "The Life Cycle Hypothesis of Saving, the Demand for Wealth and the Supply of Capital." *Social Research* 33, no. 2 (1966): 160–217.

Money Geek. "The Sobering Cost of Long-Term Care: A Guide to Paying for Care Without Breaking the Bank." Moneygeek.com. (2020). https://www.moneygeek.com/seniors/resources/paying-for-long-term-care-guide/.

"Monthly Statistical Snapshot." US Social Security Administration. (2018). https://www.ssa.gov/policy/docs/quickfacts/stat_snapshot/2018-07.pdf.

"More Than 40% of U.S. Coronavirus Deaths Are Linked to Nursing Homes." *New York Times* (September 2020). https://www.nytimes.com/interactive/2020/us/coronavirus-nursing-homes.html.

Morrissey, Monique. "The State of American Retirement Savings." Economic Policy Institute. (December 10, 2019). https://files.epi.org/pdf/136219.pdf

Moulton, Stephanie, and Donald Haurin. "Unlocking Housing Wealth for Older Americans: Strategies to Improve Reverse Mortgages." The Brookings Institution. (October 2019). https://www.brookings.edu/research/unlocking-housing-wealth-for-older-americans-strategies-to-improve-reverse-mortgages/.

Moulton, Stephanie, Donald R. Haurin, and Wei Shi. "An Analysis of Default Risk in the Home Equity Conversion Mortgage (HECM) Program." *Journal of Urban Economics* 90, no. 1 (November 2015): 17–34. doi:10.1016/j.jue.2015.08.002.

Moulton, Stephanie, Cazillia Loibl, and Donald Haurin. "Reverse Mortgages, Motivations and Outcomes." *Cityscape* 19, no. 1 (2017): 73–98. https://www.jstor.org/stable/26328299.

Mudrazija, Stipica, and Richard W. Johnson. "Economic Impacts of Programs to Support Caregivers: Final Report to the Office of the Assistant Secretary for Planning and Evaluation, U.S. Department of Health and Human Services." (January 2020). https://aspe.hhs.gov/sites/default/files/migrated_legacy_files//194136/EconImpact.pdf.

Munnell, Alicia, and Anqi Chen. "401(k)/IRA Holdings in 2016: An Update from the SCF." Center for Retirement Research at Boston College. (October 2017). https://crr.bc.edu/briefs/401kira-holdings-in-2016-an-update-from-the-scf/.

Munnell, Alicia H., and Anqi Chen. "The National Retirement Risk Index: An Update from the 2019 SCF." Center for Retirement Research at Boston College. Issue in Brief 21-2. (January 2021). https://crr.bc.edu/wp-content/uploads/2021/01/IB_21-2.pdf.

Munnell, Alicia H., and Anqi Chen. "Trends in Social Security Claiming." Center for Retirement Research at Boston College. Issue in Brief 15-8. (2015). https://crr.bc.edu/briefs/trends-in-social-security-claiming/.

Munnell, Alicia H., Wenliang Hou, and Anthony Webb. "Will the Explosion of Student Debt Widen the Retirement Security Gap?" Center for Retirement Research, Boston College. (February 2016). https://crr.bc.edu/wp-content/uploads/2019/12/IB_16-2.pdf.

Munnell, Alicia H., and Steven A. Sass. "The Government's Redesigned Reverse Mortgage Program." Center for Retirement Research at Boston College. *Issue in Brief* 14, no. 1 (January 2014): 1–6. http://crr.bc.edu/wp-content/uploads/2014/01/IB_14-1_508x.pdf.

Munnell, Alicia, and Abigail Walters. "Keeping Older People in the Labor Force." The Brookings Institution. (January 2019). https://www.brookings.edu/wp-content/uploads/2018/12/3-Munnell-Walters.pdf.

Mutual of Omaha Insurance Company. "Long-Term Care Insurance Calculator." (2020). https://www.mutualofomaha.com/long-term-care-insurance/calculator.

Nakajima, Makuto, and Irina Telyukova. "Home Equity in Retirement." Federal Reserve Bank of Philadelphia Working Paper 19-50. (December 2019). https://philadelphia fed.org/-/media/research-and-data/publications/working-papers/2019/wp19-50.pdf.

Nakajima, Makoto, and Irina A. Telyukova. "Reverse Mortgage Loans: A Quantitative Analysis." *Journal of Finance* 72, no. 2 (April 2017): 911–950. doi:10.1111/jofi.12489.

National Academies of Sciences, Engineering, and Medicine. *Social Isolation and Loneliness in Older Adults: Opportunities for the Health Care System.* Washington, DC: The National Academies Press, 2020. https://doi.org/10.17226/25663.

National Reverse Mortgage Lenders Association. "HECM Endorsement Analytics – June 2019." (Last modified July 3, 2019). https://www.nrmlaonline.org/2019/07/03/hecm-endorsement-analytics-june-2019.

Neumark, David. "Strengthening Age Discrimination Protections to Help Confront the Challenge of Population Aging." The Brookings Institution. (November 2020). https://www.brookings.edu/wp-content/uploads/2020/11/ES-11.19.20-Neumark.pdf

Oakley, Diane, Jennifer Erin Brown, and Joel Saad-Lessler. "Retirement in America | Out of Reach for Most Americans?" National Institute on Retirement Security. (2018). https://www.nirsonline.org/reports/retirement-in-america-out-of-reach-for-most-americans/.

Okun, Arthur M., William Fellner, and Alan Greenspan. "Upward Mobility in a High-Pressure Economy." *Brookings Papers on Economic Activity* (Spring 1973): 207–261. doi:10.2307/2534087.

Olsen, Skylar. "Experts: Spring's Missing Home Sales Will Be Added to Coming Years." Zillow Research. (2020). https://www.zillow.com/research/zhpe-missing-home-sales-27209/.

O'Malley Watts, Molly, MaryBeth Musumeci, and Priya Chidambaram. "Medicaid Home and Community-Based Services Enrollment and Spending." Kaiser Family Foundation. (February 2020). https://www.kff.org/report-section/medicaid-home-and-community-based-services-enrollment-and-spending-issue-brief/.

Organisation of Economic Co-operation and Development (OECD). "Revenue Statistics 2019: Tax Revenue Trends in the OECD." (2019). https://www.oecd.org/tax/tax-policy/revenue-statistics-highlights-brochure.pdf.

Oster, Emily, Ira Shoulson, Kimberly Quaid, and E. Ray Dorsey. "Genetic Adverse Selection: Evidence from Long-Term Care Insurance and Huntington Disease." Working Paper 15326, National Bureau of Economic Research. (September 2009). https://www.nber.org/system/files/working_papers/w15326/w15326.pdf.

Ott, Matt. "US Budget Deficit Climbs to Record $2.81 Trillion." *Associated Press.* (August 12, 2020). https://apnews.com/article/business-u-s-news-virus-outbreak-economy-b91e66dc273756b3fab87fe89c7cf29c.

Pacific Standard Staff. "Is It Getting Easier for Companies to Cover up Discrimination?" Pacific Standard. (March 23, 2017). https://psmag.com/news/is-it-getting-easier-for-companies-to-cover-up-age-discrimination.

Paz Garcia, Norma, Prescott Cole, and Shawna Reeves. "Examining Faulty Foundations in Today's Reverse Mortgages." Consumer Reports. (December 2010). https://advoc

acy.consumerreports.org/wp-content/uploads/2013/02/reverse-mortgage-report-2010.pdf.

Penzenstadler, Nick, and Jeff Kelly Lowenstein. "Seniors Were Sold a Risk-Free Retirement with Reverse Mortgages. Now They Face Foreclosure." *USA Today.* (December 18, 2019). https://www.usatoday.com/in-depth/news/investigations/2019/06/11/seniors-face-foreclosure-retirement-after-failed-reverse-mortgage/1329043001/.

Perl, Libby. "HUD's Reverse Mortgage Insurance Program: Home Equity Conversion Mortgages." Congressional Research Service. (March 2017). https://fas.org/sgp/crs/misc/R44128.pdf.

Perry, Mark. J. "The Main Reason for the Loss of US Steel Jobs Is a Huge Increase in Worker Productivity, Not Imports, and the Jobs Aren't Coming Back." *AEIdeas.* (March 7, 2018). https://www.aei.org/carpe-diem/the-main-reason-for-the-loss-of-us-steel-jobs-is-productivity-and-technology-not-imports-and-theyre-not-coming-back/.

Pew Charitable Trusts. "How the Market Downturn Could Affect Public Pension Funds." Pew. (April 2020). https://www.pewtrusts.org/en/research-and-analysis/articles/2020/04/23/how-the-market-downturn-could-affect-public-pension-funds.

Pew Charitable Trusts. "The State Pension Funding Gap: 2017." Pew. (July 2019). https://www.pewtrusts.org/en/research-and-analysis/issue-briefs/2019/06/the-state-pension-funding-gap-2017.

Pew Charitable Trusts. "Who's In, Who's Out: A Look at Access to Employer-Based Retirement Plans and Participation in the States." Pew. (January 2016). https://www.pewtrusts.org/-/media/assets/2016/01/retirement_savings_report_jan16.pdf.

Picchio, Matteo. "Is Training Effective for Older Workers?" IZA World of Labor, Institute of Labor Economics. (January 2015). https://ideas.repec.org/a/iza/izawol/journly2015n121.html.

Pinnacle Actuarial Resources. "Fiscal Year 2018 Independent Actuarial Review of the Mutual Mortgage Insurance Fund: Cash Flow Net Present Value from Home Equity Conversion Mortgage Insurance-In-Force." (November 2018). https://www.hud.gov/sites/dfiles/Housing/documents/ActuarialMMIFHECM2018.pdf.

Poterba, James M. "Retirement Security in an Aging Population." *American Economic Review* 104, no. 5 (2014): 1–30. doi:10.1257/aer.104.5.1.

Poterba, James M. "Retirement Security in an Aging Society." NBER Working Paper No. 19930. (February 2014). https://www.nber.org/papers/w19930.

Poterba, James M., and Todd Sinai. "Revenue Costs and Incentive Effects of the Mortgage Interest Deduction for Owner-Occupied Housing." *National Tax Journal,* 64 no. 2 (2011): 531–564. dx.doi.org/10.17310/ntj.2011.2S.05.

Poterba, James, Steven Venti, and David Wise. "Health, Education, and the Post-Retirement Evolution of Household Assets." NBER Working Paper No. 18695. (January 2013). https://www.nber.org/papers/w18695.

Raftery, Adrian. "The Dip in US Birthrate Isn't a Crisis, but the Fall in Immigration May Be." *The Conversation.* (June 21, 2021). https://theconversation.com/the-dip-in-the-us-birthrate-isnt-a-crisis-but-the-fall-in-immigration-may-be-161169.

Rasmussen, David, Isaac F. Megbolugbe, and Barbara A. Morgan. "Using the 1990 Public Use Microdata Sample to Estimate Potential Demand for Reverse Mortgage Products." *Journal of Housing Research* 6, no. 1 (1995): 1–23. https://www.jstor.org/stable/24825888.

Rau, Jordan. "Why Glaring Quality Gaps Among Nursing Homes Are Likely to Grow If Medicaid Is Cut." KHN News from the Kaiser Family Foundation. (September 28, 2017). https://khn.org/news/why-glaring-quality-gaps-among-nursing-homes-are-likely-to-grow-if-medicaid-is-cut/.

Redfoot, Donald L., Ken Scholen, and S. Kathi Brown. "Reverse Mortgages: Niche Product or Mainstream Solution? Report on the 2006 AARP National Survey of Reverse Mortgage Shoppers." AARP Public Policy Institute. (December 2007). https://www.aarp.org/money/budgeting-saving/info-2007/2007_22_revmortgage.html.

Retirement Income Journal. "One Bright Spot in First Quarter Annuity Sales." (May 21, 2020). https://retirementincomejournal.com/article/one-bright-spot-in-first-quarter-annuity-sales-limra-sri/.

Richard M. Villarreal v. R.J. Reynolds Tobacco Company, No. 15-10602. 11th Cir. (2015).

Rohwedder, Susann, and Robert J. Willis. "Mental Retirement." *Journal of Economic Perspectives* 24, no. 1 (Winter 2010): 119–138. https://doi.org/10.1257/jep.24.1.119.

Rowland, Diane. "Testimony to the Commission on Long-Term Care." Federal Commission on Long-Term Care. (August 1, 2013). https://www.kff.org/wp-content/uploads/2013/08/drowland_08-01-13-testimony-what-would-strengthen-medicaid-long-term-services-and-supports.pdf.

Ruseski, J. E., and A. A. Wadsworth. "Adverse Selection and Long-Term Care." In *Encyclopedia of Gerontology and Population Aging*, edited by D. Gu and M Dupre. Springer, Cham, 2019. https://doi.org/10.1007/978-3-319-69892-2_996-1, https://link.springer.com/referenceworkentry/10.1007/978-3-319-69892-2_996-1.

Rutledge, Robb, Peter Smittenaar, Peter Zeidman, Harriet Brown, Rick Adams, Ulman Lindenberger, Peter Dayan, and Raymond Dolan. "Risk Taking for Potential Reward Decreases across the Lifespan." *Current Biology* 26 (2016). 10.1016/j.cub.2016.05.017.

Sawhill, Isabel V., and Christopher Pulliam. "Six Facts About Wealth in the United States." The Brookings Institution. (June 2019). https://www.brookings.edu/blog/up-front/2019/06/25/six-facts-about-wealth-in-the-united-states/.

Scholz, John Karl, Ananth Seshadri, and Surachai Khitatrakun. "Are Americans Saving 'Optimally' for Retirement?" *Journal of Political Economy* 114, no. 4 (2006): 607–643. doi:10.1086/506335.

Schumacher, E. F. *Small Is Beautiful: A Study of Economics as if People Mattered.* London: Blond and Briggs, 1973.

Scott, Jason, John G. Watson, and Wei-Yin Hu. "Efficient Annuitization: Optimal Strategies for Hedging Mortality Risk." PRC WP2007-09, Pension Research Council, The University of Pennsylvania. (November 2007). https://pensionresearchcouncil.wharton.upenn.edu/wp-content/uploads/2015/09/WP09-ScottWatsonHu-11.2.07.pdf.

Shan, Hui. "Reversing the Trend: The Recent Expansion of the Reverse Mortgage Market." *Real Estate Economics* 39, no. 4 (Winter 2011): 743–768. doi:10.1111/j.1540-6229.2011.00310.x.

Sloan, Frank A., V. Kerry Smith, and Donald H. Taylor Jr. "Longevity Expectations and Death: Can People Predict Their Own Demise?" *American Economic Review* 91, no. 4 (February 2001): 1126–1134. https://www.researchgate.net/deref/http%3A%2F%2Fdx. doi.org%2F10.2139%2Fssrn.236813.

Smith, Karen, Mauricio Soto, and Rudolph Penner. "How Seniors Change Their Asset Holdings During Retirement." CCR Working Paper 2009-31. (December 2009). https://crr.bc.edu/wp-content/uploads/2009/12/wp_2009-31-508.pdf.

Social Security Administration. "Annual Statistical Supplement, 2021." (2021). https://www.ssa.gov/policy/docs/statcomps/supplement/2021/6b.pdf.

Social Security Administration. "Life Expectancy for Social Security." Social Security History. (2021). https://www.ssa.gov/history/lifeexpect.html.

Social Security Administration. "Monthly Statistical Snapshot, July 2021." (August 2021). https://www.ssa.gov/policy/docs/quickfacts/stat_snapshot/.

Social Security Administration. "Social Security Basic Facts." (2021). https://www.ssa.gov/news/press/factsheets/basicfact-alt.pdf.

Social Security Administration. "Status of the Social Security and Medicare Programs." (2020). https://www.ssa.gov/oact/TRSUM/images/LD_ChartE.html.

Social Security and Medicare Boards of Trustees. "Status of the Social Security and Medicare Programs." US Social Security Administration. (2018). https://www.ssa.gov/oact/TRSUM/tr18summary.pdf.

Society for Human Resource Management. "2017 Employee Benefits: Remaining Competitive in a Challenging Talent Marketplace." 17-0428. (2017). https://www.shrm.org/hr-today/trends-and-forecasting/research-and-surveys/Documents/2017%20Employee%20Benefits%20Report.pdf.

Spillman, Brenda C. "Why Do Elders Receiving Informal Home Care Transition to Long Stay Nursing Home Residency?" US Department of Health and Human Services, Office of the Assistant Secretary for Planning and Evaluation. (2014). https://aspe.hhs.gov/reports/why-do-elders-receiving-informal-home-care-transition-long-stay-nursing-home-residency-0.

Stark, Ellen. "Expanding Retirement Security Through Public and Private Innovation." Aspen Institute Financial Security Program. (2018). https://assets.aspeninstitute.org/content/uploads/2018/08/2018_RetirementSavingsReport.pdf.

Stark, Ellen. "5 Things You SHOULD Know About Long-Term Care Insurance." *AARP Bulletin.* (March 1, 2018). https://www.aarp.org/caregiving/financial-legal/info-2018/long-term-care-insurance-fd.html.

Statista. "Number of Retired Workers Receiving Social Security in the United States from 2010 to 2020." (2020). https://www.statista.com/statistics/194295/number-of-us-retired-workers-who-receive-social-security/.

Sullivan, Daniel, and Till von Wachter. "Job Displacement and Mortality: An Analysis Using Administrative Data." *Quarterly Journal of Economics* 124, no. 3 (August 2009): 1265–1306. https://www.jstor.org/stable/40506257.

Swagel, Phill. "CBO's Current Projections of Output, Employment, and Interest Rates and a Preliminary Look at Federal Deficits for 2020 and 2021." CBO Blog, Congressional Budget Office. (April 2020). https://www.cbo.gov/publication/56335.

Tax Policy Center. "Key Elements of the U.S. Tax System." Urban Institute and Brookings Institution. (2020). https://www.taxpolicycenter.org/briefing-book/key-elements-us-tax-system.

Tax Policy Center. "T18-0128 Tax Units with Zero or Negative Income Tax Under Current Law, 2011-2028." Urban Institute & Brookings Institution Tax Policy Center. September 2018. https://www.taxpolicycenter.org/model-estimates/tax-units-zero-or-negative-income-tax-liability-september-2018/t18-0128-tax-units.

Thaler, Richard, and Cass Sunstein. *Nudge: Improving Decisions About Health, Wealth, and Happiness.* New Haven: Yale University Press, 2008.

Thornton, Alexandra. "Taking Stock of Spending Through the Tax Code." Center for American Progress. (July 25, 2019). https://www.americanprogress.org/issues/economy/reports/2019/07/25/472678/taking-stock-spending-tax-code/.

Toossi, Mitra, and Elka Torpey. "Older Workers: Labor Force Trends and Career Options." Career Outlook, Bureau of Labor Statistics. (May 2017). https://www.bls.gov/careeroutlook/2017/article/older-workers.htm.

Tuccille, J. D. "Shaky Social Security Trust Fund May Run Out in 11 Years." *Reason.* (July 14, 2021). https://reason.com/2021/07/14/shaky-social-security-trust-fund-may-run-out-in-11-years/.

Twomey, Tara, and Rick Jurgens. "Subprime Revisited: How Reverse Mortgage Lenders Put Older Homeowners' Equity at Risk." National Consumer Law Center. (October 2009). https://www.nclc.org/images/pdf/pr-reports/report-reverse-mortgages-2009.pdf.

US Bureau of Labor Statistics. "Civilian Labor Force Participation Rate by Age, Sex, Race, and Ethnicity." (September 1, 2020). https://www.bls.gov/emp/tables/civilian-labor-force-participation-rate.htm.

US Bureau of Labor Statistics. "Displaced Workers Summary." Department of Labor. (August 27, 2020). https://www.bls.gov/news.release/disp.nr0.htm.

US Bureau of Labor Statistics. "Employment, Hours, and Earnings from the Current Employment Statistics Survey (National)." (2020a). https://data.bls.gov/timeseries/CES3000000001.

US Bureau of Labor Statistics. "Employment, Hours, and Earnings: National." Distributed by Haver Analytics. (2020b). https://www.bls.gov/ces/data/.

US Bureau of Labor Statistics. "Home Health and Personal Care Aides, Occupational Outlook Handbook." (2022). https://www.bls.gov/ooh/healthcare/home-health-aides-and-personal-care-aides.htm.

US Bureau of Labor Statistics. "Job Openings and Labor Turnover Survey." FRED. Federal Reserve Bank of St. Louis. (2020). https://www.bls.gov/jlt/.

US Bureau of Labor Statistics. "Labor Force Statistics from the Current Population Survey." Department of Labor. (2020). http://www.bls.gov/data/.

US Bureau of Labor Statistics. "The Recession of 2007–2009." BLS Spotlight on Statistics. (February 2012). https://www.bls.gov/spotlight/2012/recession/pdf/recession_bls_spotlight.pdf.

US Bureau of Labor Statistics. "Union Membership Rate Declines in 2021, Returns to 2019 Rate of 10.3 Percent." (January 25, 2022). https://www.bls.gov/opub/ted/2022/union-membership-rate-declines-in-2021-returns-to-2019-rate-of-10-3-percent.htm.

US Census Bureau. "65 and Older Population Grows Rapidly as Baby Boomers Age."

CB20-99. Census.gov. (June 2019). https://www.census.gov/newsroom/press-relea ses/2020/65-older-population-grows.html.

US Census Bureau. "Household Pulse Survey Public Use Files." (2020). https://www.cen sus.gov/programs-surveys/household-pulse-survey/datasets.html.

US Census Bureau. "Real Median Household Income in the United States." FRED. Federal Reserve Bank of St. Louis (September 10, 2019). https://fred.stlouisfed.org/ series/MEHOINUSA672N.

US Census Bureau. "Wealth, Asset Ownership, & Debt of Households Detailed Tables: 2017." (Last revised August 12, 2020). https://www.census.gov/data/tables/ 2017/demo/wealth/wealth-asset-ownership.html.

US Department of Health & Human Services. "How Much Care Will You Need?" LongTermCare.gov. (2017). https://longtermcare.acl.gov/the-basics/how-much-care- will-you-need.html.

US Department of Labor, Employee Benefits Security Administration. "Private Pension Plan Bulletin Historical Tables and Graphs 1975–2019." (January 2021). https://www. dol.gov/sites/dolgov/files/ebsa/researchers/statistics/retirement-bulletins/private- pension-plan-bulletin-historical-tables-and-graphs.pdf.

US Department of the Treasury. "General Explanations of the Administration's Fiscal Year 2017 Revenue Proposals." (February 2016). https://home.treasury.gov/policy-iss ues/tax-policy/revenue-proposals.

US Government Accountability Office. "401(k) Plans: DOL Could Take Steps to Improve Retirement Income Options for Plan Participants." GAO 16-433. (2016). https://www. gao.gov/assets/680/678924.pdf.

US Government Accountability Office. "Retirement Savings: Additional Data and Analysis Could Provide Insight into Early Withdrawals. GAO–19-179." (March 2019). https://www.gao.gov/assets/700/698041.pdf.

US Government Accountability Office. "Reverse Mortgages: FHA Needs to Improve Monitoring and Oversight of Loan Outcomes and Servicing." (September 2019). https://www.gao.gov/assets/710/701676.pdf.

US Library of Congress, Congressional Research Service. "Social Security: What Would Happen If the Trust Funds Ran Out?" RL33514. (July 2020). https://fas.org/sgp/crs/ misc/RL33514.pdf.

Urban Institute. "State and Local Government Pensions." (2021). https://www.urban. org/policy-centers/cross-center-initiatives/state-and-local-finance-initiative/state- and-local-backgrounders/state-and-local-expenditures.

Van Horn, Carl, Kathy Krepcio, Maria Heidkamp, and John J. Heldrich. "Improving Education and Training for Older Workers." AARP Public Policy Institute. (February 25, 2015). https://www.aarp.org/ppi/info-2015/improving-education-training-older- workers.html.

Venti, Steven F., and David A. Wise. "Aging and Housing Equity: Another Look." NBER Working Paper No. 8608. 2004. https://www.nber.org/papers/w8608.

Venti, Steven F., and David A. Wise. "Aging and the Income Value of Housing Wealth." *Journal of Public Economics* 44, no. 3 (April 1991): 371–397. doi:10.1016/ 0047-2727(91)90020-3.

Venti, Steven F., and David A. Wise. "Aging, Moving, and Housing Wealth." In *Issues in the Economics of Aging*, edited by David A. Wise, 9–54. Chicago: University of Chicago Press, 1990. http://www.nber.org/chapters/c11577.

Venti, Steven F., and David A. Wise. "But They Don't Want to Reduce Housing Equity." In *Issues in the Economics of Aging*, edited by David A. Wise, 13–32. Chicago: University of Chicago Press, 1990. http://www.nber.org/chapters/c7112.

Vernon, Steve, Amal Harrati, and Jialu Streeter. "Are Americans Saving Enough for an Adequate Retirement?" *Seeing Our Way to Financial Security in the Age of Increased Longevity*, Special Report from the Stanford Center on Longevity. (October 2018). http://longevity.stanford.edu/wp-content/uploads/2018/11/Sightlines-Financial-Security-Special-Report-2018.pdf.

Weir, David. "The Health and Retirement Study." The University of Michigan's Institute for Social Research. (2008). https://hrs.isr.umich.edu/welcome-health-and-retirement-study.

Willis Towers Watson. "Lifetime Income Solutions." (September 2019). https://www.willistowerswatson.com/en-US/Insights/2019/09/lifetime-income-solutions.

Wolf, Michael, Marina Serper, Lauren Opsasnick, Rachel M. O'Conor, Laura Curtis, Julia Yoshino Benavente, Guisselle Wismer, et al. "Awareness, Attitudes, and Actions Related to COVID-19 Among Adults with Chronic Conditions at the Onset of the U.S. Outbreak: A Cross-sectional Survey." *Annals of Internal Medicine* 173 (2020): 100–109. https://doi.org/10.7326/M20-1239.

Wolff, Edward N., and Maury Gittleman. "Inheritances and the Distribution of Wealth or Whatever Happened to the Great Inheritance Boom?" *Journal of Economic Inequality* 12, no. 4 (2014): 439–468. https://doi.org/10.1007/s10888-013-9261-8.

World Bank. "Database on Fertility by Country." https://data.worldbank.org/indicator/SP.DYN.TFRT.IN?locations=XU-US.

Xue, Baowen, Dorina Cadar, Maria Fleischmann, Stephen Stansfeld, Ewan Carr, Mika Kivimäki, Anne McMunn, and Jenny Head. "Effect of Retirement on Cognitive Function: The Whitehall II Cohort Study." *European Journal of Epidemiology* 33 (2018): 989–1001. https://doi.org/10.1007/s10654-017-0347-7.

Yaari, Menahem E. "Uncertain Lifetime, Life Insurance, and the Theory of the Consumer." *Review of Economic Studies* 32, no. 3 (1965): 137–150.

Zwick, Thomas. "Why Training Older Employees Is Less Effective." Centre for European Economic Research. (2011). https://ftp.zew.de/pub/zew-docs/dp/dp11046.pdf.

For the benefit of digital users, indexed terms that span two pages (e.g., 52–53) may, on occasion, appear on only one of those pages.

Tables and figures are indicated by an italic *t*, and *f* following the page/paragraph number.